D1266842

ORDERS OF KNIGHTHOOD, AWARDS AND THE HOLY SEE
– A historical, juridical and practical Compendium –

IOANNI PAULO II

Pontifici Maximo

Qui in universa Ecclesia Catholica

sub Deo

omnium Fons est Honorum

benigne annuenti

hoc quantulumcumque est opus

Hyginus Cardinale

observantissimo filii animo

inscribit

dedicat

Hyginus Eugene Cardinale

VAN DUREN
GERRARDS CROSS 1983

First published in 1983 by Van Duren Publishers
P.O. Box 1, Gerrards Cross, Buckinghamshire SL9 7AE England.

Case bound edition
ISBN: 0 905715 12 8

Leather bound, limited signed edition
ISBN: 0 905715 13 6

Set in Pilgrim 11/13 by Inforum Ltd, Portsmouth.

Printed on Henrietta Matt Coated Cartridge 115 gsm
and White Art 115 gsm by Billing & Sons Ltd, Worcester.

Produced in Great Britain

CONTENTS

DEDICATION		3
PREFACE		19
CHAPTER ONE:	THE INVOLVEMENT OF THE HOLY SEE IN THE FIELD OF CHIVALRY	21
CHAPTER TWO:	PONTIFICAL ORDERS OF KNIGHTHOOD	27
	I The Supreme Order of Christ	27
	II The Order of the Golden Spur	35
	III The Order of Pius IX	45
	IV The Order of St. Gregory the Great	53
	V The Order of Pope St. Sylvester	57
CHAPTER THREE:	OTHER PAPAL AWARDS	61
	I The Golden Rose	63
	II The Cross *Pro Ecclesia et Pontifice*	67
	III The *Benemerenti* Medal	70
	IV The Pontifical Medal	75
CHAPTER FOUR:	RELIGIOUS BUT NOT PONTIFICAL ORDERS OF KNIGHTHOOD RECOGNISED BY THE HOLY SEE	81
	I The Sovereign Military Hospitaller Order of St. John of Jerusalem, of Rhodes and of Malta	81
	II The Equestrian Order of the Holy Sepulchre of Jerusalem	93
	III The Teutonic Order – or The Teutonic Knights of St. Mary's Hospital at Jerusalem	107

CHAPTER FIVE: RELIGIOUS BUT NOT PONTIFICAL AWARDS RECOGNISED BY THE HOLY SEE 111

I The Lateran Cross 111

II The Lauretan Cross 111

III The Holy Land Pilgrim's Cross 112

CHAPTER SIX: THE PROCEDURE FOR ADMISSION TO THE ORDERS OF KNIGHTHOOD 113

and a Corollary on the Use of Titles and Style 117

CHAPTER SEVEN: DYNASTIC ORDERS OF KNIGHTHOOD 119

I: SECULAR DYNASTIC ORDERS BESTOWED BY A REIGNING SOVEREIGN 123

The Royal Victorian Order (Great Britain) 123

The Royal Victorian Chain (Great Britain) 124

The Royal Order of the Seraphim (Sweden) 125

II: CATHOLIC DYNASTIC ORDERS BESTOWED BY A REIGNING SOVEREIGN 126

The Noble Order of the Golden Fleece (Spanish Branch) 126

The Royal Order of Maria Luisa (Spain) 134

III: CATHOLIC DYNASTIC ORDERS BESTOWED BY A SOVEREIGN IN EXILE 135

The Supreme Order of the Most Holy Annunciation (The Royal House of Savoy) 135

The Order of SS. Maurice and Lazarus (The Royal House of Savoy) 137

IV: CATHOLIC DYNASTIC ORDERS OF KNIGHTHOOD BESTOWED BY A LEGITIMATE SUCCESSOR IN EXILE AND HEAD OF A ROYAL FAMILY 140

The Noble Order of the Golden Fleece (Austrian Branch) 140

and a Corollary on the Military Imperial Order of the Three Golden Fleeces planned by Napoleon in 1809 144

The Sacred and Military Constantinian Order of St. George (The Royal Houses of Bourbon of the Two Sicilies and of Spain) 145

The Royal and Illustrious Order of St. Januarius (The Royal Houses of Bourbon of the Two Sicilies and of Spain) 151

The Order of St. George, Defender of the Faith in the Immaculate Conception (The Royal House of Bavaria – Wittelsbach) 153

The Order of St. Hubert (The Royal House of Bavaria – Wittelsbach) 153

The Order of the Holy Ghost (The Royal House of Bourbon-Orléans – France) 154

The Royal and Military Order of St. Louis (idem) 155

The Order of St. Michael of France (idem) 156

The Order of the Dames of the Starry Cross (The Imperial and Royal House of Habsburg-Lorraine; H.I. and R.H. Archduke Otto of Austria) 156

The Order of St. Joseph (The Imperial and Royal House of Habsburg-Lorraine; H.I. and R.H. Archduke Godfrey of Austria) 157

The Order of St. Stephen (The Imperial and Royal House of Habsburg-Lorraine; H.I. and R.H. Archduke Godfrey of Austria) 158

CHAPTER EIGHT: STATE-FOUNDED CATHOLIC ORDERS AND THE HOLY SEE 159

Monastic-Military Orders

The Military Order of Alcantara (Spain) 161

The Military Order of Calatrava (Spain) 161

The Military Order of Montesa (Spain) 162

The Military Order of Santiago or of St. James of the Sword (Spain) 163

Orders of Merit

The Most Distinguished Order of Carlos III (Spain) 164

The Order of Cisneros (Spain) 165

The Equestrian Order of St. Agatha (Republic of San Marino) 165

The Order of St. Charles (Principality of Monaco) 166

The Military Order of St. Ferdinand (Spain) 168

The Royal and Military Order of St. Hermenegildus (Spain) 169

The Order of Isabella the Catholic (Spain) 169

The Civil and Military Order of San Marino (Republic of San Marino) 171
The Order of the Cross of St. Raymond of Peñafort (Spain) 172

CHAPTER NINE: EXTINCT CATHOLIC ORDERS AND THE HOLY SEE 173
I: Short-lived Orders of Knighthood 177
The Order of St. Mark
The Order of St. Anthony of Vienna
The Order of SS. John and Thomas
The Order of the Militia of Jesus Christ, or of St. Dominic
The Order of Mercy
The Order of the Glorious St. Mary
The Order of St. James, or of the Shell
The Order of the Dove
The Order of St. Anthony of Hainault
The Order of St. John Lateran
The Order of Our Lady of Loreto
The Order of Jesus and Mary
The Order of the Immaculate Conception
The Order of the Celestial Collar of the Holy Rosary
The Order of Brotherly Love
The Order of St. Bridget of Sweden
II: Long-lived Orders of Knighthood 178
The Mediaeval Period
The Order of the Knights Templars 178

The Order of the Ancient Nobility of the Four Emperors (Empire) 182
The Order of the Defeated Dragon (Empire) 182
The Order of the Fleet, or of the Two Moons (France) 183
The Order of the Hacha [Hatchet] (Spain) 183
The Order of the Holy Ghost of Montpellier (France) 183
The Order of the Holy Vial (France) 183
The Order of the Military Cincture (Sicily) 184
The Order of Montjoie (France) 184
The Order of Our Lady of Bethlehem (Papal) 185
The Sacred and Military Order of Our Lady of Mercy (Spain) 185
The Order of St. George of Alfama (Spain) 185
The Order of St. George of Burgundy (Belgium) 186
The Order of St. George in Carinthia (Empire) 186
The Order of St. Hubert of Lorraine, or of Bar (France) 187
The Order of St. James of Altopascio (Tuscany) 187
The Order of St. Michael's Wing (Portugal) 188
The Order of the Swan (Brandenburg) 188
The Order of the Sword Bearers (Lithuania) 188
The Order of the White Eagle (Poland) 189

Modern Times 190
The Order of Our Lady of Guadalupe (Mexico) 190
The Order of Our Lady of Mount Carmel and the Order of St. Lazarus of Jerusalem [amalgamated] (France) 191
The Order of Our Lady of Vila Viçosa (Portugal) 191
The Order of St. Anne (München) 192
The Order of St. Anne (Würzburg) 192
The Order of St. Charles (Mexico) 193
The Order of St. Elizabeth (Sultzbach) 193
The Imperial Order of St. Faustin (Haiti) 194
The Order of St. Ferdinand and of Merit (Two Sicilies) 194
The Order of St. George of Ravenna (Papal) 195
The Order of St. George of the Reunion (Two Sicilies) 195
The Military Order of St. Henry (Poland – Saxony) 196
The Royal Military Order of St. Henry (Haiti) 196
The Order of St. Isabella (Portugal) 196
The Order of St. Louis (Parma) 197
The Order of St. Margaret (France) 198
The Order of St. Mary Magdalene (Haiti) 198
The Order of St. Michael (Bavaria) 198

	The Order of St. Rose and Civilisation (Honduras)	199
	The Royal Hungarian Order of St. Stephen (Empire)	200
	The Order of the Slaves of Virtue (Empire)	200
CHAPTER TEN:	ORIGINALLY CATHOLIC ORDERS OF KNIGHTHOOD STILL BESTOWED AS SECULAR ORDERS BY SOVEREIGN STATES	201
I	The Military Order of Avis, or the Military Order of St. Benedict of Avis (Portugal)	202
II	The Most Honourable Order of the Bath (Great Britain)	204
III	The Military Order of Christ (Portugal)	207
IV	The Order of the Dannebrog, or the Order of the Flag of the Danes (Denmark)	209
V	The Order of the Elephant (Denmark)	212
VI	The Most Noble Order of the Garter (Great Britain)	213
VII	The Military Order of St. James of the Sword (Portugal)	220
VIII	The Most Ancient and Most Noble Order of the Thistle (Great Britain)	222
IX	The Grand Collar of the Three Orders (Portugal)	224
X	The Military Order of the Sword, or the Order of the Yellow Ribbon (Sweden)	225
XI	The Military Order of the Tower and the Sword, of Valour, Loyalty and Merit (Portugal)	226

XII The Imperial Society of Knights Bachelor (Great Britain) 227

CHAPTER ELEVEN: AUTONOMOUS AND SELF-STYLED ORDERS OF KNIGHTHOOD 231
– The historical and juridical situation – 231
– A Corollary on the Association of the Knights of Columbus – 237

CHAPTER TWELVE: THE SUPERNATURAL IN THE ORDERS OF KNIGHTHOOD 239
The Deity
A Chivalrous Register of Saints
The Blessed Virgin Mary
St. Michael the Archangel
The Saints

CHAPTER THIRTEEN: THE SPIRIT OF CHRISTIAN CHIVALRY TODAY 267

ACKNOWLEDGEMENTS 271

APPENDICES 273

BIBLIOGRAPHY 313

INDEX 315

COLOUR PLATES

Between pages 72 and 73

PLATE I	The Supreme Order of Christ
PLATE II	The Order of the Golden Spur
PLATE III	The Order of Pius IX
PLATE IV	The Order of St. Gregory the Great
PLATE V	The Order of Pope St. Sylvester
PLATE VI	The Cross *Pro Ecclesia et Pontifice* The Medal *Concilium Oecumenicum Vaticanum II* The Medal *Anno Iubilaei Romae MCMLXXLV*
PLATE VII	The *Benemerenti* Medal
PLATE VIII	The Golden Rose The Pontifical Medal

Between pages 96 and 97

PLATE IX	The Sovereign Military Order of Malta
PLATE X	Orders of Merit of the Sovereign Military Order of Malta
PLATE XI	The Order of the Holy Sepulchre of Jerusalem
PLATE XII	Orders of Merit of the Order of the Holy Sepulchre of Jerusalem

Between pages 120 and 121

PLATE XIII	The Noble Order of the Golden Fleece
PLATE XIV	The Collar of the Sacred Military Constantinian Order of St. George
PLATE XV	The Sacred Military Constantinian Order of St. George
PLATE XVI	The Order of SS. Maurice and Lazarus The Royal and Illustrious Order of St. Januarius

Between pages 216 and 217

PLATE XVII The Royal Victorian Order

PLATE XVIII The Order of Isabella the Catholic

PLATE XIX The Grand Collar of the Three Orders
The Military Order of the Tower and the Sword, of Valour, Loyalty and Merit

PLATE XX Ceremonial Dress of Orders of Knighthood:
A Knight of the Most Noble Order or the Garter
A Knight of the Most Honourable Order of the Bath
A Knight Commander of the Order of Pius IX
A Knight Commander of the Order of St. Gregory the Great

PREFACE

There is a great need for a reliable guide concerning Orders of Knighthood and Awards conferred by the Holy See and the Holy See's attitude towards other Orders. To my knowledge there are few publications which deal chiefly with honours bestowed by the Holy See, and then only with regard to specific Orders and their different classes. Unfortunately such publications usually treat the subject in general terms and cannot always claim accuracy as their distinguishing mark.

The present work is intended to be an answer to that need. Having been involved in various capacities in the granting of pontifical honours in my service of the Holy See, I am pleased to place the result of my personal experience and interest at the disposal of those who are concerned with the matter.

My main purpose in writing this book was therefore a practical one. In doing so, I was solicitous to provide the reader with a treatise which, though it can never be exhaustive, would be fully adequate to its aims. This work contains all the historical, juridical and practical information about each Pontifical Order and Award relevant in this connexion. It also deals with other Catholic or originally Catholic Orders of Knighthood with which the Holy See continues to have or has had a special relationship. It is quite obvious that we shall use the term "Catholic" in this context not in its theological or canonical sense but in its historical, social and practical application.

I am personally responsible for the views expressed in this work, particularly with regard to issues on which the Holy See has not made any public authoritative pronouncement. The demands of my several missions in the service of the Holy See restricted the time and attention I could personally give to certain aspects of my inquiry and detail. I therefore gladly accepted the help and assistance of several experts in the varied field of research in this vast subject. Their collaboration has proved especially helpful.

In fact, as soon as it became known that this work was in the process of being prepared for publication, an unexpectedly great number of autonomous and self-styled Orders of Knighthood expressed a desire to be mentioned in this book. This has been done, but in a separate chapter, so as to avoid any possible misunderstanding that their inclusion be interpreted as an *ipso facto* recognition of their alleged and pretended approval or acknowledgement.

It is my hope that this book will be useful to those who desire to become better acquainted with the Holy See's ancient practice of bestowing Knighthoods and Awards and with its attitude to other Orders of Knighthood, and furnish the information so often sought from Apostolic Nunciatures, Delegations and even from the Papal Secretariat of State.

+ H. E. Cardinale

CHAPTER ONE

THE INVOLVEMENT OF THE HOLY SEE IN THE FIELD OF CHIVALRY

The granting of papal honours to members of the laity for distinguished service and as a means of recognising and rewarding loyalty is a very ancient custom in the Catholic Church. These honours were once conferred mainly in the framework of the Orders of Christ and of the Golden Militia. Noble lineage was then normally required in the recipients. If this could not be proved, the recipients were ennobled by the Orders into which they were admitted.

In the sixteenth century the Papacy founded several *Collegia Militum* (Colleges of Militia), all of them short-lived. Thus, among others, we find the *Collegium Sancti Petri* (College of St. Peter), established by Leo X (1513–1521) in 1520. It possessed the characteristics of chivalry but in reality it was a society of gentlemen engaging themselves to give financial help to the Roman Curia and receiving, in return, honours and tributes. In 1540 Paul III (1534–1549) set up the *Collegium Militum Sancti Pauli* (College of St. Paul's Militiamen) and in 1546 the Knights of the Lily. Pius IV (1559–1565) founded the Pian Knights in 1559. In 1586 Sixtus V (1585–1590) established the Lauretan Knights whose aim it was to defend the Holy House of Loreto against piratical assaults from the Adriatic Sea. The Holy House of Loreto is the reputed house of the Holy Family at Nazareth, which according to tradition was translated to Fiume in Illyria in 1291, thence to Recanati in 1294 and finally to the estate of a certain Lady Lauretta, who gave the name to the town of Loreto, situated three miles from the Adriatic in central Italy. Many miracles are recorded as having taken place at the Holy House.

There is a connexion between the shrines of Loreto and of Walsingham, England. The latter was built in the early thirteenth century as a memorial of the same mystery of the Annunciation, first enacted in the Holy House of Nazareth, now revered at Loreto.

In the two following centuries and in the early 1800s several other minor institutions, all short-lived, appeared in the Papal States, mostly of an honorary kind. Among these were the Equestrian Order of the Moretto, founded by Pius VII (1800–1823) to honour the chairmen of the *Accademia di San Luca*, an academy of painters, sculptors and architects; and the Equestrian Order of St. Cecilia, established by Pius IX (1846–1878) in 1847, to be awarded to the four guardians, the chairman, the secretary and the *camerlengo* of the Musical Academy of St. Cecilia. Following the suppression of nobility and the privileges associated with it in the nineteenth century, and the increase of abuses perpetrated in the bestowal of awards, nobiliary titles, privileges and favours of all kinds by delegated bodies or individuals, as well as the appearance of State Orders of Merit in Europe, the Papacy decided to reform its own system of conferring honours on well-deserving persons, basing it on the new criterion of personal merit and worth. Gradually the term 'Order' was loosely applied to the insignia and decorations themselves. It thus no longer implied submission to a rule or statute, of which the knight was proud to carry some sign on his surcoat so as to give public witness of his allegiance.

Pius VI (1800–1823) started off the reform by suppressing the title of Count Palatine attributed to members of the Golden Militia. Great confusion persisted in connexion with the existing papal titles and decorations until Pius X (1903–1914) established a certain uniformity by an Apostolic Letter of 7 February 1905 *Multum ad excitandos*, by which the arrangement and constitution of Pontifical Orders were remodelled. The Pope defined Pontifical Orders of Knighthood as corporations instituted by the Roman Pontiffs to reward persons who deserved special recognition on account of the services rendered by them to the Church and society. These Orders are called 'Pontifical' because they are founded and awarded by the Sovereign Pontiff either directly (*motu proprio*) or indirectly, following a request submitted to the Secretariat of State. Pius X confirmed the Supreme Order of Christ, the Order of the Golden Militia, the Order of Pius IX, the Order of St. Gregory the Great and the Order of Pope St. Sylvester. Only the Order of Pius IX continued to confer nobility, in different degrees, upon its knights of the first and the second classes. This privilege, as we shall see, was completely suppressed by Pius XII (1939–1958) on 11 November 1939.

During the second half of the pontificate of Pius XII the Holy See began to restrict the bestowing of titles of nobility in general. The reason for this measure is to be found in the Holy See's desire to adapt its practices as much as possible to commendable attitudes of present day society. Another reason is that in recent years the Sovereign Pontiffs have tended more and more to minimise the temporal aspect of their exercise of sovereignty, which some jurists felt was reflected in the concession of titles of nobility. These titles are now given with extreme parsimony and discretion. As a result, pontifical decorations have attracted more attention and are in greater demand.

Pius VII began the reform of the Pontifical Orders of Knighthood.

The main decoration of Pontifical Orders of Knighthood normally consists of a cross, except for the Order of Pius IX which has a star. The trophy is generally added for the sole military division, where it exists.

There is a fundamental difference between the Pontifical Orders of Knighthood and the Religious-Military, but not Pontifical, Orders of Knighthood, such as the Sovereign Military Order of Malta, the Equestrian Order of the Holy Sepulchre, and the Teutonic Order. Their foundation was a result of private initiative, later approved by the Papacy, but from their very beginning, like the other early monastic-military Orders of Knighthood, they were naturally oriented towards the Church by reason of their very constitution and motivation. The aforesaid Orders, as we shall see later on, are fully recognised by the Holy See in their respective different status.

Pius X defined the Pontifical Orders of Knighthood as 'corporations'. This is to be understood loosely, as a group of persons belonging to a certain body, and not in the strict sense of the term as a body corporate legally authorised to act as a single individual or having the capacity of perpetual succession.

As a group, the members of the Pontifical Orders of Knighthood have the right to use their titles and to wear their uniforms and decorations for ecclesiastical purposes. They also have a special place in papal *cortèges*. Where permitted, they may use their titles and insignia for civil purposes. In certain countries authorisation may be required to accept and

Opposite: A decorative shield, (20th century), depicting a knight praying before a statue of the Blessed Virgin in the upper half, and St. George slaying the dragon in the lower half of the shield. In the bordure above are the words: *REGINA EQUITUM CHRISTIANORUM O.P.N.* [Queen of Christian Knights, pray for us]. The bordure is decorated with Catholic Orders of Chivalry which are (clockwise starting on the right): The Supreme Order of Christ (Holy See); The Order of Pius IX (Holy See); The Order of St. Gregory the Great (Holy See); The Order of Pope St. Sylvester (Holy See); The Order of the Holy Sepulchre; The Sacred and Military Constantinian Order of St. George (Two Sicilies and Spain); The Sovereign Military Order of Malta; [The Papal Insignia]; The Order of St. Hubert (Bavaria); The Royal and Illustrious Order of St. Januarius (Two Sicilies and Spain); The Noble Order of the Golden Fleece (Spain and Austria); The Military Order of Calatrava and Alcantara (Spain); The Military Order of Santiago (Spain); The Order of SS. Maurice and Lazarus (Savoy); The Order of the Golden Spur (Holy See). [*W.E. Maitre Sculp. – Valdausa Invent.*]

Courtesy: Marquess di Lorenzo

LEMAITRE SCULP
JESUIS LIMMACULEE CONCEPTION

wear decorations of foreign Orders in public, and to make public use of the titles that go with them. As regards Great Britain, it was confirmed in the *London Gazette* of 3 May 1968 that decorations conferred in the Pontifical Orders of Knighthood by His Holiness the Pope could be worn without restriction by United Kingdom citizens who were not servants of the Crown.

The other Orders mentioned above, instead, form a corporation in the legal sense of the word: if properly instituted they have a corporate life, with corporate rights, privileges, duties and activities. They are recognised as a corporation even under civil law where they have registered as such. The activities of these Orders are of a ceremonial, cultural, medical, social and benevolent character. These Orders consist of a federation of moral persons, represented by their respective Grand Priories, Priories, Lieutenancies, Delegations and Associations, legitimately established according to canon and civil law, governed by a constitutional charter approved by the Holy See and having a central authority invested in the Grand Master who under the Pope is the supreme head of the Order.

It is interesting to note that the Pontifical Orders of Knighthood, generally speaking, do not derive from ancient monastic-military institutions but belong rather to the category of the secular Orders of Merit. Apart from the Supreme Order of Christ and the Order of the Golden Spur, which possess an eminently religious character, they may be bestowed on non-Christians, and indeed on non-believers as well. In a way, they are even more secular than the Orders of Merit founded and sponsored by the various modern States, in that the members of the clergy and the religious of both sexes are excluded from their membership.

The only partial exception to this rule was the Order of the Golden Militia to which for several centuries ecclesiastics were admitted. During the eighteenth century their membership entailed the title of Protonotary Apostolic. Such a custom ended entirely with the reform by Gregory XVI (1831–1846) in 1841.

Finally, before attempting our subject, it may prove useful to recall that, according to international practice, the Holy See recognises legitimately instituted Orders of Knighthood as juridical persons under public law in the various States as it also recognises the awards conferred by them. The Orders and awards bestowed by the Holy See are likewise generally recognised by different States which have chivalric institutions and grant marks of distinction to meritorious individuals.

Chapter Two

PONTIFICAL ORDERS OF KNIGHTHOOD

I

THE SUPREME ORDER OF CHRIST

(THE MILITIA OF OUR LORD JESUS CHRIST)

This is the highest of the five Pontifical Orders of Knighthood now in existence. It was founded on 14 August 1318 under the name of THE MILITIA OF JESUS CHRIST by Denis I and St. Isabella King and Queen of Portugal (1279–1326), with the aim of defending the country against the Moorish invaders, in replacement of the Supreme Order of the Templars, which had been suppressed by Clement V (1305–1314) in 1312. The new Order was approved and confirmed by John XXII (1316–1334) from Avignon, by the constitution *Ad ea ex quibus* of 14 March 1319. The Pope, in fact, had been its inspirer as a religious Order. He became its patron and gave it the rule of the Cistercians. The Order was endowed with the properties of the extinct Order of the Templars and additional means of subsistence. It immediately extended to Spain, France, Italy and Germany, and gained the support of subsequent Pontiffs. In 1499 Alexander VI (1492–1503) and later Julius II (1503–1513) freed the knights from the obligation of taking solemn vows. The Order thus lost its monastic character, but continued to recognise the reigning Pope as its supreme head. The Pope appointed the Portuguese Sovereign as his administrator for the affairs of the Order in Portugal. In 1522 the Order was definitively divided into two separate branches, one, essentially religious, under the Pope, and the other, as a distinct civil Order, under the Portuguese Sovereign exclusively, as they subsist today. While the latter, having lost its original religious character in 1789, was conferred to a great number of persons, the former was gradually reserved for very exceptional cases, until it went practically into disuse. After undergoing a certain reform in 1878, the Pontifical Order was restored and completely reorganised by Pius X on 7 February 1905 (*Multum ad excitandos*). On 15 April 1966 Paul VI (1963–1978) decreed in *Equestres Ordines* that the Supreme Order of Christ and that of the Golden Militia, known also as the Order of the Golden Spur, and granted only for extraordinary reasons, would henceforth be awarded to Heads of State only on the occasion of very important celebrations at which the Sovereign Pontiff is personally present, or of exceptionally momentous events. Because of the strongly religious character of these two Orders, the former bearing the title of Our Lord Jesus Christ and the latter being instituted to honour the Blessed Virgin Mary, they would be reserved exclusively for Heads of State professing the Christian faith.

Cross with Crown and Trophy

The jewelled Star

The Supreme Order of Christ has only one class. Its decoration consists of a long red Latin cross, on which is superimposed a smaller red and white enamel cross, surmounted by a crown and a military trophy, hanging from a golden chain, worn round the neck. The use of the chain was introduced when courtly Orders replaced the early monastic-military Orders, whose knights wore their badge as a large fabric cross applied to their cloak and were distinguished by the form of the cross and the colour of the cloak. The knight would use the cross borne on his surcoat as his personal emblem, found also on his shield and his seal. Courtly Orders adopted the ornamental chain, also known as the Grand Collar, for the highest rank of the order, which often consisted only of one class. The chain was symbolic of the sterling attachment, subjection

Ceremonial uniform of a Knight of the Supreme Order of Christ.

and loyalty of the knight to his master. This chain is composed of interlacing plaquettes connected with golden knots and representing the cross of the Order and the papal emblems alternatively. It is accompanied by a badge, consisting of a silver eight-rayed star, ornamented with jewels and bearing the cross of the Order in the centre, encircled by a crown of oak leaves. The Order has its own uniform worn only for State occasions. It is of a bright scarlet fabric with facings of white cloth and rich gold embroideries on the collar, breast and cuffs. Knee breeches of white smooth silk with gold side stripes, shoes of white silk with gold buckles, hat with white plumes and ornamented with a knot of twisted gold cord terminating in tassels of gold. A sword with a gold and mother-of-pearl hilt and pendant tassels of twisted gold cord complete the costume.

The conferring of this Order is made *motu proprio* (at his own initiative) by the Sovereign Pontiff himself. The criterion of bestowal remains very restrictive.

At the Inauguration of John Paul I on 3 September 1978, three Sovereign Heads of State, wearing Pontifical Orders of Knighthood reserved for Sovereigns and Heads of State: King Baudouin (Belgium), the Supreme Order of Christ; King Juan Carlos (Spain), the Golden Collar of the Order of Pius IX; and Grand Duke Jean (Luxembourg), the Order of the Golden Spur.

Courtesy: Felici, Pontificia Fotografia, Rome

H.M. King Baudouin of the Belgians, Knight of the Supreme Order of Christ (1961).

Courtesy: Felici, Pontificia Fotografia, Rome

President Charles de Gaulle of France, Knight of the Supreme Order of Christ with John XXIII (1959).

Courtesy: Felici, Pontificia Fotografia, Rome

President Antonio Segni of Italy became a Knight of the Supreme Order of Christ in 1963, having already been made a Knight of the Order of the Golden Spur in 1962. Both Orders were conferred by John XXIII.

Courtesy: Felici, Pontificia Fotografia, Rome

It may cause some surprise to discover among the members of this Order, previous to the revision by Paul VI, the names of certain personages who were indeed outstanding in one way or another, but who were neither Catholics nor benefactors, even in a general manner, of the Catholic Church. Such is the name of the German Chancellor, Prince Otto von Bismarck on whom Leo XIII conferred the Order of Christ on 31 December 1885. This he did as a token of gratitude for the important part the Chancellor had played in solving the dispute between Germany and Spain about the possession of the Caroline Islands, the arbitration of which had been confided to the Holy See. One must remember, in this connexion, that the Order of Christ became 'Supreme' under Pius X, in 1905, when it was thoroughly reformed. This explains why the Order was formerly given rather lavishly. This lavishness however did not disappear immediately after its reform, though it was reserved for Catholics, all of whom, however, cannot be described as practising, nor were they all Sovereigns or Heads of State. Closer to our time one can note the following, among the latter, on whom the Order was conferred:

Epitacio da Silva Passoa, President of Brazil (1922);
Augusto B. Leguia, President of Peru (1928);
Victor Emmanuel III, King of Italy (1932);
William Miklas, Federal President of Austria (1933);
Albert I, King of the Belgians (1934);
Agustin P. Justo, President of Argentina (1934);
Albert Lebrun, President of France (1935);
Francisco Franco Bahamonde, Head of State of Spain (1953);
René Coty, President of France (1957);
Giovanni Gronchi, President of Italy (1959);
General Charles De Gaulle, President of France (1959);
Baudouin, King of the Belgians (1961);
Eamon De Valera, President of Ireland (1962);
Antonio Segni, President of Italy (1963); [see Order of the Golden Spur];
Giuseppe Saragat, President of Italy (1966).

Grand Duke Jean of Luxembourg, Knight of the Order of the Golden Spur, in audience with John Paul II after the Pope's Inauguration in 1978.

Courtesy: Felici, Pontificia Fotografia, Rome

II

THE ORDER OF THE GOLDEN SPUR

(THE GOLDEN MILITIA)

This Order of Knighthood is one of the most ancient. It was instituted – not as an Order but as an honour – at an uncertain date in the early Christian centuries. Some writers believe that it is an extension of the Knights of Emperor Constantine, who formed the Golden Militia and to whom Pope St. Sylvester I gave the rule of St. Basilius. The members of the Order of the Golden Spur, however, are thought to be the predecessors of the Crusader Knights and to have given an origin to several other Orders of Knighthood, such as the Sacred and Military Constantinian Order of St. George. The members of the Order were called Knights of the Golden Spur because of their use of gilt spurs, with which they were presented during the dubbing ceremony as a symbol of the rank and office they had gained. They were also called Knights of the Golden Militia because of their marked military character.

It is interesting to note that in Welsh poetry of the late fifteenth century, such as in the works of Gutur Owain, Gwaith Tudor Aled and Guto'r Glyn, there are many references to golden spurs. "To gild the feet" of someone is to give him golden spurs, and "to make someone's spurs golden" is to promote him to a higher rank in the knighthood. Those who were thus knighted were called *equites aureati* [golden knights], and were highly respected.

As from Pius IV (1559–1565) and up to Benedict XIV (1740–1758) the recipient of the Order of the Golden Spur was usually awarded the title of *Palatini et Aulae Nostrae Lateranensis Comes et Miles Nobilis* (Count of the Palatine and of Our Lateran Palace and Noble Soldier). Order and title continued to go together in many instances until 1815, when Pius VII abolished the custom. This title was always personal, unless it was stated differently in the Brief of conferment. In the former case the recipient was a *comes palatinus minor* (minor count palatine) and in the latter, *comes palatinus major* (major count palatine). The Order itself conferred nobility also to the descendants of its members.

The title of Count Palatine was reminiscent of functions and honours attributed to the *comes palatii*, who was a count attached to the imperial palace in the later Roman Empire. The term 'palatine' recalls one of the Seven Hills – the Palatine Hill – upon which the original city of Romulus was built and to which he later united the Capitoline and the Quirinal.

The Caelian, Aventine, Esquiline and Viminal Hills were added still later to form the city. The Palatine Hill became the site of the palace (hence the origin of the word) of the Caesars.

The Order of the Golden Spur as it was conferred until 1932, when a gold chain was substituted for the red ribbon with the silver borders.

Under the Frankish kings of the Merovingian dynasty, who preserved many of the ancient Roman appellations, Counts Palatine enjoyed supreme judicial authority in causes that came to the Sovereign's immediate attention. They were also sent to various parts of the empire as judges and governors. By extension the term came to designate the districts over which palatine powers were exercised. In England it was applied to counties outside ordinary administration. It was even taken to some of the possessions in America, such as Maryland and Maine.

Under the Holy Roman Emperors, who had constituted themselves as successors of the Roman Emperors after the decline of the latter, and who were popularly known as the German Emperors and who disappeared in 1806, a Count Palatine enjoyed the prerogative of exercising jurisdiction in his own fief or province in Germany.

This title is not to be confused with that of Count of the Holy Roman Empire, which was bestowed exclusively by the Emperor.

Starting with Charles V King of the Romans (1519) and Emperor (1519–1556) the title of Count Palatine gradually became honorary and was conferred with great profuseness by the Emperor and the Pope. It was attached to some offices in both the imperial and the papal courts to increase the honour of their incumbents, without jurisdictional or territorial significance, and was not transmissible, unless otherwise established by the Sovereign. As regards the papal court, whatever power and privileges a Count Palatine enjoyed came to him from the membership in the Order of the Golden Spur.

The prestige of this title gradually declined because of lavish and indiscriminate bestowal and inheritance deriving from concessions made by those of the Pope's and the Emperor's delegates who had been given the privilege of conferring the title. As regards the Papacy, the power to create members of the Order and to attribute the title of Count Palatine was delegated first of all to the Marquis of Ferrara (1367); subsequently, among others, it was delegated to Papal Legates, Nuncios and Patriarchs, to Archbishops and Bishops Assistant at the Papal Throne, to the College of Abbreviators and finally to the House of the Dukes of S. Fiora, Sforza-Cesarini, as a mark of recognition for their support of the Papacy. These delegates also had the power to appoint Protonotaries Apostolic.

The abuses began with the Sforza-Cesarini family after 1539 and were extended when these privileges were granted to other leading families. In every case, the delegated power was restricted to a certain number of concessions, depending on the exalted status and merits of the delegate.

This liberality entailed much confusion, which Popes found it hard to suppress. Pius VII made a first attempt at reforming the Order and abolishing the title of Count Palatine in 1815, but with little success. Gregory XVI (1831–1846), on 31 October 1841 (*Cum hominum mentes*), finally withdrew all the delegated powers and succeeded in renewing the Order, giving it the name of "the Order of St. Sylvester and of the Golden Militia", and reserving its bestowal to the Holy See exclusively.

It was only under Pius X (*Multum ad excitandos*) that the Order underwent a really radical transformation. It thus became the Order of the Golden Militia, while the Order of St. Sylvester was reinstated as a separate entity. It was placed under the patronage of the Blessed Virgin Mary to mark the fiftieth anniversary of the proclamation of the Dogma of the Immaculate Conception. The Holy See was thus endowed with an Order of Chivalry dedicated to Our Lady. The membership of the Order was restricted to one hundred knights who were expected to be 'champions and defenders of the Church of God', distinguishing themselves in the most eminent manner for that cause. All titles of nobility it previously conferred were suppressed for the future; now it is bestowed only by papal *motu proprio*. It was also decided that it would comprise only one class and take second place among the Pontifical Orders of Knighthood, coming immediately after the Supreme Order of Christ.

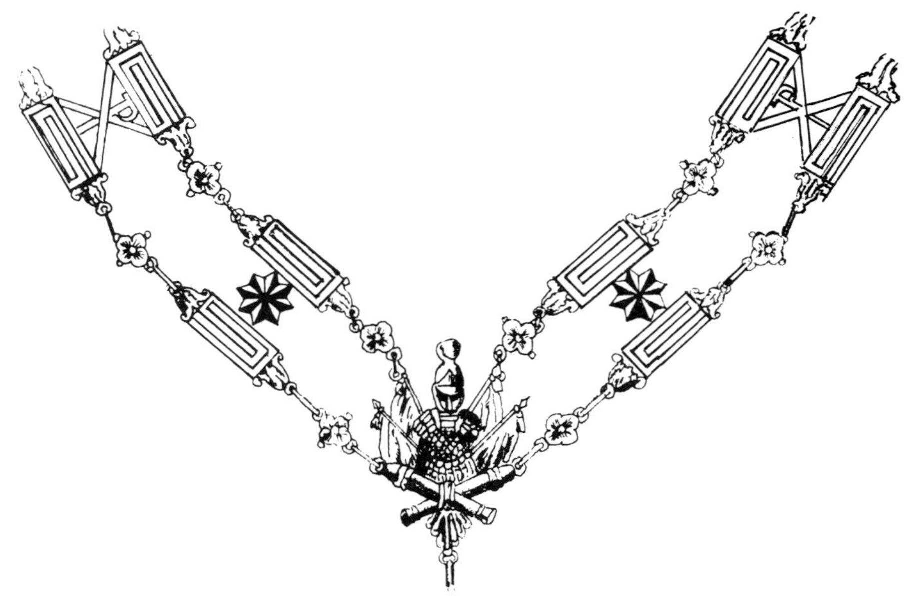

The Chain with Trophy

Pope Saint Pius X.

The Order underwent further restrictions on 15 April 1966 (*Equestres Ordines*) when Paul VI established that it would henceforth be awarded only to Christian Sovereigns and Heads of State. It is interesting to note that the Pontiff mentions it only by the name of the Golden Militia, while the *Annuario Pontificio*, the official pontifical yearbook, continues to call it "Order of the Golden Spur (Golden Militia)".

The badge of the Order consists of an eight-pointed yellow and gold enamel cross, without rays, surmounted by a gold military trophy with a gold spur hanging from the inner sides of its bifurcated foot.

From 1905 until 1932 this badge was worn suspended from a red and silver ribbon. This was later replaced with a gold collar, which is an ornamental chain identical to the collar formerly used for the Order of St. Sylvester combined with that of the Golden Militia.

This change took place in 1932 when the Order was bestowed on the Italian Premier, Benito Mussolini, as a token of gratitude for the goodwill shown in concluding the Lateran Treaty and thus putting an end to the long dispute between the Holy See and Italy following the annexation of the Papal States (1870–1929).

On the same occasion King Victor Emmanuel III of Italy and Crown Prince Umberto received the Supreme Order of Christ. The silver-bordered red ribbon of the Golden Spur was since then substituted with a gold chain so as to avoid the impression that the rank bestowed upon Benito Mussolini was simply that of a Commander, who usually wears his badge suspended from a ribbon.

The obverse of the badge is superimposed on a silver, eight-pointed star, which is worn on the left breast of the tunic.

The Order has its own uniform, which is worn only on State occasions; it consists of a red tunic with two rows of gilt buttons, the collar and cuffs of which are black velvet, embroidered with threads of gold. The trousers are long, of black cloth with gold side stripes. The epaulettes are ornamented with gold fringes and surmounted with the emblem of the Order, gold spurs, an oblong two-peaked hat fringed with gold and adorned with a gold knot displaying papal colours; a sword whose hilt is a gilded cross and scabbard black, hanging from a gilded sword belt with red fringe complete the uniform.

In going through the list of members of this Order, one finds eminent personages of the world of the arts and science, such as Wolfgang Amadeus Mozart, the Austrian composer; Antonio Canova, the Italian sculptor; Christoph Willibald Gluck, the German composer; and Gaetano Donizetti, the Italian operatic composer; all in the seventeenth

Ceremonial uniform of a Knight of the Golden Spur with the insignia on the ribbon instead of the chain.

and eighteenth centuries. It is amazing once again to come across certain names of personages, some of whom cannot be considered as "champions and defenders of the Catholic Church" and others are not even Christians. This explains the reason for the stringent measures of Paul VI. Among the members of the Order in the last sixty years or so, one finds the following Heads of State:

Fouad I, King of Egypt (1927)
Amanullah, King of Afghanistan (1928)
Ahmad Pasha, Bey of Tunis (1931)
Nicholas Horty de Nagybanya, Regent of Hungary (1936)
Paul Kara-Georgevitch, Prince of Yugoslavia (1939)
Mohamed Reza Pahlavia, Shahinshah of Iran (1948)
Luigi Einaudi, President of Italy (1948)
Theodor Heuss, President of the Federal Republic of Germany (1957)
Paul, King of the Hellenes (1959)
Antonio Segni, President of Italy (1962)*
Frederick IX, King of Denmark (1964)
Hussein I, King of Jordan (1964)
Jean, Grand Duke of Luxembourg (1965)

The reason for such lavishness is to be found in the fact that it had become quite normal to confer this Order on Heads of State and of Government when it was impossible to bestow the Supreme Order of Christ, which since the reforms introduced by Pius X and until the revisions of Paul VI included a profession of the Catholic Faith.

* President Antonio Segni received the Order of the Golden Spur in 1962 and was decorated with the Supreme Order of Christ on 30 April 1963. This is one of the very rare cases where a Head of State, at such a short interval, received the two highest Orders. The Chancellor of the Federal Republic of Germany, Dr. Konrad Adenauer, also received both Orders though he was not a Head of State and does therefore not appear in the above lists.

King Frederick IX of Denmark, was made a Knight of the Order of the Golden Spur in 1964 by Paul VI.

Courtesy: + B.B. Heim

Paul VI made King Hussein of Jordan a Knight of the Order of the Golden Spur in 1964.

Courtesy: Felici, Pontificia Fotografia, Rome

King Juan Carlos of Spain, upon whom Paul VI conferred the Golden Collar of the Order of Pius IX in 1977.

Courtesy: Felici, Pontificia Fotografia, Rome

III

THE ORDER OF PIUS IX

(THE PIAN ORDER)

This Order was instituted by Pius IX on 17 June 1847 (*Romanis Pontificibus*). Hence the name of the Order which in the Pope's intention was to be reminiscent of the Pian Knights founded by Pius IV in 1560, and endowed with many privileges of the nobility and the personal title of Count Palatine (*Pii patris amplissimi*).

Pius IX (Giovanni Maria Mastai Ferretti) was born at Senigallia (Italy) on 13 May 1792. He was ordained a priest in 1819, served as *auditeur* at the Apostolic Delegations of Chile and of Peru, was named bishop of Spoleto in 1827 and became bishop of Imola in 1832 and Cardinal in 1840. He was elected Pope in 1846. He inherited a most difficult task, the political situation of the Papal States being one of great confusion. He was compelled to leave Rome in 1848, taking refuge first at Gaeta and then at Portici. He returned to Rome in 1850, where he was confronted with many problems. Despite his strenuous efforts, he was overcome by the political events culminating in the occupation of all the Papal States and Territories, including Rome, by the victorious Italian Army in 1870. Pius IX was tireless in promoting all sacred disciplines and dealt with many doctrinal questions and theological disputes. He convoked the First Vatican Council in 1868. He died on 7 February 1878 in odour of sanctity. His successor, Leo XIII, (1878–1903), authorised the introduction of his cause of beatification, which however is still under discussion.

Pius IV (Gian Angelo Medici), whose name is also connected with the Pian Order, was born at Milan on 31 March 1499. He was an experienced administrator and became governor of several provinces, commissioner for the Papal Army in Hungary and Transylvania, vice-legate to Bologna, archbishop of Ragusa (1545), cardinal (1549) and Pope in 1559. He was an eminent jurist but a modest politician. He endeavoured to improve the religious situation in France, convoked the third and final session of the Council of Trent in 1560, reformed the Roman Curia, the Missal and the Breviary, launched the Catholic Reformation (also referred to by historians as "Counter Reformation"), and promoted the arts and sciences. He died on 9 December 1565. The Order of the Pian Knights, founded by him, scarcely survived his pontificate.

Ceremonial uniform of a Knight Commander with Star of the Order of Pius IX.

Since the Gregorian Reform only the Order of Pius IX, among the different Orders of Knighthood founded by the Popes, once conferred nobility upon its members. This privilege, obviously derived from the ancient Pian Order, was transferable by right of primogeniture in the male line for the Knights Grand Cross and personal, that is non-transferable, for the Commanders with Star and ordinary Commanders. Its object was and remains fittingly to reward conspicuous deeds of merit in Church and society. The Order was reformed by Pius XII on 11 November 1939 (*Litteris suis*), when the Pontiff established that it would no longer confer nobility, in any way, on its recipients, so that personal merit and worth would henceforth be the only title to honour. On 25 December 1957 Pius XII added another class to the three existing ones, that of Knights Golden Collar, which was to be reserved for Sovereigns and Heads of State and exceptionally for some other very high authorities. In view of their prevalently religious character, the Supreme

H.M. Gustav Adolf VI, King of Sweden, Knight of the Golden Collar of the Order of Pius IX, with Paul VI in 1967. Courtesy: +B.B. Heim

H.M. Olav V, King of Norway, Knight of the Golden Collar of Pius IX, being accompanied to the papal audience by S.E. Mgr. Nassalli Rocca di Corneliano, Maestro di Camera di Sua Santità. Courtesy: +B.B. Heim

Pius IX.

Courtesy: Felici, Pontificia Fotografia, Rome

Pius XII, who also prepared several reforms which were implemented by his successor.

Courtesy: Felici, Pontificia Fotografia, Rome

Order of Christ and the Order of the Golden Spur were from then on to be restricted to Christians. Paul VI on 15 April 1966 (*Equestres Ordines*) decreed that the Golden Pian Collar should be reserved exclusively for Sovereigns and Heads of State, and given on the occasion of official visits to the Sovereign Pontiff.

Among the recipients of the Golden Collar of the Order of Pius IX since the revision by Paul VI are the following Heads of State:

Artur Da Costa e Silva, President of Brazil (1966)
Gustav Adolf VI, King of Sweden (1967)
Olav V, King of Norway (1967)
Cevedet Sunay, President of Turkey (1967)
Hailé Sellasié, Emperor of Ethiopia (1970)
Urho Kekonen, President of Finland (1971)
Gustav Heinemann, President of the Federal Republic of Germany (1973)
Juan Carlos, King of Spain (1977)
Antonio Ramalho Eanes, President of Portugal (1980)

President Antonio Ramalho Eanes, President of Portugal, upon whom John Paul II conferred the Golden Collar of Pius IX in 1980.

Courtesy: Felici, Pontificia Fotografia, Rome

The Order of Pius IX has three other classes: Knights Grand Cross, Commanders with Star and Commanders, and Knights. It rates third among the Pontifical Orders of Knighthood and is granted also to non-Catholics for outstanding deeds performed for Church and society.

The Golden Collar of the Order consists of a gold ornamental chain to be worn round the neck, with a star to be pinned to the left side of the breast. The decoration for the other classes is a golden star with eight blue enameled rays and a white enamel medaillion in the centre bearing the words *ORDO PIANUS* and around it, in an inner white circle, the words *A PIO XII AUCTUS* (Enlarged by Pius XII). The older decorations have in the inner white circle the name *PIUS IX* and the motto *VIRTUTI ET MERITO* (for virtue and merit), which is repeated in the second, third and fourth class. The ribbon is dark blue silk, bordered with red stripes. The badge is a large silver star-shaped medal. The Order has its own uniform, consisting of a dark blue evening dress coat closed in front by one row of gilded buttons. The collar, cuffs and breast of the coat are covered with golden embroideries more or less elaborate, according to the grade or class of the wearer. Golden epaulettes, white trousers with gold side stripes, a bicornered hat with plumes and a knightly sword complete the official dress.

Manuscript dating from the 10th or 11th century depicting Pope St. Gregory the Great sending the first missionaries to England.

IV

THE ORDER OF ST. GREGORY THE GREAT

This Order was founded by Gregory XVI on 1 September 1831 (*Quod summis quibusque*) for the purpose of honouring loyal and well-deserving citizens of the Papal States. The Pontiff placed it under the patronage of the great Pope, whose name it bears. He established four classes for the Order, but these were reduced to three in 1834; he also established two divisions, civil and military, for its members. Pius X reformed the Order on 7 February 1905 so as to adapt it to the new circumstances of the Church and society.

Gregory XVI (Bartolomeo Alberto Cappellari) was born at Belluno (Italy), on 18 September 1765. He entered the Camaldolite Monastery of St. Michael at Murano in 1783. Ordained a priest in 1787, he became professor of philosophy and science in 1790, and abbot of St. Michael's Monastery in 1805. In 1814 he was called to Rome for the service of the Holy See. He was made a cardinal and prefect of the Sacred Congregation for the Propagation of the Faith in 1825. He was elected Pope in 1831. He fought strenuously for the defence of the religious and civil liberties of the Papacy, the Church and the faithful, which were being attacked and denied in many countries by insurgent liberalism, that kept gaining ground both in the political and theological spheres. He gave new impulse to the missions and to the propagation of the faith in general. Gregory XVI was throughout his pontificate confronted with grievous political problems in the Papal States. He died on 1 June 1846.

Pope St. Gregory the Great, whom Gregory XVI intended to honour by the institution of this new Order, was born in Rome about the year 540. After studying law and jurisprudence, he entered the public service and was appointed a prefect of the city of Rome. Feeling the call to the religious life, he surrendered wealth and power together with a brilliant civil career, and entered the Benedictine Monastery of St. Andrew on Clivus Scauri, where he was ordained a deacon. Pelagius II (579–590) sent him as his representative with the title of *aprocrisarius* to the Court of the Byzantine Emperor Tiberius II at Constantinople in 579, where he remained until 585, showing much diplomatic expertise. Having returned to his Roman monastery, Gregory became very active in the pastoral life. Elected Pope on 3 September 590, he emerged as a true pastor in the administration of the Universal Church and the diocese of Rome, the care of the poor, the love for the liturgy and the spreading and consolidating of the faith in Rome, Italy and and world then known. In

Gregory XVI.

Courtesy: Biblioteca Apostolica Vaticana

596 he sent St. Augustine from the Monastery of St. Andrew in Rome to preach the Gospel in England, where he founded the See of Canterbury, of which Augustine became the first archbishop. Gregory wrote many works on faith and morals and is one of the great Doctors of the Latin Church. He was the first to adopt the title of *Servus Servorum Dei* (the Servant of the Servants of God). He died in 604, a clear model of devotion to the duty of one's state.

The Order of St. Gregory the Great, intended to reward civil and military service, is now bestowed on persons who distinguish themselves for conspicuous virtue and notable accomplishment on behalf of the Church and society, regardless of their religious belief. It has civil and military divisions, and has retained its original three classes: Knights

Ceremonial uniform of a Knight Commander with Star of the Order of St. Gregory the Great.

Grand Cross, Commanders with Star and Commanders, Knights.

The Order of St. Gregory the Great takes fourth place among the Pontifical Orders of Knighthood.

The decoration of the Order is an eight-pointed cross, of red enamel, with a medallion bearing the image of St. Gregory the Great in the centre and the words *Pro Deo et Principe* on the reverse side, hanging from a red ribbon with orange borders. The cross of the civil division is surmounted by a crown of green oak leaves, while the cross of the military division carries a military trophy. The badge consists of the cross of the Order, surrounded with silver rays. The Order has its own uniform. It is a dress coat of dark green fabric, open in front and covered at the collar, on the breast and the back with embroideries of silver oak leaves more or less elaborate according to the grade or class of the wearer. The buttons are embossed with the emblem of the Order. White trousers with silver side stripes, a bicornered ornamental hat with a plume and a court sword complete the official dress.

Left: Rudolf Niedballa, engraver of the seals of four Popes and many dignitaries, wearing the insignia of a Knight Commander of the Order of St. Gregory the Great. Right: The Cross of a Knight Commander, Military Division, which hangs from a military trophy instead of the laurel wreath of the Civil Division.

V

THE ORDER OF POPE ST. SYLVESTER

This Order was instituted by Gregory XVI on 31 October 1841 (*Cum hominum mentes*). Though originally intended to absorb the Order of the Golden Spur, it actually remained adjoined to it. Pius X detached it from the latter and made it a distinct Order with the title of Pope St. Sylvester on 7 February 1905 (*Multum ad excitandos*).

St. Sylvester was born in Rome in the latter part of the third century. He was elected Pope in 314. He ruled the Church during the reign of the Emperor Constantine the Great (288–306–337). In 337 he baptised the Emperor, who, by the Edict of Milan (313) had freed the Church from persecution and legal discrimination and disabilities thus allowing her to spread rapidly throughout the Roman Empire. During Pope Sylvester's pontificate, the Church suffered from the spread of the Donatist schism and the Arian heresy. Arianism was eventually condemned by the Council of Nicaea in 325, when the divinity of Christ was also defined, thus setting a clear rule of faith for the Church of the future. Pope Sylvester is remembered for having established several liturgical and juridical institutions and he distinguished himself in drawing up the original form of the Nicene Creed and building places of worship, especially in Rome. He died in 335 and was buried in the cemetery of Priscilla on the Via Salaria.

The Order of St. Sylvester ranks fifth among the Pontifical Orders of Knighthood. It was especially created to reward laymen who are active in the apostolate in particular in the exercise of their professional duties and masters of the different arts. It is also conferred on well-deserving non-Catholics and it comprises three classes: Knights Grand Cross, Commanders with Stars and Commanders, Knights. The Order has only a civil division.

The emblem of the Order is an eight-pointed, white enamel cross, bearing the image of Pope Sylvester in the centre and surmounted by a papal tiara and the keys, hanging from a black silk ribbon with three narrow red stripes.

The Order has its own uniform which consists of a black tail-coat closed by one row of gilt buttons embossed with the emblem of the Order. The collar and cuffs are of black velvet, and the tail-coat is embroidered with gold laurel leaves more or less elaborate according to the grade or class of the wearer. The black trousers have gold stripes, and the bicornered hat of rough silk is adorned with a cockade in the papal colours. A court-sword with a mother-of-pearl hilt, ornamented with gold and the emblem of the Order and worn in a sheath suspended from a gilt belt with a sword knot completes the official dress.

Pope Sylvester entering the City of Rome after it was conquered in 312 by the Emperor Constantine, who gave freedom to the Christians by the Edict of Milan in 313.

Ceremonial uniform of a Knight Commander with Star of the Order of Pope St. Sylvester.

Leo XIII.

CHAPTER THREE

OTHER PAPAL AWARDS

Other papal awards, as distinct from Pontifical Orders of Knighthood, are also conferred as a reward for services rendered to the Church and society, especially in the direct exercise of the apostolate. These decorations are not normally awarded to members of the clergy, but only to practising Catholic laymen and laywomen. They may however be given to religious sisters and brothers, who like priests and bishops are never given a decoration pertaining to a Pontifical Order of Knighthood, whose members are exclusively laymen. The possibility of awarding Pontifical Orders of Knighthood also to women, with the title 'Dame' and the corresponding equestrian rank has been repeatedly under study, but a final decision has not yet been reached. Thus recourse is made to other marks of distinctions especially when decorations are requested for women. However, the Grand Cross of the Order of Pius IX was given to Her Excellency Miss Lombe Phyllis Chibesakunda when she left her post as Ambassador of Zambia to the Holy See in 1981. She thus became the first female recipient of a pontifical equestrian decoration.

Apart from Pontifical Orders of Knighthood, the main awards are THE GOLDEN ROSE, the Cross *PRO ECCLESIA ET PONTIFICE* (for Church and the Pontiff), and the Medal *BENEMERENTI* (for a well-deserving person).

Both these latter honours owe their permanent character to Leo XIII (1878–1903) who, though he came from a patrician family, showed far greater interest in this form of recognition based on personal merit than in that of Pontifical Knighthoods of a nobiliary character.

Leo XIII (Vincenzo Gioacchino Pecci) was born at Carpineto, Italy, on 2 March 1810. He was educated by the Jesuits at Viterbo and Rome. After winning his doctorate in theology, he entered the *Accademia dei Nobili Ecclesiastici* at Rome, where Church diplomats are trained, and he was ordained a priest on 31 December 1837. In 1841 he was appointed legate to Perugia, where he was soon recognised as a social and municipal reformer. Subsequently he was sent to Bologna and Spoleto in the same capacity. Consecrated a bishop on 17 February 1843, he was sent to Brussels as Apostolic Nuncio. There he was confronted with the raging education controversy and the dispute between the Jesuits and the Catholic University of Louvain. Before returning to Perugia as archbishop in 1864, he visited London, where he was introduced to Queen

Victoria by her uncle, King Leopold I of the Belgians (1831–1865) and was warmly received by the Queen at Buckingham Palace. He also visited Paris and other northern capitals. He became a cardinal on 19 December 1853. Spirituality, learning and social reform were the keynotes of his thirty-two years episcopate at Perugia. In 1877 he was named *Camerlengo* of the Holy Roman Church. Elected Pope on 20 February 1878, he set about at once to reform the papal household and to secure a better theological training of the clergy on the lines laid down by St. Thomas Aquinas, encouraging the rise of neo-thomism. He threw open the Vatican archives and library, established voluntary schools, wrote encyclicals of prime and lasting importance such as: *Aeterni Patris, Libertas, Rerum Novarum* and many others. Especially concerned about the return of the Anglicans to communion with Rome, he addressed a letter *Ad Anglos* on 14 April 1895, followed by an encyclical on the unity of the Church, *Satis Cognitum*, on 29 June 1896; he also appointed a commission to consider Anglican ordinations, the result of which was the publication of *Apostolicae Curae* (1896). The Scottish Diocesan Hierarchy was re-established under him. He showed great statesmanship in his determination to heal the breach between the Church and the modern States without any sacrifice of principle. His general policy with the Italian government was conciliatory, though he protested against the loss of temporal power and warned Italian Catholics to abstain from political activities until this was restored. He supported governments outside Italy wherever they represented social order, persuaded Chancellor von Bismarck to put an end to the German *Kulturkampf*, successfully arbitrated between Germany and Spain in a dispute over the Caroline Islands and condemned the Irish *Plan of Campaign* in 1888. In 1887 Pope Leo XIII exchanged diplomatic courtesies with Queen Victoria on her jubilee and again in the same year on the occasion of his own priestly jubilee. In 1903 he received King Edward VII at the Vatican.

He worked for the reunion of the Oriental Churches with Rome, endeavoured to secure better conditions of religious freedom for Catholics in Russia, China, Japan and Persia and he beatified Sir Thomas More, who was canonised by Pius XI in 1935.

Simple and frugal in his private life, he was most liberal and generous with others. He died on 20 July 1903, after leading the Church with exceptional ability for twenty-five years.

I

THE GOLDEN ROSE

The Golden Rose is a mark of distinction of the highest class which is now conferred by the Sovereign Pontiff on Catholic female Sovereigns as a sign of recognition for services rendered to the Catholic Church. It is in a way equivalent, as an honour for women, to the Supreme Order of Jesus Christ, which is reserved for male Sovereigns and Heads of State alone.

This distinction is also given to important shrines, especially those dedicated to the Blessed Virgin Mary.

In the past, the Golden Rose was bestowed as well on very eminent men, mostly of imperial, royal and princely rank, and also on important cities on the occasion of historical events having a special religious significance.

The origin of the blessing and sending of some such symbol is lost in history. The earliest verifiable reference we have is a document of Leo IX (1049–1054) dated 1049 regarding a commitment taken upon themselves by the nuns of the Holy Cross convent of Tulle in Alsace, to present a Golden Rose to the Pope every year as a token of gratitude for the exemption they had been granted from the jurisdiction of the local Ordinary. The Golden Rose is referred to in the relative document as something well known. The first historical instance of the conferring of the Golden Rose by the Pope is of 1096, when Urban II (1088–1099), passing through Angers during the preaching of the First Crusade, bestowed this distinction on the Count Fulco d'Angiò. Since the period of the Popes' stay at Avignon many instances of such a custom are recorded. The recipients were individual personages of both sexes, churches and cities.

Among male personages we find various Emperors on the occasion of their coronation in the church of Santa Maria in Cosmedin at Rome, several Kings of France, such as Louis VIII, Charles VI and VII, and other Kings and leaders. Thus Don Manuel, King of Portugal received the Rose for having paved the way to the propagation of the Faith in the Indies (1513); Alphonse, King of Naples and of Aragon, for his victory over the Turks (1451) and John of Austria, famous for his part in the Lepanto victory (1567). Last among men to receive the Golden Rose was the Doge of Venice, Francis Loredan, in 1759 from Clement VIII (1758–1769). From then on the Golden Rose was reserved exclusively for female personages.

Among the first Queens to receive the Golden Rose was Casimira of

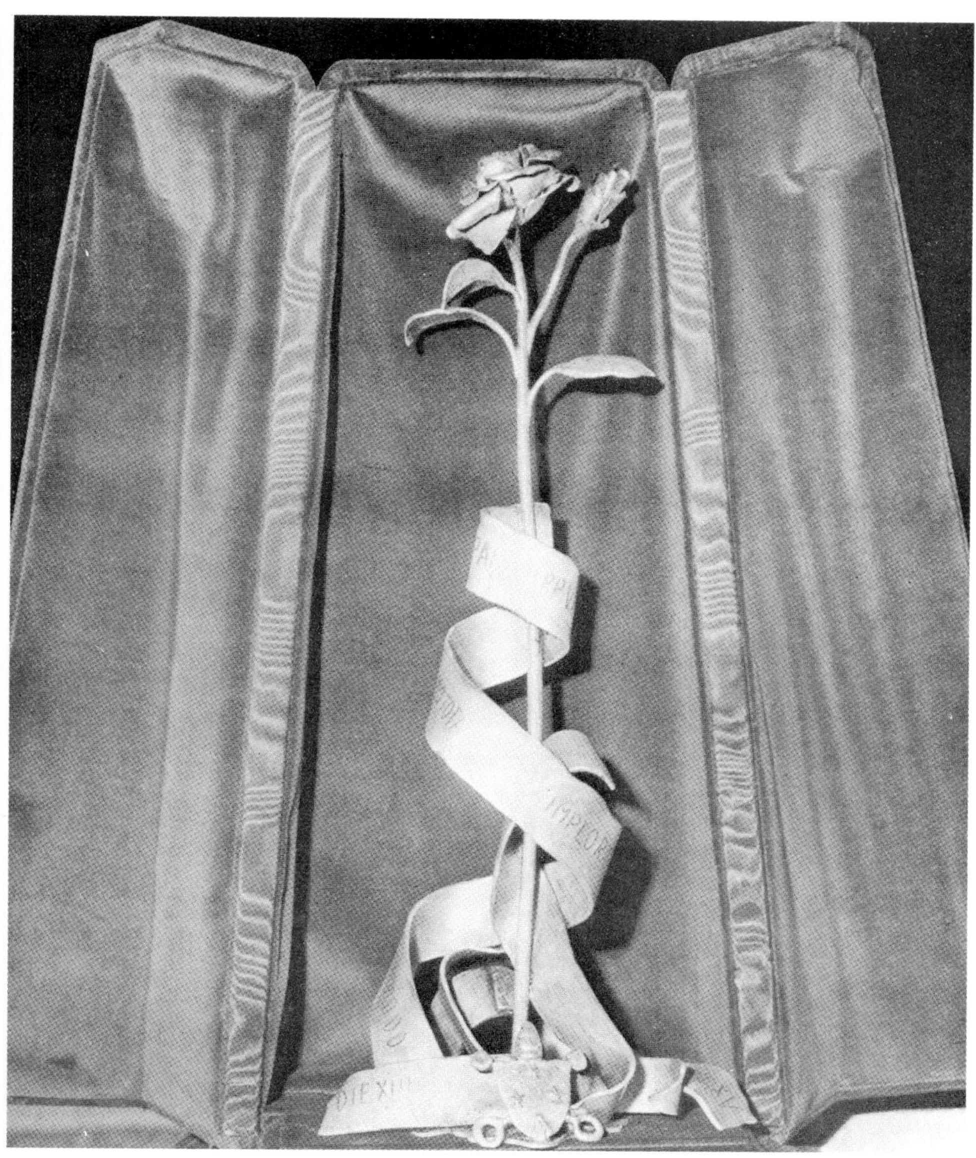

Opposite: A Golden Rose conferred by Pius XII. Above: The Golden Rose bestowed on the Shrine of Our Lady of Fatima by Paul VI. According to Innocent III (1198–1216), the Golden Rose is meant to express Christian love exhaling the fragrance of all virtues ("the odour of sanctity"). The Golden Rose was carried in procession, after its blessing by the Pope at the Lateran Basilica, to the nearby Basilica of the Holy Cross in Jerusalem, which had been built to hold the relics of the True Cross Empress Helena had brought back from the Holy Land.

Courtesy: Felici, Pontificia Fotografia, Rome

Poland (1684) for the Vienna victory. Other ladies were Queen Maria Theresa of Sardinia (1825); the Queens of Spain, Isabella II (1868) and Maria Christina (1886); the Empress Eugénie of France (1856) –[the Rose is preserved in the Farnborough Abbey, England]; Empress Elizabeth of Brazil (1888); Queen Amelia of Portugal (1892); Queen Marie Henriette of the Belgians (1893). Closer to our time are Queen Elizabeth of the Belgians (1925); Queen Victoria Eugenia of Spain (1925); Queen Elena di Savoia of Italy (1937), which was the fifth time that such a distinction was given to the Royal House of Savoy; and the Grand Duchess Charlotte of Luxembourg (1956).

The Golden Rose was also given to Maria Pia, Royal Princess of the Kingdom of Sardinia (1848) and Maria Grazia Pia, Royal Princess of the Kingdom of the Two Sicilies (1849) on the occasion of their baptism, at which Pope Pius IX acted as Godfather.

The most important churches and shrines which received the Golden Rose are the Basilica of St. Peter in Rome (five times); the Basilica of St. John Lateran in Rome (four times); the Basilica of St. Mary Major in Rome (twice); the Marian Shrines of Our Lady of Loreto; Santa Maria del Fiore at Florence; Our Lady of Lourdes; Our Lady of Fatima; Our Lady of Guadalupe, Mexico; Our Lady of Aparecida, Brazil; the Image of the Holy Infant, Bethlehem, and finally the Shrine of St. Francis Xavier in Goa.

Among the cities to which the Golden Rose was given are Venice, Bologna, Siena, Savona and Lucca.

The ornament itself has been of different forms. The design finally adopted by Sixtus IV (1471–1484) is a thorny branch with several leaves and flowers, the petals of which are decked with gems, usually sapphires. It is surmounted by a principal rose, containing a receptacle into which balsam and musk are poured. The ornament is made of solid gold.

The Golden Rose is blessed with great solemnity by the Sovereign Pontiff at the Vatican, usually on *Laetare* Sunday, the fourth Sunday in Lent, also known as 'Sunday of the Rose' and as 'Mothering Sunday' in England from the ancient custom of visiting the oldest church in a district or the cathedral, considered as the Mother Church of the diocese.

The presentation of the Golden Rose is performed with great pomp and ceremony. If the recipient is in Rome, it is customary for the Sovereign Pontiff himself to confer it in the Sistine Chapel. Otherwise, a Special Mission is entrusted with the presentation of the Rose and the accompanying Apostolic Brief announcing the bestowal and giving the reason for sending it and recounting the merits and virtues of the recipient.

At the conferment of the Golden Rose on Her Royal Highness Charlotte, the Grand Duchess of Luxembourg, in 1956, the Apostolic Nuncio to Luxembourg was named Head of the Mission, which included four prelates and four lay dignitaries. The presentation took place in the Cathedral of Luxembourg, in the presence of the members of the Grand-Ducal family, the members of the Government of Luxembourg and of the Diplomatic Corps accredited to the Grand Duchy. A Pontifical Mass was celebrated, followed by the formal presentation of the Golden Rose by the Apostolic Nuncio, who announced that the Sovereign Pontiff had deigned to accord a plenary indulgence, in the normal terms, to all those present at the ceremony. The Golden Rose was exposed at the Cathedral during the whole day.

Because of the world situation at the time, the custom of bestowing the Golden Rose was interrupted during the pontificates of Pius X and Benedict XV and resumed under Pius XI. One would expect the presentation ceremony to be much simplified if the Rose were once again conferred on a personage. It is quite normal that the presentation to a shrine should be entirely of a religious character, accompanied by a certain solemnity.

II

THE CROSS *PRO ECCLESIA ET PONTIFICE*

The Cross *Pro Ecclesia et Pontifice* (For the Church and the Pontiff), was instituted on 17 July 1888 (*Quod singulari Dei concessu*) to mark the golden priestly jubilee of Leo XIII. It was bestowed on those who had contributed in any significant way to the success of the jubilee celebrations and of the Vatican Exhibition organised on that occasion. It has continued to be awarded as a sign of the Pontiff's recognition of distinguished service to the Church and to the Papacy.

The form of the metal cross, which was originally stamped in gold, silver and bronze, and is today stamped only in gold (for very important presentations) or gilt plate (for normal presentations), and the images engraved on it have undergone some changes. It is now a Greek-shaped four-pointed cross, bearing in its centre the images of the Princes of the Apostles, Peter and Paul, and the words *Pro Ecclesia et Pontifice* and the name of the reigning Pontiff.

The Cross is suspended from a yellow and white ribbon and is worn on the left breast.

The Cross *Pro Ecclesia et Pontifice* (left) which was awarded in gold, silver and bronze since its institution in 1888 by Leo XIII, until Paul VI changed it to a simple gilt Greek-shaped cross, more in keeping with the Pope's liking for modern art forms.

The original Cross *Pro Ecclesia et Pontifice*, which was made a permanent distinction in October 1898, was a cross made octangular in form by *fleurs-de-lis* fixed in the angles of the cross in a special manner. The extremities of the cross were of a slightly *potence* form. In the centre of the cross was a small medal with an image of its founder, and encircling the image were the words *LEO XIII P.M. ANNO* X. On the reverse side were the papal emblems in the centre, and in the circle surrounding the emblems the motto *Pro Ecclesia et Pontifice*. On the obverse surface of the Cross were comets, which with the *fleurs-de-lis* formed the coat of arms of the Pecci family. The Cross was suspended from a deep red ribbon with delicate borders in the papal colours.

Paul VI.

Two special medals struck under Paul VI. Left: the Cross *Concilium Oecumenicum Vaticanum II* in bronze, pending from a ribbon in the papal colours, and right: the Medal in silver for meritorious services during the Holy Year 1975. Such medals are only given for a limited period of time and for a specific purpose. On occasion they take the place of the *Benemerenti* Medal.

III

THE *BENEMERENTI* MEDAL

A *Benemerenti* Medal was first awarded by Pius VI (1775–1799) and intended to recognise military merit. Other such medals have continued to be bestowed by subsequent Pontiffs on men and women distinguishing themselves for special service or accomplishment.

In 1831 under Gregory XVI, a special *Benemerenti* Medal was struck to reward those who had fought with military daring and courage in the

Left: The *Benemerenti* Medal in the traditional form was awarded since 1891 by successive pontiffs. Right: a modern design adopted by Paul VI towards the end of his pontificate, having used the traditional design for several years.

papal army at Ferrara, Bologna and Vienna. Pius IX also struck several medals of the kind to be conferred on soldiers who had remained loyal to the Papacy in those difficult years for the Papal States. Such were the Medal *Pro Petri Sede* (For the See of Peter), to honour the veterans of the Castelfidardo battle (1860), and the Medal *Fidei et Virtuti* (For Faith and Valour) to reward the veterans of the battle of Mentana (1867). Pius XI instituted two special *Benemerenti* Medals in 1925 in recognition of distinguished service to the Holy See on the occasion of the celebration of the Holy Year and of the opening of the Missionary Exhibition organised by the Vatican. A special *Benemerenti* Medal was struck as a means of rewarding the loyalty and faithful service of members of the Palatine Guard of Honour, under Paul VI. The same Pontiff ordered another medal

COLOUR PLATES

PLATE I — The insignia of the Supreme Order of Christ.

Courtesy: Secretariat of Stat

PLATE II — The insignia of the Order of the Golden Spur. This decoration wa worn pending from a silver-bordered red ribbon until 1932 whe the golden chain was substituted for the ribbon.

Courtesy: Secretariat of Stat

PLATE III — The Collar of the Order of Pius IX, instituted by Pius XII in 1957
The insignia of a Knight Grand Cross of the Order of Pius IX.
The insignia of a Knight Commander with Star of the Order of Piu IX.

Courtesy: Secretariat of Stat

PLATE IV — The insignia of the Order of St. Gregory the Great:
(From top left, clockwise) Knight Grand Cross with Star Miniature and Lapel Button; Knight Commander with Star Miniature and Lapel Button; Knight Commander, Miniatur (which has a golden tiara and crossed keys on the ribbon), an Lapel Button; Knight of the Order of St. Gregory, Miniature an Lapel Button.

Courtesy: Giovanni Johnso

PLATE V — The insignia of the Order of Pope St. Sylvester:
(From top left clockwise) Knight Grand Cross with Star Miniature and Lapel Button; Knight Commander with Star Miniature and Lapel Button; Knight Commander, Miniature an Lapel Button; Knight of the Order of Pope St. Sylvester, Miniatur and Lapel Button.

Courtesy: Giovanni Johnso

PLATE I

PLATE II

PLATE III

ORDO A PIO XII AVCTVS PIANVS
ANNO MCMLVII
ORDO A PIO XII AVCTVS PIANVS
VIRTVTI ET MERITO PIVS IX
ANNO MDCCCXLVII
VIRTVTI ET MERITO PIVS IX
VIRTVTI ET MERITO PIVS IX
VIRTVTI ET MERITO PIVS IX
ANNO MDCCCXLVII

PLATE IV

PLATE V

PLATE VI

PRO ECCLESIA ET PONTIFICE
PAULUS VI PP
PRO ECCLESIA ET PONTIFICE
IOANNES PAULUS II PP
CONCILIUM OECUMENICUM VATICANUM
PAULUS VI PONT MAX

PLATE VII

PLATE VIII

COLOUR PLATES

PLATE VI Top row: *The Cross Pro Ecclesia et Pontifice*; left: the Cross as it was instuted and awarded under successive Popes until Paul VI changed the cross and ribbon; centre: the cross as awarded by Paul VI; it bears a small shield of Paul VI's coat of arms; the papal colours of the ribbon are reversed, though not intentionally; right: the Cross bearing the armorial shield of John Paul II.
Bottom row: Medals to commemorate special occasions; left: the Medal *Concilium Oecumenicum Vaticanum II* in bronze, pending from a ribbon in the papal colours; right: The Medal *Anno Iubilaei Romae MCMLXXV* in silver, awarded for meritorious services during the Holy Year 1975.

PLATE VII The *Benemerenti* Medal as it was awarded since 1891 (Leo XIII) by successive Pontiffs. Left to right: the medals bearing the portraits of Pius XII, John XXIII and Paul VI.
Bottom row: The *Benemerenti* Medal as adopted during Paul VI's pontificate, and the medal bearing the arms of John Paul II.

PLATE VIII Top: The Golden Rose which was conferred in 1956 on H.R.H. Charlotte, Grand Duchess of Luxembourg, by Pius XII*.
Bottom: The Pontifical Medal struck by the Vatican to commemorate the pastoral visit of John Paul II to Great Britain in 1982. The obverse bears the portrait of the Pontiff and the date of his visit; on the reverse are the symbols of England, Scotland and Wales and the emblem of unity with the words *Ut Unum Sint*. This medal was awarded in connexion with the Holy Father's visit for meritorious services to individuals and corporations such as British Rail for organising the train services, British Leyland for building the special vehicles used by the Pope and his entourage and Police Authorities**.

*Photo: N. Manderscheit, courtesy: H.R.H. The Grand Duchess Charlotte of Luxembourg

**Courtesy: Colin P. Smythe

to be struck and to be awarded to those who had well deserved during the 1975 Holy Year celebrations.

All these medals were obviously of a temporary character and not intended to be awarded indefinitely. The *Benemerenti* Medal instituted by Pope Leo XIII in 1891 was meant to be of a permanent kind and has in fact been confirmed as such by the subsequent Pontiffs. Originally struck in bronze only, in 1912 Pius X had it also stamped in silver. It ranks second after the Cross *Pro Ecclesia et Pontifice* and it is bestowed upon Catholic men and women who have rendered minor but significant service to the Church and society. The *Benemerenti* Medal made permanent by Leo XIII retained practically the same form until Paul VI in the latter years of his pontificate decided to adapt it to his more modern artistic taste. At present it is made of gold plate and consists of a lozenge-shaped cross, bearing the figure of Our Lord in the centre, the papal tiara on the left and the reigning Pontiff's armorial shield on the right. On the reverse side are the words *Benemerenti*.

The Cross *Pro Ecclesia et Pontifice* and the Medal *Benemerenti* can be awarded to religious sisters and brothers for outstanding services. (Left to right): Sr. Adelbert (Bibi), M.M.M., Sr. Helena, M.M.M., and Sr. Adrienne Mary, O.S.U. were honoured by the Pope with the Cross *Pro Ecclesia et Pontifice* after his visit to Great Britain. Sister Bibi had already received the Medal *Benemerenti* in the reign of Paul VI.

Courtesy: Fr. Kieran Conry

The original *Benemerenti* Medal in bronze gilt bore the likeness of the reigning Pontiff surrounded by a crown of laurels, suspended from the papal emblems, the tiara and keys and hanging from a ribbon of the papal colours. On the reverse side, surrounded by a crown of laurels was the inscription *Benemerenti*.

IV

THE PONTIFICAL MEDAL

The Pontifical Medal is not a decoration, though it is often awarded as a sign of grateful recognition or of special esteem for the recipient. It is made in gold, in silver and in bronze by the Mint of the State of Italy, for the Holy See. The complete set of the Pontifical Medal in gold, silver and bronze, of the current year of the pontificate is usually presented by the Sovereign Pontiff as a gift to a visiting Sovereign or Head of State.

The form of the Pontifical Medal has been practically the same for several centuries, starting with Nicholas V (1447–1455). It is circular, of about one inch and a half diameter, or even larger, reaching three inches, occasionally, to mark very special events, with a symbol of the event on one side and the Pope's image, name and the date on the other. Pope Paul VI, who was an admirer of modern art, introduced several new forms which recall a combination of both ancient and contemporaneous styles.

Pontifical Medals are of great value, artistically, iconographically and historically speaking. Their collection represents the highlights of the history of the Church and of the Papacy.

Other medals are struck *Sede Vacante*, that is during the vacancy of the See of Peter, following the death of the Pontiff, such as the medal marking the interim, and the personal medal of the Cardinal *Camerlengo* of the Holy Roman Church, who together with the College of Cardinals, as first among peers, manages the current affairs of the Church until the newly elected Pope takes over.

Six of the Pontifical Medals struck during the pontificate of Paul VI, who introduced many new forms which recall both ancient and contemporaneous styles. For example, the medal reproduced bottom left (ANNO V) shows on the

everse the images of SS. Peter and Paul as they have always appeared on a Papal Bull. The medal reproduced bottom right (ANNO VII) recalls on the reverse the mportant encyclical letter of that year, *Humanae Vitae*.

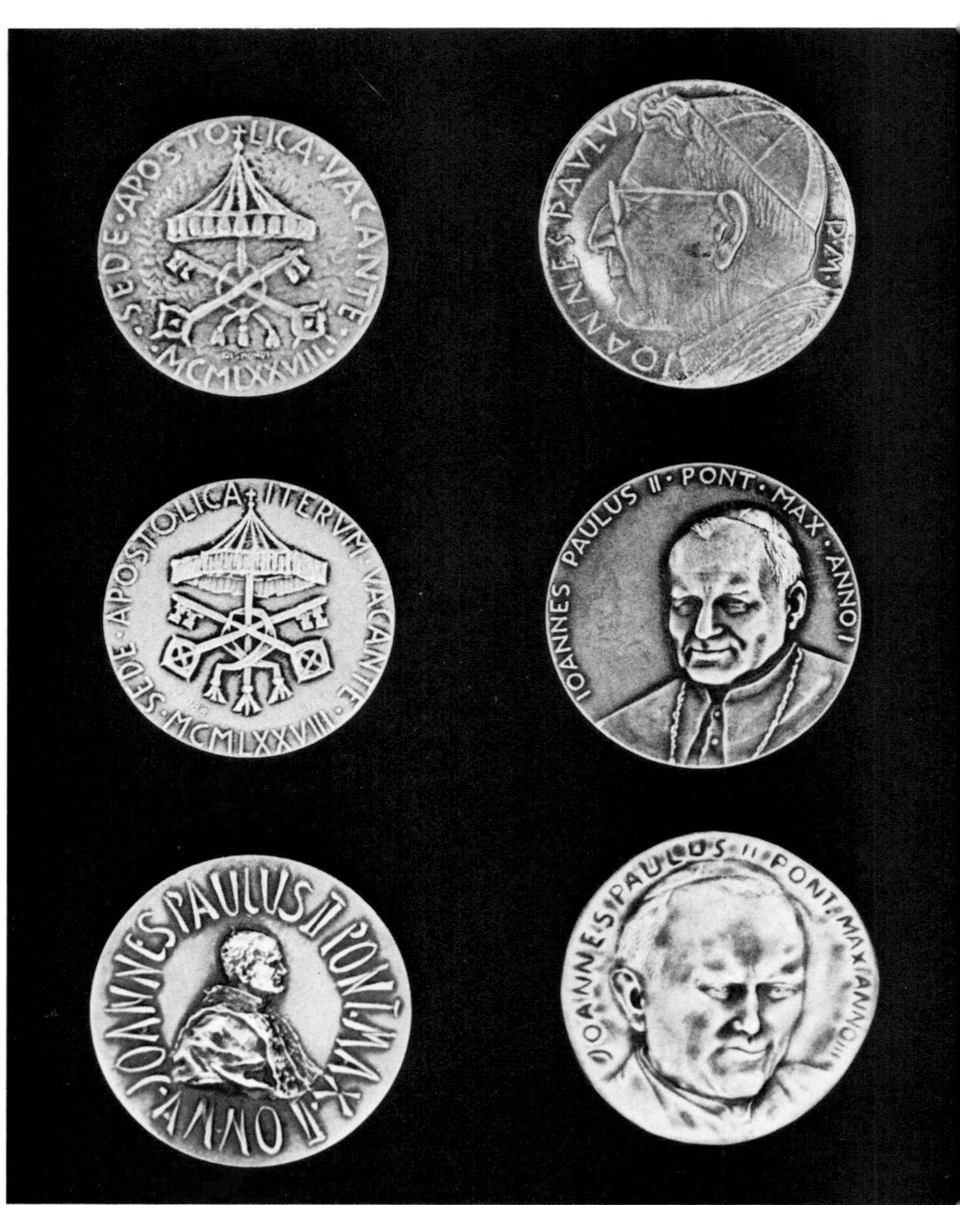

Above left: The Medal *Sede Vacante* struck after the death of Paul VI in 1978. Right: The Medal commemorating the short reign of John Paul I. Centre Left: The Medal *Sede Iterum Vacante*, struck after the death of John Paul I in 1978. Centre right and bottom row: the medals commemorating the first three years of the pontificate of John Paul II.

The Medals *Sede Vacante* and *Sede Iterum Vacante* were struck by order of the Camerlengo. Jean Cardinal Villot was Camerlengo on both occasions and the medals bear his coat of arms on the reverse. The Pontifical Medal ANNO I always bears the new Pontiff's arms.

The Prince and Grand Master, and the Sovereign Council of the Sovereign Military Order of Malta (S.M.O.M) in audience with John Paul II in 1981.
Courtesy: Felici, Pontificia Fotografia, Rome

King Edward VII of Great Britain during his visit to Malta in 1907, wearing the Cross of Honour and Devotion of the S.M.O.M. Courtesy: Kenneth Rose, London

His Most Eminent Highness Frà Angelo de Mojana di Cologna, Prince and Grand Master of the Sovereign Military Order of Malta.

Chapter Four

RELIGIOUS BUT NOT PONTIFICAL ORDERS OF KNIGHTHOOD RECOGNISED BY THE HOLY SEE

There are three Orders of Knighthood of ancient origin still in existence which are religious but not pontifical. In other words, they are inspired by the principles of the Gospel and profess the Catholic Faith in communion with and in submission to the Holy See, but have not been founded by the Papacy. They do, however, enjoy the official recognition of the Holy See from their earliest beginnings. They are now fraternal and charitable societies with the aim of manifesting the impact of the Christian Faith on society by uniting laymen and ecclesiastics in corporate religious and civic unity and usefulness. They once embodied the medieval conception of the ideal life, where service to Christ and to the less fortunate, honour, valour, courtesy, generosity and dexterity in arms were the summit of man's attainment. They now strive to foster those traditional ideals of chilvalry in the context of the present world.

Membership in these Orders, in different capacities and ranks, is open to ecclesiastics as well as laymen and laywomen.

These Orders are *THE SOVEREIGN MILITARY HOSPITALLER ORDER OF ST. JOHN OF JERUSALEM, OF RHODES AND OF MALTA*, often briefly referred to as the *ORDER OF MALTA*; *THE EQUESTRIAN ORDER OF THE HOLY SEPULCHRE OF JERUSALEM*, referred to simply as the *ORDER OF THE HOLY SEPULCHRE*; and, on a different plane, *THE TEUTONIC ORDER*.

I

THE SOVEREIGN MILITARY HOSPITALLER ORDER OF ST. JOHN OF JERUSALEM, OF RHODES AND OF MALTA

The Sovereign Military Hospitaller Order of St. John of Jerusalem, of Rhodes and of Malta, which for practical purposes we shall refer to simply as the Order of Malta, is the most ancient religious Order of Chivalry in Christendom.

It is an Order of Chivalry, composed of not only professed but also of secular knights and of other associates.

It is a religious Order, whose membership is made up of lay brothers and of chaplains, the aims of which are the glorification of God through the sanctification of its members, service to the Faith and to the Holy See, and welfare work in the whole world. As a religious Order, it follows the principles of the Gospel and of Canon Law, and the teachings of the *Magisterium* of the Church, which inspire its constitutional charter. Its professed members, its churches, chapels and conventual institutions are exempt from the jurisdiction of local Ordinaries and are placed under the authority of their own Prelate.

Furthermore, it is a sovereign entity, that is an international person, a subject of international law, and is governed in accordance with its own Code of Laws, approved by the Holy See. The Order's sovereignty, resulting from official recognition by the Holy See in the first place, but also by other subjects of international law, including numerous sovereign states, does not depend on territory, though the Order did once hold territory, as described in its official appellation, in sovereign possession. This sovereignty however is not to be taken in a plenary sense, in that in practice the Order does not exercise all the attributes of sovereignty in the present circumstances of its existence.

The religious and sovereign aspects of the Order are integrally related and connected. Thanks to its sovereign, and therefore supra-national character, it is able to pursue its religious and charitable mission on a world-wide scale. It dedicates itself especially to aiding the sick, among whom the victims of leprosy have pride of place, emigrants, refugees and exiles, abandoned children and the destitute, those stricken by natural disasters and war casualties, and ministers to the spiritual development of all these needy people as well.

Traditionally the Order is a nobiliary body, and one of the conditions for admission is nobility of sixteen quarterings. Today, thanks to the appointments of Knights of Magistral Grace, however, its membership is open in some measure to all well-deserving Catholics of a respectable position, especially in those countries where nobility no longer exists as an institution.

The uninterrupted history of the Order goes back to the First Crusade. It began in 1070 as a hospice-infirmary, *sacra domus hospitalis*, whence the word 'hospitaller' in the official title, for Amalfi pilgrims in Jerusalem. The construction of the hospital was authorised by the Fatimid Caliphs, masters of Palestine. Its founder and first head was the Blessed Gerard (+1120) who gave the hospice the name of St. John the Baptist. The rule of the confraternity in charge was a variant of that of St.

Augustine. In 1113 the new institution was approved by Paschal II (1099–1118) and placed under the protection of the Holy See. It also had the favour and approval of Christian rulers. In 1126 this religious confraternity assumed military-chivalric functions as well, with the aim of protecting the sick and the pilgrims, and of defending the Christian nations in the Levant and especially the Holy Places against Muslim attacks. Indeed, the chief strength of the Christian Kingdom of Jerusalem lay in the support it received from the Hospitallers and the Templars.

Rector Gerard was succeeded by Raymond de Puy in 1128. He was the first head of the Order to receive the title of Grand Master. He divided the Order into three classes: Knights, Chaplains and Serving Brothers and introduced the famous eight-pointed cross, so typical of the Order. He was succeeded by Auger de Balbens in 1169.

Following the Muslim conquest of all the Holy Land, the Order was compelled to leave Palestine. Subsequently it moved to Cyprus in 1291 and established its headquarters at Limasol, under the protection of the Lusignan Kings. In 1310 the Order acquired the island of Rhodes and was thus able to guarantee its independence from political rulers through the possession of territorial sovereignty. At Rhodes the Order became an international naval Power of no mean importance and took part in several Crusading campaigns for the defence of Christendom.

It was here that the formation of the *Langues* took place, that is the organisation of independent national branches headed by a Bailiff, to which the Knights were allotted and from which they could not transfer to another *language*. Expelled from Rhodes in 1522 by the assaults of the Muslims on the island and their final victory, the Order took up its residence in Malta which it had received in sovereign fief with Gozo and Comino, together with Tripoli (abandoned in 1551) from Emperor Charles V in 1530, with the approval of Clement VII (1523–1534). Thanks to its vigilant and militant presence in Malta, the Order halted the advance of Islam towards the heart of Christendom. In 1575 it built a very efficient hospital in Malta, consisting of eleven wards for five-hundred patients, with a School of Anatomy and Surgery, a School of Pharmacy and an illustrious medical team, which was a remarkable enterprise of world-wide renown, the first international hospital in history. Since 1581 the Grand Master wears a special crown. In 1607 the Grand Master was granted the title of "Prince of the Holy Roman Empire" by Emperor Rudolph II (1576–1612), whose successor, Ferdinand II (1619–1637), granted him the title of "Most Serene Highness", still used by the reigning Princes. In 1630, Urban VIII (1623–1644) accorded him a rank equal to that of a Cardinal of the Holy Roman Church and the style of "His Most Eminent Highness".

In 1798 Malta capitulated to the French invaders, lead by Napoleon Bonaparte, on their way to Egypt. The Order was thus compelled to surrender its territories, army, fleet and possessions, and to leave the island, which it eventually lost to the advantage of Great Britain, following the Treaty of Paris in 1814, though the Treaty of Amiens of 1802 had established that the island was to be restored to the Order. Since then the Order has been in exile, especially at St. Petersburg in Russia where it enjoyed the protection of Czars Paul and Alexander successively.

After facing innumerable vicissitudes, it finally retired to Rome, thanks to the welcome extended by Gregory XVI in 1834, and the Order established its headquarters there, where they continue to exist, with the good will of the Italian State. Though twice in immediate danger of collapsing, and even without territorial power, it has retained the title and status of sovereign in international law. This is to be understood in the sense that the Order is a subject of international law.

The international personality of the Order of Malta was upheld by the Italian Court of Cassation in a decision given in 1935. In 1959 the Office of the Legal Adviser of the U.S. Government asserted that ". . . the United States, on its part, does not recognise the Order as a State". It is obvious that he was confusing the concept of State and that of a subject of international law. The Order does not presume to be a State, but it is a full-fledged subject of international law, enjoying and exercising the pertinent prerogatives in all normality. This is recognised not only by the States entertaining diplomatic relations with the Order, but also by international organisations and agencies such as U.N.O., U.N.E.S.C.O., and the Council of Europe. "Sovereignty", as the Italian Court of Cassation put it, "is a complex notion, which international law, from the external standpoint, contemplates, so to speak, negatively, having only in view independence *vis-à-vis* other States. . . . It is impossible to deny to other international collective units a limited capacity of acting internationally within the ambit and the actual exercise of their own functions, with the resulting international juridical personality and capacity which is its necessary and natural corollary." (*cf.* Nanni and Others, v. Pace and the S.O. of M., Court of Cassation of Italy, Mar. 13, 1935 [1935–1937] Ann. Dig. 2, 4–6 [no.2]).

The position of the Order with regard to the Holy See is defined by the judgement of the Tribunal of Cardinals, instituted by Pius XII in 1951, which was promulgated on 24 January 1953. According to the Tribunal's decision,

> 1) the sovereign quality of the Order, repeatedly recognised by the Holy See, consists in the enjoyment of certain prerogatives inherent in the Order itself as a subject of international law. Said prerogatives are proper to sovereignty, in harmony with international law, and have been recognised by a number of States, following the example of the Holy See. They do not, however, constitute in the Order the ensemble of powers and prerogatives which belong to sovereign bodies in the full sense of the word; and
> 2) it is also a religious Order, approved by the Holy See, pursuing the sanctification of its members and other religious and charitable ends. (*cf. Acta Apostolicae Sedis, vol. XX, 1953, pp. 765–767*).

All this goes to show that the Order of Malta is indeed a unique subject of international law. It is, in fact, the second oldest in existence after the Holy See.

The Order now numbers almost ten-thousand members, located in five Grand Priories, three sub-Grand Priories, and thirty-seven National Associations, in Europe and in the Americas.

It may be useful to recall at this point that during the Reformation a Protestant group at Brandenburg – where a Bailiwick had existed from 1350 to the Reformation – constituted itself into a body resembling that of the Sovereign Order of Malta, and taking the name of St. John. This group was closely associated with the House of Hohenzollern, ruling over

Knight of Justice

Johanniterorden, Prussia

Knight of Honour

Brandenburg and later over Prussia. In 1812 King Frederick William III of Prussia, after suppressing the Protestant Bailiwick of Brandenburg, founded the Royal Prussian Order of St. John, which in 1852 was abolished by King Frederick William IV of Prussia, who created an Order of St. John along the lines of the ancient Bailiwick with Prince Karl as Grand Master. The Bailiwick of Brandenburg continues to exist with the same name or that of "Johanniterorden" with associations affiliated to it in Germany, Switzerland, Finland, Hungary and France. In 1920 a Swedish Order of St. John, with the King of Sweden as its Patron, came into existence, and in 1945 the Netherlands followed suit with an Order called "Johanniter".

In 1888 Queen Victoria (1837–1901) influenced by Prince Edward, granted a royal charter to the floundering British Priory of the Order, which had been founded in 1831 – the first after the abolition of the ancient Sovereign Military Order of Malta by Henry VIII (1509–1547), apart from a short revival under Queen Mary (1553–1558). In 1858 the British Priory had declared itself totally independent from the Sovereign Order, after failing to obtain affiliation with the same because of its interdenominational character. Thus patronised and legalised by the Crown, the Order was incorporated under the name of "The Most Venerable Order of the Hospital of the Order of St. John of Jerusalem in the British Realm", and has also received several privileges under the royal signature. The Order obtained its actual arms on 1 February 1926.

There also exists another "Sovereign Order of St. John of Jerusalem" which came into existence at the initiative of several hereditary Commanders of the Russian Orthodox Grand Priory of the Order of Malta,

The Venerable Order of St. John
Badge and Star of a
Knight of Justice

who had taken refuge in the United States of America following the Communist Revolution in Russia in 1917. This quite autonomous Order has set up Grand Priories in the United States, Europe (Malta, England), and the Pacific (Australia). This independent Order of St. John of Jerusalem, which also adds the style "sovereign" to its name, is neither patronised nor acknowledged by the Holy See.*

We draw special attention to the Holy See's announcement concerning the "Sovereign Order of St. John of Jerusalem" which was published in *L'Osservatore Romano* and is reproduced in Chapter Eleven which deals with autonomous and self-styled orders. None of these bodies enjoy sovereignty or the status of subject of international law.

Grand Cross of Honour and Devotion (SMOM)

Johanniterorden, Austria

Grand Cross of Professed Bailiff

Grand Cross of a Knight of Grace

In 1963 a joint statement was signed between the British Venerable Order of St. John and the Sovereign Military Order of Malta underlining the common purpose of charity towards the poor and the sick, and their intention to collaborate to promote God's glory and to alleviate the sufferings and miseries of mankind. It is in this same spirit that the other Protestant Orders of St. John in Europe collaborate with the ancient

* Under the heading "*MALFAITEURS EN MANTEAU ROUGE*" the monthly review HISTORIA Spécial 403bis, Paris, pp. 100–101, publishes a list of fourteen self-styled Orders of Malta throughout the Western world. Most of them were founded between 1960 and 1975.

Order wherever and however circumstances render this possible, thus making a valuable contribution to the promotion of both the causes of social welfare and ecumenism.

According to its constitutional charter of 24 June 1961, approved by John XXIII, the members of the Sovereign Military Hospitaller Order of Malta, who must belong to the Catholic Faith, are divided into the following classes: the Knights of Justice and the professed Conventual Chaplains; the Knights of Obedience and the Donats; lay members and Honorary Chaplains (*ad honorem*); Knights and Dames of Honour and Devotion; Magistral Chaplains; Knights and Dames of Magistral Grace; Donats of Devotion.

There is also an Order of Merit, with both a civil and military division, attached to the Order of Malta. It is destined for persons who have acquired special merit in the affairs of the Order. Its decorations are conferred on benefactors, independently of their origin, as a recognition of conspicuous works of charity. They are not accompanied by a profession of faith and they do not imply membership in the Order as such. The recipients must be persons of flawless integrity. If they do not belong to the Catholic Faith, it is up to the Sovereign Council to consider whether the conferring is appropriate.

The Order of Merit comprises three ranks: the Collar, consisting of one class, generally reserved for Heads of State; the Cross, with civil and military divisions (the latter with swords), consisting of five ranks: Grand Cross of Merit, Grand Officer, Commander, Officer and Cross of Merit. All have equivalent ranks for ladies. Furthermore, reserved for the clergy are the Grand Cross and the Cross *pro piis meritis*, for pious merit.

There is also a special Medal, divided into three ranks: gold, silver and bronze. Other Medals are struck to mark important historical events in

Ribbon to Grand Cross (SMOM)

Spanish *Langue* of the Sovereign Order

Original Badge of German *Langue*

The ceremony of Solemn Profession of Frà Andrew Bertie, who was the first Professed Knight of Justice of the Sovereign and Military Order of Malta in England since the Reformation.

Courtesy: S.M.O.M. British Association

H.E. the President of the British Association of the Sovereign Order, Viscount Monckton (centre right) in procession. Viscount Furness, Regent of the Sub-Priory of the Blessed Adrian Fortescue, (second from left) is also in the procession.

Courtesy: S.M.O.M. British Association

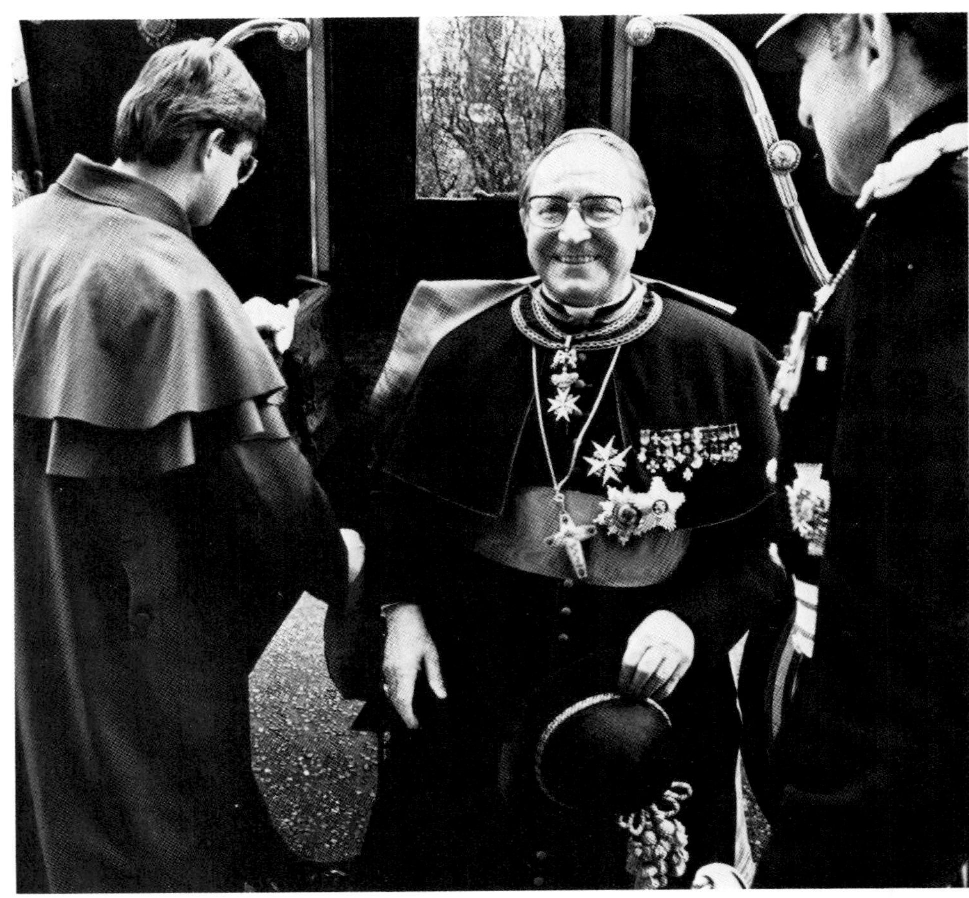

Archbishop B.B. Heim, first pro-Nuncio to the United Kingdom, returning from Buckingham Palace in March 1982 where he had presented his credentials to H.M. the Queen. Among his decorations he wears the Collar of a Knight Grand Cross of Magistral Grace, S.M.O.M., and below, above the other stars, the insignia of a sub-Prelate of the Venerable Order, the Protestant counterpart of the S.M.O.M. Courtesy: The Times, London.

which the Order was able to play a significant charitable rôle and are conferred upon benefactors.

The badge of the Order is an eight-pointed, white enameled cross, known as the Maltese Cross, with the extremity of each arm indented by two points. The arms are narrow where they meet and gradually expand. The symbol placed between the arms of the cross varies according to the *Langue* or national branch to which the recipient belongs. Most countries follow the Maltese pattern of having slightly differing versions of *fleurs-de-lis*, as one can note, for example, in the French, the Spanish and the British branches among others. The English *Langue* ranked sixth in the order of seniority when it was abolished by Henry VIII in 1534. Many of the five-hundred Knights belonging to the *Langue* at that time died on the scaffold, having refused to give up their Catholic faith.

When the formation of the *Langues* took place at Rhodes, all the Knights retained their original insignia, the white cross of eight points but in the centre of the cross those of the German *Langue* had a golden crown and a black eagle, whereas those of the French *Langue* had a golden *fleur-de-lis*.

Later the national differences became more prominent; the German *Langue*, for example, adopted a double-headed crowned eagle in gold instead of the *fleur-de-lis*.

The cross is surmounted by a crown, suspended from a shield with a Latin cross in the centre and a military trophy of flags and arms for Knights of Justice and Knights of Honour and Devotion, while Knights of Grace have a gold bow.

The star consists of an eight-pointed, white enameled Maltese Cross; the ribbon is of black watered silk, The badge and star for members of the Order of Merit are somewhat different in form and the ribbon is of crimson watered silk with two bordering white stripes.

The uniform of a Knight of Magistral Grace consists of a red cloth jacket, with cuffs, lapels and collar of black velvet, and closed in front by twelve buttons embossed with the Cross of the Order. The trousers are dark blue and long, with a golden braid and red stripes applied on the sides. The belt is embroidered with gold lace. The shoulders are fringed. A cocked hat and spurs complete the uniform.

A Knight Grand Cross of Magistral Grace has the same uniform, but with gold embroidered cuffs, lapels and collar.

A Knight of Honour and Devotion has the same uniform, except for the different motif embroidered on the facings of the cuffs, lapels and collar.

The mantle for all Knights is a long black cloak reaching below the knee, with silk lapels, velvet collar, and a golden chain fastening in the middle. The Cross of the Order is embroidered in red and white yarn on the left side.

The cowl is a sort of tunic of light woollen fabric, with white silk cuffs and the Cross of the Order embroidered in front.

The seat of the government of the Order is situated in Rome. Since the eighteenth century the Prince and Grand Master of the Order has been named by the reigning Pontiff.

II

THE EQUESTRIAN ORDER OF THE HOLY SEPULCHRE OF JERUSALEM

The origin of this Order, as we know it today, can be traced back to Godefroy de Bouillon, leader of the First Crusade, who captured Jerusalem from the Saracens in 1099. From its beginnings, the aim of the Order was the protection of the Holy Places and of the pilgrims who visited them.

The first period of the long and chequered history of the Order extends up to the loss of St. John of Acre in 1291 and coincides with the history of the Crusader Kingdom of Jerusalem. Godefroy de Bouillon founded the Order with a body of Crusader knights for the purpose of assisting the Chapter of Canons who watched over the Holy Sepulchre under the direction of a Guardian and the authority of the Patriarch of Jerusalem. As their emblem these knights adopted the coat of arms of the other Crusaders, but in red rather than gold. Their foundation finally received the approval of Callistus II (1119–1124) in 1122. The main aim of the knights was to defend the Church Universal, protect the city of Jerusalem, guard the Basilica of the Holy Sepulchre, look after the pilgrims and fight the Muslims. After incessant battles the knights were compelled to withdraw from Jerusalem completely in 1244 and to take refuge at St. John of Acre, until this fortress town also capitulated in 1291.

The second period of the Order's history goes from 1291 to 1847. During this time the Franciscan Custody of Mount Sion was established in Jerusalem and the Guardian, also known as the Custodian, was the sole authority representing the Holy See in the Holy Land (1333). The Guardian was authorised to dub the knights in the Basilica of the Holy Sepulchre. Meanwhile, the knights joined the many priories of the Order

(Opposite, top): The Grand Master, Grand Prior, Governor General and other members of the Grand Magistry of the Equestrian Order of the Holy Sepulchre in audience with John Paul II.
(centre): Members of the Grand Magistry and Lieutenants followed by hundreds of Knights and Dames of the Order enter St. Peter's in Rome during the Holy Year 1975. The procession wound across St. Peter's Square and down the Via della Conciliazione.
(bottom): The Members of the Grand Magistry and the Lieutenants inside St. Peter's. The occasion coincided with the Order's International General Assembly.

Courtesy: Felici, Pontificia Fotografia, Rome

in Europe, while the Franciscans remained in the Holy Land, displaying great faith and tenacious courage. After twice overcoming the threat of suppression by the Pontiffs, the Order, which had been provisionally united to that of the Knights of St. John and of Rhodes by Innocent VIII (1484–1492) in 1489, was re-established in its independent existence by Alexander VI (1492–1503) in 1496. This Pope also reserved for himself and for his successors the title of Grand Master of the Order, confirmed the Custodian's right of dubbing the knights, renewed the conditions required for the investiture. The Order's position and privileges were approved by subsequent Pontiffs. It would be impossible to describe the incredible vicissitudes the Order was exposed to, without, however, collapsing under the weight of the events.

The third period of the Order's history opens in 1847 and continues to our present day. Following a pact with the Sublime Porte, Pius IX reinstated the Latin Patriarchate of Jerusalem in 1847. The Patriarch once again became the 'ecclesiastical authority' of the Order with the title of Grand Master. He immediately helped the Order to expand throughout the whole world by authorising certain knights to dub other knights in whatever country they were, outside the Holy Sepulchre Basilica, regardless of their origin. In 1868 Pius IX instituted three classes of knights: Grand Cross, Commanders and simply Knights. In 1871 the first woman was received into the Order as a member in the person of the Countess Mary Frances Lomas. In 1888 Leo XIII formally approved the admission of women in the three classes, with grades equivalent to those of the knights.

In 1907 Pius X again reserved for the Pope the office of Grand Master to which he added that of 'Protector of the Order', but in 1928 Pius XI relinquished the Grand Mastership in favour of the Patriarch of Jerusalem. In 1931, at the request of the Holy See, the Order replaced the attributes '*Sacred*' and '*Military*' with '*Equestrian*'. In 1940, in view of the difficulties arising from the political situation, Pius XII entrusted the interests of the Order to Cardinal Canali as its Protector.

New constitutions were promulgated in 1949 which made the Order a legal person under canon law. The Cardinal Protector became Grand Master of the Order, with the power of governing it. In 1945 the seat of the Order was transferred from Jerusalem to Rome, in the Church and Monastery of S. Onofrio (St. Humphrey), on the Janiculum Hill, where the well known Italian poet Torquato Tasso (1544–1595), who composed his famous poem on the liberation of Jerusalem, is buried in the adjoining cloister. In 1962 John XXIII authorised the updating of the Order, con-

Jnder the new constitution promulgated in 1949, Pius XII appointed the Cardi-
ıal Protector of the Equestrian Order of the Holy Sepulchre of Jerusalem as its
Grand Master. Since then the Grand Master is always a cardinal named by the
overeign Pontiff.

Courtesy: Felici, Pontificia Fotografia, Rome

COLOUR PLATES

PLATE IX THE SOVEREIGN MILITARY ORDER OF MALTA

A: Sash of a Professed Bailiff
Grand Cross of a Professed Bailiff
Breast Cross of a Professed Bailiff
Breast Cross of a Knight of Justice
Breast Cross of a Knight of Obedience
Breast Cross of a Donat of Justice
Cross of a Conventual Chaplain
Rosette for Bailiff and Knight Grand Cross of Obedience

B: Sash of a Knight of Honour and Devotion
Grand Cross of a Knight of Honour and Devotion
Cross of a Knight of Honour and Devotion
Cross of a Knight of Grace and Devotion

C: Sash of a Knight Grand Cross of Grace and Devotion
Grand Cross of a Knight of Grace and Devotion

D: Sash of a Knight Grand Cross of Magistral Grace
Grand Cross of a Knight of Magistral Grace
Cross of a Conventual Chaplain '*ad honorem*' and a Knight of Magistral Grace
Cross of a Donat of Devotion 1st class and a Donat of Justice
Cross of a Chaplain of Magistral Grace
Cross of a Donat of Devotion 2nd class
Cross of a Donat of Devotion 3rd class

PLATE IX

A B

C D

PLATE X

A B

C D

PLATE XI

A

B

C

D

PLATE XII

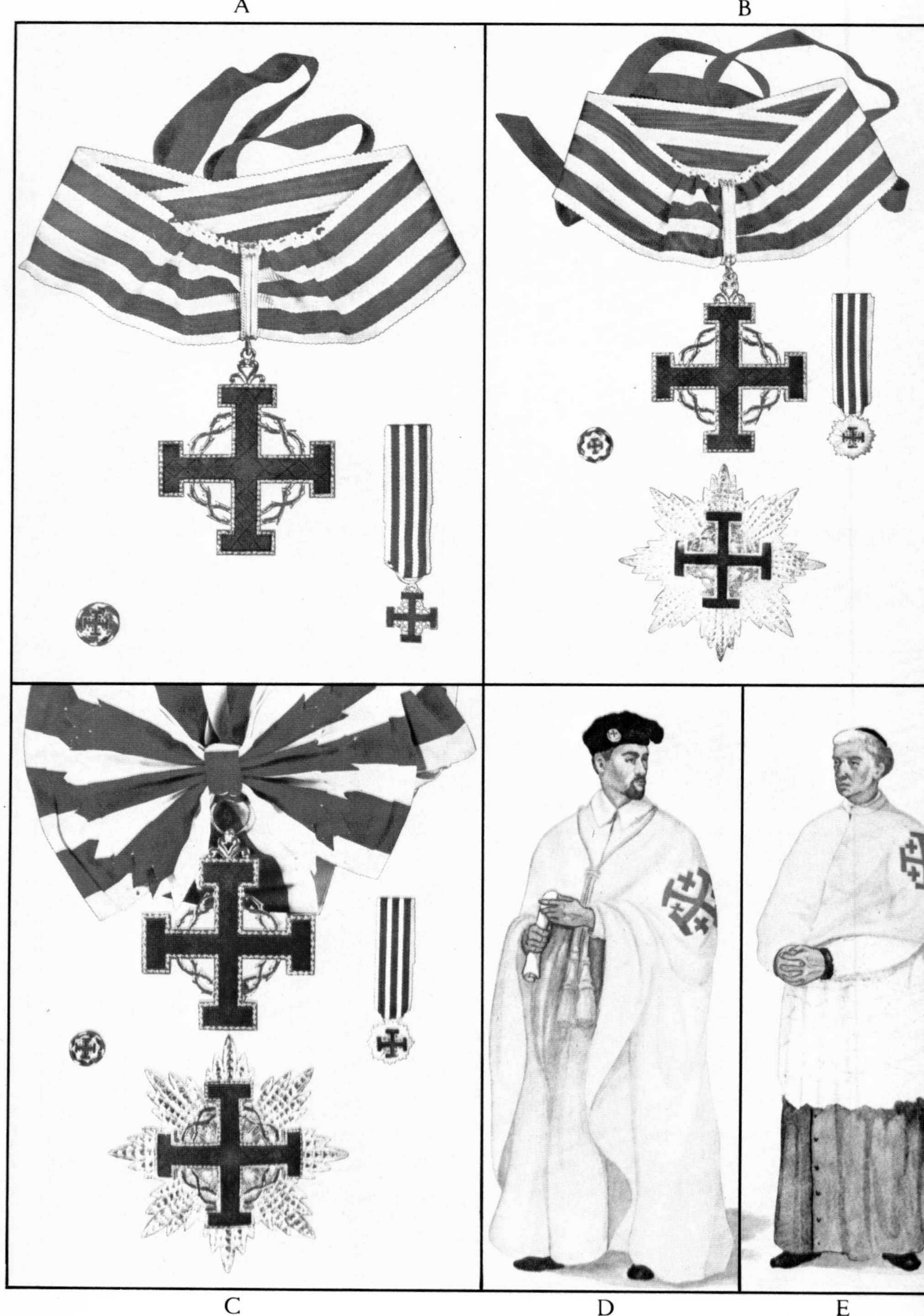

A B C D E

COLOUR PLATES

PLATE X ORDERS OF MERIT OF THE SOVEREIGN MILITARY ORDER OF MALTA

A: Gold Chain and Star for Heads of State

ORDERS OF MERIT FOR GENTLEMAN

CIVIL CLASS

B: Sash of Special Class of Grand Cross and to Grand Cross of Merit
Star of Special Class of Grand Cross of Merit
Star of Cross of Grand Officer
Star of Grand Cross of Merit
Cross of Officer
Cross of Commander
Cross of Merit

MILITARY CLASS

C: Sash of Grand Cross of Merit
Star of Grand Cross of Merit
Cross of Grand Officer and of Commander
Star of Grand Officer
Cross of Officer
Cross of Merit

D: ORDER OF MERIT FOR LADIES

Sash of Grand Cross of Merit
Star of Grand Cross of Merit
Star of Cross of Merit
Cross of Merit with Crown
Cross of Merit with Shield
Cross of Merit

Plates IX and X reproduced courtesy: H. Kirchner and G. v. Truszczynski, Malteser Hilfsdienst e.V.Köln

COLOUR PLATES

PLATE XI THE ORDER OF THE HOLY SEPULCHRE OF JERUSALEM

A: Collar and Star of a Knight or Dame of the Collar
The Palms of the Order
The Pilgrim's Shell

B: Insignia of a Knight of the Order
Insignia of a Dame of the Order
Cross of a Knight Commander and of a Grand Officer
Star of a Grand Officer, of a Dame Grand Cross and of a Dame Commander with Star
Cross pending from a riband tied in a bow of a Dame Commander of the Order
Star of a Knight Grand Cross
Sash and insignia of a Knight Grand Cross
Sash and insignia of a Dame Grand Cross

C: Insignia of rank worn by Knight on the ceremonial hat
Badge of a Knight
Badge of a Knight Commander
Badge of a Knight Commander with Star (Grand Officer)
Badge of a Knight Grand Cross
Badge of a Knight of the Collar

D: Ceremonial dress of a Dame and a Knight of the Order or the Holy Sepulchre of Jerusalem

PLATE XII ORDERS OF MERIT OF THE ORDER OF THE HOLY SEPULCHRE OF JERUSALEM

A: Cross of Merit, Miniature and Lapel Button
B: Cross of Merit with Silver Star, Miniature and Lapel Button
C: Grand Cross of Merit with Gold Star, Miniature and Lapel Button
D: Ceremonial Dress of a Dignitary of the Order of the Holy Sepulchre of Jerusalem
E: Prelate wearing the Mozzetta of the Order of the Holy Sepulchre of Jerusalem

Plates XI and XII reproduced courtesy: D. Jenkins, Esq., K.C.S.G., Member of the Grand Magistry of the Order of the Holy Sepulchre of Jerusalem

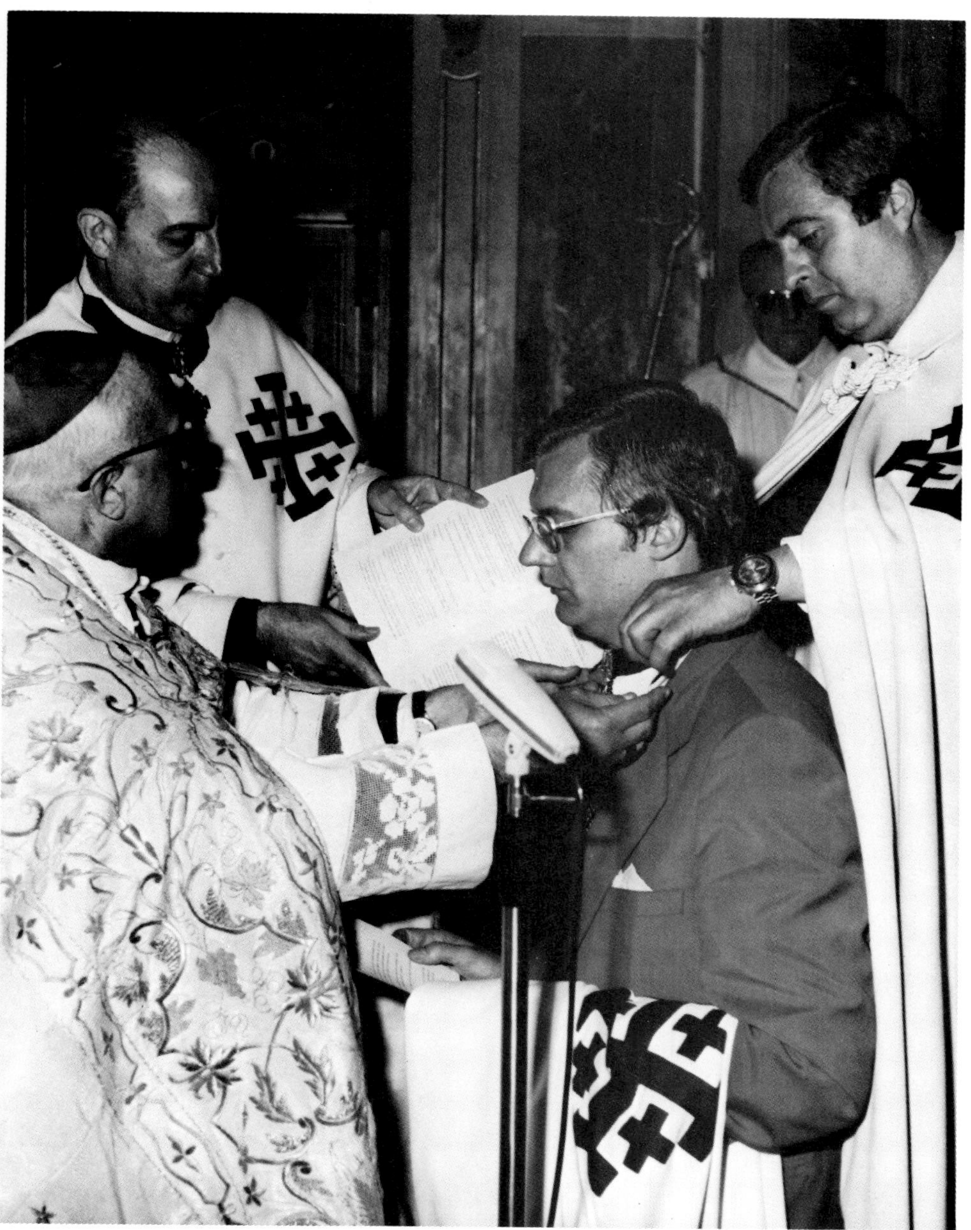

The induction ceremony of a Knight into the Order of the Holy Sepulchre. S.E. Mgr. Liverzani, Grand Prior of the Lieutenancy of Italy, presides over the ceremony.

His Eminence Maximilien Cardinal de Fürstenberg, Grand Master of the Equestrian Order of the Holy Sepulchre of Jerusalem.

Courtesy: Lieutenancy of Central Italy

(Opposite): Douglas Jenkins, Esq., K.C.S.G., G.C.H.S., for many years Lieutenant of the Order for England and now Lieutenant of Honour and Member of the Grand Magistry of the Order.

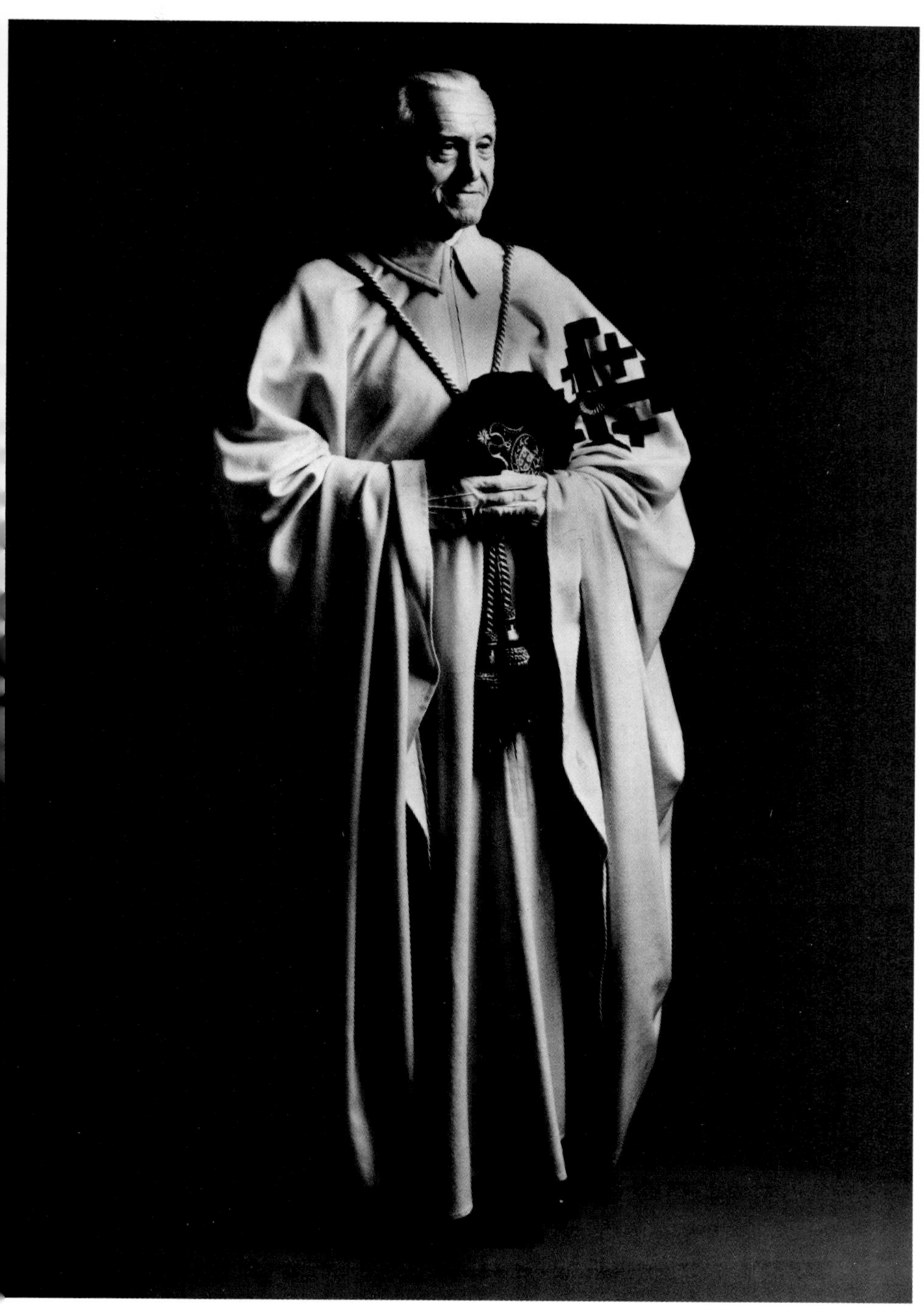

firming that it had its headquarters in the Vatican City and enjoyed th protection of the Holy See, as had been already decided by Pius XII. I 1977 Paul VI finally approved the constitutions in their final edition. Th Order sets for itself the aim "to revive in modern form the spirit and ideal of the Crusaders with the weapons of faith, the apostolate and Christia charity", close collaboration with the Hierarchy and the Latin Patriarc of Jerusalem in particular, especially on behalf of the schools and charit able institutions of the Holy Land. The objects of the Order are clearl spelled out in the constitutions. They are:

1. the practice of the Christian life in filial love towards th Papacy and the Church;
2. the conservation and propagation of the Faith in the Hol Land;
3. the protection and upholding in the Holy Places of th sacred, indefeasible rights of the Catholic Church.

There are more than ten-thousand Knights in the differen Lieutenacies and Delegations scattered in many countries of the old an the new world.

S.E. le général de Chizelle, Lieutenant of the Order for France in audience wit John Paul II in 1981.

Courtesy: Felici, Pontificia Fotografia, Rom

His Beatitude Mgr. Giacomo Giuseppe Beltritti, Patriarch of Jerusalem, Grand Prior of the Equestrian Order of the Holy Sepulchre.

The Order now comprises five classes: Knights of the Collar, a rank established by Pius XII in 1949, and of whom there are twelve in number Knights Grand Cross; Commanders with Star, who are also called Grand Officers, an honour given for "special merit"; Commanders; simply Knights. All these classes are also given to women in separate divisions Dame of the Collar; Dame Grand Cross; Dame Commander with Star Dame Commander and Dame. Some countries prefer the title Lady to Dame. Only Catholics can be members of these classes, since the apposite investiture ceremonies include a profession of faith and a pledge of exemplary Christian life and loyalty to the Papacy. The members do not take vows, and this is the reason that the Order of the Holy Sepulchre does not fall under the competence of the Sacred Congregation for the Religious.

The Order has also a Cross of Merit which may be conferred on non Catholics who have helped the various works. It has five ranks: Knigh

The Lieutenancy of Switzerland has been one of the most active in various spheres since its foundation in 1947. It owes its foundation to Mgr. Albert Oesch and Count Galeazzi, Personal Counsellor to Pius XII. Above, Herr Dr. H. Schnyder von Wartensee von Segesser, and his wife Hilda. He became the first Regent and later Lieutenant for Switzerland.

Captain Louis de Wohl, who served during the Second World War as Head of the Department for psychologica warfare in the British Intelligence Corps, and a well known literary figure, was a Grand Officer of the Orde in the Swiss Lieutenancy. The Lieutenancy counts among its members several influential industrialists, bankers and economists.

Painting: C.T. von Blaa

Mme. Ruth M.M. de Wohl is inducted into the Order and during the religious ceremony pledges her allegiance before the Bishop.

As Dame Commander of the Order Mme. de Wohl joined Mme. Hilda von Schnyder von Wartensee, Dame Commander with Star, in presenting a new candidate to the Bishop.

Grand Collar; Knight Grand Cross; Commander with Star; Commander; and Knight. The Order of Merit is also conferred on women who are titled "Dames" plus the respective rank.

The emblem of the Order from the very outset has been that of the Crusaders and of the Kings of Jerusalem. It is in reality of a much more ancient origin: in the year 800 Charlemagne received the emblem of Jerusalem, sent to him by Patriarch Thomas of Jerusalem. It consists of five red and gold crosses, with a Gallow Cross in the centre, inset at the intersections with four small Greek Crosses, representing the five wounds of Our Lord, all surmounted by a Crown. It is worn as a badge on the left breast and also appears on the white cloak. As a decoration it pends from a military trophy, attached to a black watered silk ribbon.

The religious men and women of the Priories of the Holy Sepulchre, associated with the history of the Order, adopted the Patriarchal Cross, known also as the Cross of Lorraine, as their insignia, because of its more direct religious connotation and reference to the Patriarchate of Jerusalem.

The uniform is a white dress coat with collar, cuffs and breast facings of black velvet with gold embroideries, epaulettes of twisted gold cord, white trousers with gold side stripes, a sword and a plumed hat. Pius X added to the uniform a large white woollen mantle with a red Jerusalem Cross on the left breast.

The Dames wear the emblems of their rank always on the left side of the breast. They have a long cloak of black cloth with facings of black silk and the Cross of the Order on the left side in red fabric, outlined in gold.

The Holy Land Pilgrim's Cross which, as we shall see further on, is granted by the Father Custodian of the Holy Land to pilgrims to the Holy Places, is not an equestrian decoration but a symbolic testimonial, remembering the hardships endured by the faithful over the centuries to protect and to visit the Holy Places.

The Order is recognised in Italy and some other countries by governmental decree; however, it is not a subject of public international law, such as the Order of Malta, though it has a place among the persons of public law enjoying international recognition.

The motto of the Order is the battle cry given by Urban II (1088–1099) to the first Crusaders: *Deus lo vult* (God wills it).

The legal seat of the Order is situated in the Vatican City State and the Order has also offices in Rome. The Grand Master is a Cardinal and he is named by the Sovereign Pontiff.

The origins of the castle of Alden Biesen in Belgium go back to 1220 when the Teutonic Knights set up a hostel there along the great east-west connexion from Cologne to Flanders via Brabant. Alden Biesen became soon the Landcommandery of the Netherlands, recognised in a Papal Bull of 1227 by Gregory IX. The castle ceased to be the property of the Order after the annexation of the area by Napoleon in 1797, resulting in the discontinuance of the Order in the French Empire in 1809.

Courtesy: H. Vandekackhove & J. Jans

III

THE TEUTONIC ORDER

or

THE TEUTONIC KNIGHTS OF ST. MARY'S HOSPITAL AT JERUSALEM

The Teutonic Order, or the Teutonic Knights of St. Mary's Hospital at Jerusalem, is one of the three great military and religious Orders which were founded in the Holy Land at the time of the Crusades. Its beginnings go back to the third Crusade when in 1190 certain pious merchants from Bremen and Lübeck laid the foundations of a hospital in a vessel which they had drawn ashore during the siege of Acre, attended by privations and plague. The foundation was shortly after attached to the German Church of St. Mary at Jerusalem and in 1198 the brethren of the hospital company were raised to the rank of an Order of Knighthood. Being thus ennobled, membership in the Order was henceforth reserved only for German subjects of noble birth.

The Order subsequently developed into a military body and eventually ended up as a sort of chartered society with territorial possessions on the eastern frontier of Europe, having lost every connexion with the Holy Land. It thus began to exercise sovereign rights on the troubled confines of Christendom without however entirely giving up its original charitable purpose. The Teutonic State in the Baltic was to become the historical claim to sovereignty by Prussia. In 1234 it became independent of all

Grand Cross and Star of the Grand Master

authorities except the Papacy, because of its religious character. It then surrendered its territories to the Holy See, which restored them to the Order as a fief with the privileges of the Crusaders for its members. The character of the Order was fundamentally changed by the accession of many territories and the statutes were adapted to the new conditions. The Order prospered during the fourteenth and fifteenth centuries, thanks to its concord with the towns and the Hanse. Its decline began when this was broken. The French Revolution deprived the Order of all its estates and, indeed, of its very existence in 1809. At Utrecht the Knights joined the Dutch Reformed Church branch of the Order which had been founded at the time of the Reformation. Eventually suppressed in 1840, the Order was resuscitated in Austria as a semi-religious Order of Knighthood by Archdukes Francis I in 1834 and Ferdinand I in 1840. It remained closely connected with the Dynasty of Habsburg until 1918.. Archduke Eugene maintained its Grand Mastership until 1923, when it passed to the Bishop of Brno, Dr. Norbert Klein. Because it was also a Religious Order, it survived the Act of Suppression of all the other Orders of Chivalry in Austria after the First World War.

The question may be asked why the Teutonic Order has not retained its international personality, such as the Order of Malta. This was because it lost its lands before the modern system of international law really developed; because it was never truly cosmopolitan being confined to the

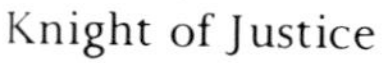

Knight of Justice

Knight of Honour

Cross of Chaplains

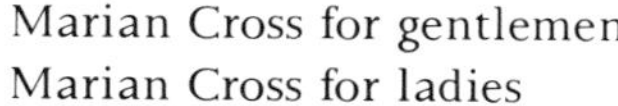

Marian Cross for gentlemen
Marian Cross for ladies

Teutonic race; and because the Reformation, with its antagonism to non-territorial sovereignty, dealt it a blow from which it has never recovered [*cf.* Farran, *The Sovereign Order of Malta: a Supplementary Note, 4 International and Comparative Law Questions* (1955) 308–309].

The Order is composed of male and female religious, but it now has professed and honorary members as well. It is under the protection of the Holy See which recognised its new Statutes on 22 September 1965. The monastic character of the Order was established by a Decree of the Sacred Congregation of the Religious on 27 November 1929. Because of its ancient chivalric traditions, the Supreme Master was authorised to maintain the faculty of conferring the dignity of knight and the title of Knight of Honour and Dame of Honour on those who have acquired very special credit in respect of the Church and especially of the Order. He may also confer the Marian Cross on meritorious men and women who become *Familiars* of the Order. Nobility is no longer required for membership.

The decoration for the Knights and Dames of Honour consists of a black enamel cross with gold edgings, pending from a black watered-silk ribbon, worn around the neck. The same cross is worn on the white cloak. The *Familiars* have a similar cross, surmounted by a small shield with another cross in the centre attached to a ribbon with vertical white and black stripes. The cloak is black.

The investiture ceremony is performed during a religious service. The insignia are used only at religious ceremonies of the Order or when the recipients join in a procession as a group.

The seat of the Order is in Vienna, Austria, with a Procurator General in Rome. The Order comes under the jurisdiction of the Sacred Congregation for the Religious.

H.R.H. Archduke Eugen of Austria, who resigned as High Master of the Teutonic Order in 1923 rather than allow malicious rumours to damage the Order. Hostile elements towards the Teutonic Order had spread, without any justification, the rumour that the property of the Order belonged to the Royal House of Habsburg.

CHAPTER FIVE

RELIGIOUS BUT NOT PONTIFICAL AWARDS RECOGNISED BY THE HOLY SEE

There are several marks of distinction which were instituted by the Papacy but are not conferred by the Holy See, their bestowal having been delegated to certain agents. These marks of distinction cannot therefore be qualified as pontifical.

The most important of these awards are the Lateran Cross, the Lauretan Cross and the Holy Land Pilgrim's Cross.

I

THE LATERAN CROSS

The Lateran Cross was instituted by Leo XIII on 18 February 1903. The original intention was to award it to benefactors who had contributed to the repairs of the roof of the Archbasilica of St. John Lateran. It was later given as a mark of gratitude to the faithful of both sexes who had rendered services to the Holy See and especially to the Archbasilica, and to its Chapter, to which the bestowal of the Cross was entrusted. In recent years it has practically fallen into desuetude, especially since the lavishness with which it was being conferred provoked several warnings of the Secretariat of State of His Holiness. *L'Osservatore Romano* of 30 December 1954 stated that it cannot be considered as a pontifical award.

The badge, worn on the left breast, consists of a bezant cross, with the images of St. John the Baptist, St. John the Apostle, SS. Peter and Paul on the extremity of the arms and the image of the Redeemer in the centre. On the reverse of the badge are the words *Sacrosancta Lateranensis Ecclesia, omnium Urbis et Orbis Ecclesiarum Mater et Caput* (Most Holy Lateran Church, Mother and Head of all the Churches in Rome and in the World). The Lateran Cross has three classes: gold, silver and bronze. It hangs from a red ribbon with two bordering blue stripes.

II

THE LAURETAN CROSS

Though devised by Paul III in 1547, it was Sixtus VI who, as we have already explained, actually instituted the Order of the Knights of Loreto in 1586 to defend the Holy House of Loreto and the pilgrims visiting the shrine.

The Order was short-lived. On the occasion of the third centenary of its foundation on 26 November 1888, Leo XIII created the Lauretan Cross in its memory and authorised the bishop (now prelate) of Loreto to bestow the Cross on the benefactors of the Holy House. The right of bestowal was subsequently transferred to the Father Guardian of the Holy House and Rector of the Universal Congregation of the Holy House in 1906. The Cross ceased to be conferred in recent times.

The Lauretan Cross, comprising three classes, was founded to reward both men and women for their benefactions and was enriched with many spiritual favours, the only award ever to enjoy such a prerogative, which was however granted to certain ancient Orders of Chivalry.

The badge is a copy of the medal of the ancient Knights, inset in an eight-pointed blue enamel cross with the words in gold *Benemerentibus quibus cordi est decor Domus Lauretanae* (to those who have well-deserved having at heart the beauty of the House of Loreto). It is worn on the left breast, suspended from a white ribbon with seven stripes, red-yellow-red-blue-red-yellow-red.

III

THE HOLY LAND PILGRIM'S CROSS

The Holy Land Pilgrim's Cross was established by Leo XIII in 1901 to encourage pilgrimages to the Holy Land and as a symbolic testimonial of the pilgrimage. The Pope entrusted the bestowal of the Cross to the Father Custodian of the Holy Land, as a remembrance of the important rôle he once played in the Order of the Holy Sepulchre.

Originally a natural or metal shell, then a silver or bronze palm were given to the pilgrims as a souvenir. Emblematically the shell was a symbol of a pilgrim since it was used as a glass and a plate on a pilgrimage. The Palm was a symbol of Christian triumph and victory. Since the sixteenth century it is a Jerusalem Cross made of metal. Leo XIII retained the latter form in instituting the award. It has the image of the Pope in its centre and the words *LEO XIII P.M. creavit AN. MCM* (Established by Leo XIII Sovereign Pontiff in the year 1900). On the reverse side are the words *Signum Sacri Itineris Hierosol* (Souvenir of the holy pilgrimage to Jerusalem). On the arms of the Cross are the words *Amor – Crucifixi – Traxit – Nos* (the love of the crucified Lord has attracted us). The Holy Land Pilgrim's Cross is awarded in gold, silver and bronze and is given with a special diploma.

CHAPTER SIX

THE PROCEDURE FOR ADMISSION TO THE ORDERS OF KNIGHTHOOD

Admission to the Pontifical Orders of Knighthood is not the result of application but of presentation. In other words, one does not apply directly to be admitted into one of these Orders, but is presented, or sponsored for admission by a responsible authority, unless the conferring is made directly by the Sovereign Pontiff, at his own initiative and by his own choice and will (*motu proprio*), as is the case for the Supreme Order of Christ, and for the Order of the Golden Spur, and may be the case also for other Orders of Knighthood.

The Orders of Pius IX, of St. Gregory the Great and of Pope St. Sylvester, as well as the Cross *Pro Ecclesia et Pontifice* and the *Benemerenti* Medal are granted by request of the bishop of the diocese of the candidate, addressed to the Secretariat of State, which in turn submits it to the Sovereign Pontiff's attention. The name is put forward to the Secretariat of State by the bishop of the diocese where the candidate is domiciled, even if he is a non-Catholic. The name itself may be recommended to the

The Association of Papal Knights in Great Britain organises the representation of Papal Knights in ceremonial uniform at important eccesiastical functions. Here three of the Knights of St. Gregory, including the Association's Secretary, Mr. G. Goddard, wearing the uniform of a Knight Commander of the Order of St. Gregory the Great, walk in procession between the Knights of the Order of the Holy Sepulchre of Jerusalem and the Knights of the Sovereign and Military Order of Malta, with whom such functions are always planned in close collaboration.

Courtesy: J.F. O'Shea, London

bishop by the parish priest of the candidate or any other responsible Catholic cleric or layman. The bishop will always be asked to express his view on the merits of the proposition. The endorsement of someone other than the diocesan bishop, however exalted he may be, will not suffice. The petition must state the name, place and date of birth, address and brief history of the life of the candidate, bringing out his or her special merits and the service it is intended to reward so as to justify the conferring of the papal distinction which is requested. Decorations already in possession of the candidate must also be indicated, so as to help the Secretariat of State to decide the Order and the rank which are to be granted. A candidate already possessing a pontifical decoration may, for additional merits, be awarded a higher decoration in the same Order or a different one.

Further investigation may be made by the competent offices. Once completed, the dossier will be submitted to the Sovereign Pontiff with the pertinent suggestions, for his final decision. This will be communicated to the bishop of the diocese of the candidate, and if it is in the affirmative, he will receive the apposite documents. Except in the case when the decoration is conferred *motu proprio* by the Sovereign Pontiff, a modest chancery fee is requested on receipt of the honour, and the appropriate insignia are to be sought at one of the Medal Shops in Rome or elsewhere.

John XXIII during the reception of the Special Missions which had come to Rome to attend the celebrations of the Pope's eightieth birthday. The author (on the right of the Holy Father) was then Chief of Protocol in the Secretariat of State of His Holiness, and here he introduces Heads of Government and Members of the Special Missions.

Courtesy: Felici, Pontificia Fotografia, Rome

The Papal Secretary of State, His Eminence Agostino Cardinal Casaroli. It is the Secretary of State who signs the *biglietto* of appointment of Pontifical Knights. Cardinal Casaroli defined the spirit of Chivalry and particularly the *rôle* of a Pontifical Knight thus: "Becoming a Knight means taking on a mission, before God and man."

Courtesy: *L'Osservatore Romano*

The bestowal document of the Supreme Order of Christ, of the Order of the Golden Spur, of the Golden Rose and of the Grand Collar and Grand Cross is the Apostolic Brief, signed by the Sovereign Pontiff or on his behalf. The *Biglietto* (billet, note), signed by the Cardinal Secretary of State, is used for the other ranks of the Pontifical Orders of Knighthood, and the *Diploma*, signed by the *Sostituto* (Substitute) of the Secretariat of State, for the Cross *Pro Ecclesia et Pontifice* and the *Benemerenti* Medal.

No dubbing ceremony takes place on the bestowal of any of the Pontifical Knighthoods, since they are all now considered to be in the category of Orders of Merit. The formula once prescribed for the solemn investiture of a Knight of the Supreme Order of Christ or of the Order of the

Golden Spur was suppressed, because of deference for their eminent recipients, when these Orders were reserved for Sovereigns or Heads of State. A ceremony of some kind, for which there is no set pattern, may however accompany the publication of the appointment.

The Heads of a diplomatic mission accredited to the Holy See usually receive a high decoration, such as the Grand Cross of the Order of Pius IX, two years after the presentation of their credentials to the Pontiff. The other diplomatic members of the mission are awarded a decoration, according to their respective ranks, when they relinquish their post at the Vatican. There may be an exchange of decorations on the occasion of State Visits to the Holy See, though the Supreme Pontiff does not accept any decorations.

Likewise, decorations may be given, as they were regularly in the past, on very solemn occasions to the members of Special Missions sent to the celebration of an extraordinary event, such as the crowning of the Pope, replaced at present by an official inauguration of the new Pontiff's pastoral ministry. This, however, was not done in 1978, probably owing to the expressed wish of the Pontiffs to simplify the ceremony. The members of these missions were given special souvenirs and not a pontifical decoration.

It is understood that all this takes place with due respect for the regulations in force in the diplomat's country. These may not authorise the diplomat to accept a decoration from a foreign country. Thus in the British Foreign Service, since 1930 the rules have become even more stringent than in the past: members of the Service cannot generally expect to be allowed to wear the decorations of foreign Orders, except when they are conferred for distinguished efforts displayed in the saving of life. British Heads of Mission are not permitted to accept decorations when leaving their posts on final retirement, nor indeed while they are still there. Members of British Embassies are given permission however to wear medals given by a foreign Head of State when they attend ceremonies commemorating an important event so as to avoid any appearance of discourtesy. With regard to other British subjects, the government's permission by Royal Warrant is required for the wearing of any foreign Order of Knighthood at court; regulations were first published in 1911 and revised in 1969. Rules in this connexion are also very stringent in the United States of America. In Italy a special request must be submitted to the Italian government and appropriate taxes must be paid to accept and wear foreign decorations, including those of the Pontifical Orders.

The admission procedure differs when dealing with the Order of Malta and the Order of the Holy Sepulchre, in which decorations are also bestowed upon petition, but always with a sponsor and subject to the existing rules. The dossier is not submitted to the Holy See but merely to the authorities of the Order. Because of the religious character of these Orders, an inquiry is made normally through the appropriate ecclesiastical channels to insure that the candidate is worthy of the honour which is being requested for him, and that he or she possesses the necessary qualifications. After the concession of the decoration by the Grand Master together with his Council, the Grand Priory, Priory, Lieutenancy, National Association or Delegation is contacted for the transmission of the relative documents and the insignia. The interested party is expected to show his or her gratitude in a practical and appropriate manner, by making a contribution towards the good works of the Order which rely almost entirely on the benefactions of their members to fulfil their charitable aims.

A Corollary on the Use of Titles and Style

The recipients of honours in the Pontifical and Religious Orders of Knighthood, as also in other chivalrous non-British Orders for that matter, are not given the distinctive style of "Sir" to be prefixed to their forename. In fact, the ascribing of this title and form of address is a typical British custom of great antiquity, restricted to members of British sovereign Orders of Knighthood who are British subjects, to Baronets and to Knights Bachelor, though the latter dignity is not an Order.

The Order of Merit which ranks immediately after the Most Noble Order of the Garter, the Most Ancient and Noble Order of the Thistle and after Knights Grand Cross of the Most Honourable Order of the Bath, and above all the other degrees of Knighthood, and the Order of the Companions of Honour, which ranks above several chivalric classes, do not confer any special title. Members of all sovereign Orders of Knighthood who are not British subjects are entitled to append the initials of the Order and rank behind their surname.

For internal purposes only, some higher ranking officials of the Sovereign Military Order of Malta and of the Equestrian Order of the Holy Sepulchre are addressed as "His Excellency". Such is the case for the members of the Grand Magistry, the Councillors and the Lieutenants of these Orders. Nevertheless it would be preferable not to make public use of such a style where local customs advise against it. All members of the Orders in question are however entitled to use the initials of their respective rank after their family names, or even spell it out in full, provided there is no local indication to the contrary.

The Chief of Protocol at the Belgian Court, H.E. Eugene Rittweger de Moor, greets the author, Apostolic Nuncio to Belgium, Luxembourg and the European Community. Monsieur de Moor became the Belgian Ambassador to the Holy See.

Courtesy: The Protocol Department of the Belgian Cour

Chapter Seven

DYNASTIC ORDERS OF KNIGHTHOOD

Dynastic Orders of Knighthood are a category of Orders belonging to he heraldic patrimony of a dynasty, often held by ancient right. They re sometimes called Family Orders, in that they are strictly related to a oyal Family or House. They differ from the early military and religious rders and from the later Orders of Merit belonging to a particular State, aving been instituted to reward personal services rendered to a dynasty r an ancient Family of princely rank. These Orders are the exclusive roperty of a Sovereign, and they remain such even if he goes into exile, nd are transmissible to his legitimate successor and Head of the Family. urists generally believe that even if a Sovereign abdicates of his own free vill, he does not renounce his right to the Grand Mastership of an xisting Dynastic Order belonging to his Family, unless he does so xplicitly. But even then his renunciation will be of a personal character nd such as not to involve his successors who have an inborn right to the rand Mastership and cannot be deprived of it. A Sovereign in exile and is legitimate successor and Head of the Family continue to enjoy the *ius ollationis* (the right to confer honours) and therefore may bestow onours in full legitimacy, provided the Order has not become extinct. hey cannot however found new Dynastic Orders. No authority can eprive them of the right to confer honours, since this prerogative elongs to them as a lawful personal property *iure sanguinis* (by right of lood), and both its possession and exercise are inviolable.

This is especially true when the Orders in question have been solemnly ecognised by the Supreme Authority of the Holy See. No political uthority has the right to suppress this recognition, declared by highly fficial documents, such as Papal Bulls by a merely unilateral act of bolition. So long as the recognition is not revoked by the Holy See itself, he Order cannot be considered canonically extinct. This does not mean owever, that the new political authority is not entitled to forbid the ublic use of the insignia and titles of such Orders according to its own ules in the matter of decorations.

We are here speaking strictly of Dynastic or Family Orders which elong exclusively to a Royal House and which have not been given to he State so as to form an Order of the Crown. In this case the Order takes ts place in a category distinct from the State Orders and from Dynastic-

COLOUR PLATES

PLATE XIII CATHOLIC DYNASTIC ORDERS OF KNIGHTHOOD

The Collar of the Noble Order of the Golden Fleece worn by Hi Majesty King Juan Carlos of Spain

The Golden Fleece worn suspended from a crimson ribbon by Hi Majesty King Juan Carlos of Spain

Courtesy: The Count de Sierragorda and with permission of His Majesty the King of Spa

PLATE XIV A CATHOLIC DYNASTIC ORDER OF KNIGHTHOOD

The Collar of the Grand Master of the Sacred and Militar Constantinian Order of St. George, Royal House of Bourbon o the Two Sicilies, and a reliquary of St. George (centre).

Courtesy: The Marquess di Loren

PLATE XV A CATHOLIC DYNASTIC ORDER OF KNIGHTHOOD

The insignia of a Knight of Grace and Star (which is also the Sta of a Knight Grand Cross) of the Sacred and Militar Constantinian Order of St. George. (Royal House of Bourbon o the Two Sicilies)

Courtesy: P.B.v.

PLATE XVI CATHOLIC DYNASTIC ORDERS OF KNIGHTHOOD

The insignia of the Order of SS. Maurice and Lazarus 1st clas (Royal House of Savoy)

Courtesy: H. E. Archbishop Hei

The insignia of the Royal and Illustrious Order of St. Januarius (Royal Houses of Bourbon of the Two Sicilies and of Spain) worn by H.R.H. the Duke of Castro, Grand Master of th Sicilian branch of the Order

Courtesy: The Marquess di Loren

PLATE XIII

PLATE XIV

PLATE XV

PLATE XVI

H.M. Queen Elizabeth II
overeign of the Royal Victorian Order, Dynastic Order of the Royal House of Vindsor, and of all British Orders of Knighthood. Photo: the late Peter Grugeon: Courtesy: the Peter Grugeon Studio, Reading

H.M. King Carl Gustav XVI of Sweden
Sovereign of the Royal Order of the Seraphim, and H.M. Queen Silvia, both wearing the insignia of the Dynastic Order which had its origin in the twelfth or thirteenth century and which was revived in 1748 by when it had lost its Catholic character.
Courtesy: The Royal Swedish Embassy in London

amily-Orders, but retains some characteristics of the latter in that it is reely granted by the Sovereign even though it actually belongs to the atrimony of the State.

I

Secular Dynastic Orders Bestowed by a Reigning Monarch

THE ROYAL VICTORIAN ORDER

Great Britan

The Royal Victorian Order was instituted by Queen Victoria 1837–1901) on 21 April 1896 with the object of rewarding outstanding nd personal service rendered to the Sovereign and to the Royal Family. he Order has always enjoyed great repute apart from the time of the eign of King Edward VII (1901–1910), when its value was slightened by he King's lavishness in awarding it to his friends. In 1936 King Edward /III (1936) made his mother, Queen Mary, a member of the Order. She hus became the first lady to be admitted to the Order as a Dame Grand ross. The Order has five classes: Knights Grand Cross, Knights Comnander, Commanders and Members of the IV and V class. Its badge is a vhite enameled, gold-rimmed, eight-pointed cross with the imperial nonogram of Queen Victoria portrayed on the red enamel centre medalion. The number of the badge appears on the reverse. A special Royal 'ictorian Medal in three classes is also given by the Monarch.

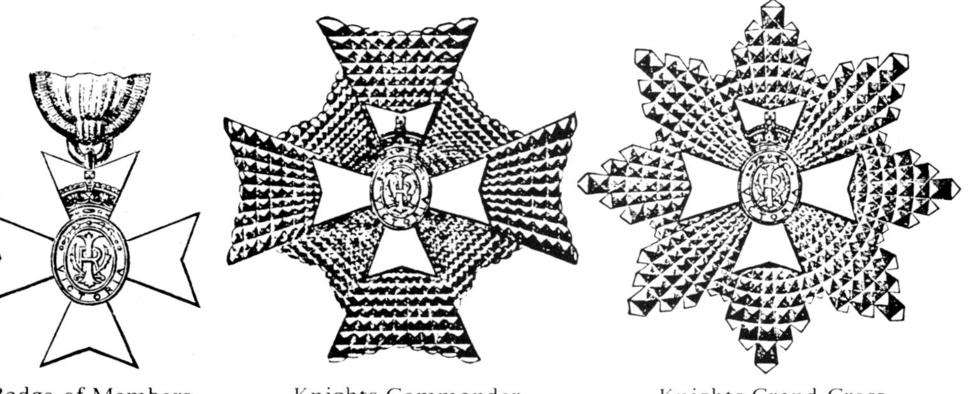

adge of Members — Knights Commander — Knights Grand Cross

THE ROYAL VICTORIAN CHAIN

GREAT BRITAIN

King Edward VII instituted the Royal Victorian Chain as an independent Order with no links, either in statutes or as an Order, with the Royal Victorian Order. The Order grants neither precedence nor any special title or rank. Its sole purpose is to enable the Monarch to show his esteem and bestow an extraordinary sign of his favour on the recipient. The Royal Victorian Chain can be conferred on members of the Royal Family, foreign Heads of State and outstandingly meritorious personages of British and foreign nationality.

Insignia of the Order

The Order has one class; gentlemen wear a chain around the neck an ladies wear the Order on a riband tied in a bow on the left shoulder. Th chain consists of three Tudor roses, two thistles, two shamrocks and tw lotus flowers, representing England, Scotland, Ireland and India. In wreath are the initials of the reigning Monarch who bestowed this hig distinction. The riband for the bow worn by ladies is blue with white an red borders. The same emblems as in the chain appear on the bow.

The cross is the Commander's Cross of the Royal Victorian Orde which hangs from the chain or from the smaller chains fastened on th bow.

The Royal Victorian Chain has to be returned to the reigning Monarc on the death of the recipient.

The two foregoing Orders are given here only as examples. No link xists between them and the Holy See, by which, of course, they are ecognised and highly esteemed.

THE ROYAL ORDER OF THE SERAPHIM

Sweden

The Royal Order of the Seraphim of Sweden may be placed in the same :ategory. The circumstances of its foundation are not certain. Some ›elieve it was instituted by King Magnus I of Sweden between 1260 and 285; others maintain it was founded by Magnus IV Eriksson in 1334 in emembrance of the siege of Upsala and to provide the State with a nilitia able to defend its Catholic faith. The Order went into abeyance ıntil King Frederick I (1720–1750) revived it in 1748. It had by then lost ts Catholic character. Subsequently renewed by Charles XIII

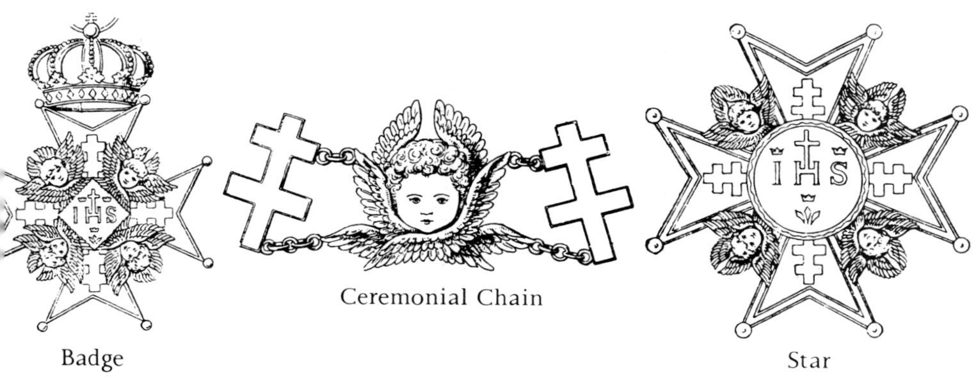

Badge

Ceremonial Chain

Star

1809–1818) in 1814, it remained Sweden's highest ranking Order. It has nly one class and is composed of thirty-two Knights, of whom eight are ›reigners, besides the members of the Royal Family and Heads of Foreign tates. Its name derives from the seraphic heads which adorn the collar nd the eight-pointed, white enameled, gold-edged cross. In the centre of ıe cross is a dark blue enameled medallion bearing the letters I.H.S., ırmounted by a cross and surrounded by three nails and three small rowns. I.H.S. is derived from the Greek IHSous for Jesus. The dash of the I evolved into a cross. In 1347 St. Bernadine of Siena interpreted it as *:sus Hominum Salvator* (Jesus the Saviour of men). Later it came to ıean *In hac Salus* (Salvation is in this, i.e. the cross).

II

Catholic Dynastic Orders Bestowed by a Reigning Sovereign

All Dynastic Orders, whether attached to the person of the Sovereign or of his legitimate successor or to the State, generally enjoy interna tional recognition. Some jurists tend to place the former under privat law and the latter under public law. The Holy See recognises all legiti mate Dynastic Orders which correspond with the requirements of inter national norms, whether they are granted by a reigning Sovereign or by Sovereign in exile or his legitimate successor and Head of the Roya Family and House.

We shall deal from here on only with Catholic Dynastic Orders.

THE NOBLE ORDER OF THE GOLDEN FLEECE

An example of this category is the Spanish branch of the Dynasti Order of the Golden Fleece, which is bestowed by a ruling Sovereign King Juan Carlos of Spain, and which is quite distinct from the Austria branch of the Order, as we shall see further on. To understand the origin nature and development of the Order, it will prove useful briefly to recal its historical background, shared by both branches from 1430 to 1683.

THE NOBLE ORDER OF THE GOLDEN FLEECE was founded in Bruge on 10 January 1430 by Philip the Good, Duke of Burgundy (1396–1467), t mark the occasion of his marriage to Isabella, Infanta of Portugal. It objects were the glory and praise of God Almighty, the honour of Hi glorious Mother the Virgin Mary and of all the celestial Army, and th protection and defence of the Christian faith, especially by undertakin a Crusade to liberate the Holy Places in Jerusalem. It was also intended t honour the Apostle St. Andrew, Patron of the House of Burgundy, and t promote the spirit and cause of Christian chivalry, to stimulate th practice of virtue and good behaviour, and to ensure the tranquillity o the Duchy.

The founder reserved the "extraterritorial" sovereignty of the Orde for himself and his successors, in whose hands the Knights were to swea indefectible fidelity to the Christian faith and to the Sovereign. H assured himself of the absolute loyalty of the most influential feuda Lords by binding them to his person by means of a special oath.

hilip the Good who founded the Noble Order of the Golden Fleece in Bruges in 430. (From a hand-coloured nineteenth century print of the fifteenth century *hronique du Hainaut*, a manuscript in the Bibliothèque de Bourgogne.)

Courtesy: The Count de Sierragorda

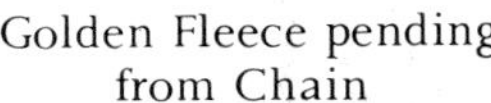

Golden Fleece pending from Chain

Golden Fleece pending from crimson ribbon

The number of Knights was originally thirty-four, and later thirty-one together with the Head and Sovereign of the Order. Emperor Charles V (1519–1556) raised the number to fifty-one, and King Philip IV of Spain (1605–1665) finally fixed it at sixty-one. The Knights were to be Gentlemen-at-Arms, belonging to the most ancient nobility. In order to avoid conflicting loyalties, they could not be members of other Orders of Knighthood, except in the case of Sovereigns who were already Heads of other Orders. They were to form a company of friends, owing each other "love and brotherliness". The Order itself was to "outshine" that of the Garter.

Charles the Bold, Duke of Burgundy and second Head and Sovereign of the Order (1433–1467–1477), included his brother-in-law, Edward IV King of England (1461–1483) and the Kings Ferdinand I of Naples (1458–1494) and John II of Sicily (1458–1479) among the first fifteen Knights he elected between 1468 and 1473.

On the death of Charles the Bold, the Order went to Archduke Maximilian of Austria and later Emperor (1459–1519), who assumed its Sovereign Mastership in place of his wife, Marie de Bourgogne, daughter of Charles the Bold, since according to the then existing rules of chivalry women could not be Sovereign Masters of an Order of Knighthood.

Chapter Meeting of the Knights of the Golden Fleece under Charles the Bold in 1473 when Edward IV, King of England, and the Kings of Naples and Sicily were among the first fifteen Knights Charles the Bold elected to the Order.

Courtesy: Fitzwilliam Museum, Cambridge

Maximilian was followed by Philip the Handsome, second Head and Sovereign of the House of Habsburg (1478–1506) when the latter attained his majority in 1494. During his reign he proceeded to the election of thirty-one Knights, among whom were Henry VII, King of England (1491), and his fourteen year old son Henry (1505) who became King Henry VIII in 1509.

In 1516 Charles V, Holy Roman Emperor, King of Spain and third Head and Sovereign of the House of Habsburg (1500–1558), became Sovereign Master and enriched the Order with many privileges, making it the most important of the time. This had the full approval of the Papacy who granted it special spiritual privileges. Charles V included among the Knights the King of France, Francis I, the Kings of Portugal, Hungary, Scotland and Poland together with the Dukes of Bavaria, Saxony, Florence, Savoy and Denmark. On his abdication in 1555, Charles V was succeeded by his son Philip II, King of Spain and fourth Head and Sovereign of the House of Habsburg (1527–1598), who in 1577 obtained from Gregory XIII (1572–1585) the exclusive right to appoint Knights to vacant posts, thus putting an end to election by co-optation, which threatened to spoil the quality of the Order's membership. He thus conferred the Order on the Kings of France, Francis II and Charles IX, the future Emperors Rudolph, Mathias and Ferdinand and many Lords in the Lowlands, the Holy Roman Empire, Spain and Italy. He retained the Sovereign Mastership of the Order until 1598 when he passed the sovereignty of the seventeen Provinces to his daughter Isabella and the Sovereign Mastership of the Order to Philip III, King of Spain and fifth Head and Sovereign of the House of Habsburg (1578–1621). He was succeeded by Philip IV (1605–1665) and Carlos II (1661–1700) in the same capacity.

The death of Carlos II marked the end of the Spanish branch of the House of Habsburg. The sovereignty of the throne of Spain was then claimed by Louis XIV for a member of the House of Bourbon, Philip d'Anjou, while Emperor Leopold demanded the succession for a member of the House of Habsburg. Philip d'Anjou actually became King of Spain and first Head and Sovereign of the House of Bourbon in 1701 while the new Emperor, Charles VI, eighth Head and Sovereign of the House of Habsburg (1685–1740), received the Low Countries, Sardinia, Naples and Milan. Both claimed the Sovereign Mastership of the Order of the Golden Fleece for themselves, Philip V because he was King of Spain and Charles VI because, thanks to the Treaty of Utrecht (1713), he had become ruler of the Low Countries. As a result the Order was divided into two different

Holbein painted Henry VIII, King of England, wearing the Catholic Order of the Golden Fleece in 1536, three years after the King's excommunication by Clement VII. The Order was bestowed on Henry in 1505, when he was fourteen years old, by Philip the Handsome. Courtesy: National Portrait Gallery, London branches, the Spanish and the Austrian. Since the sovereignty of the Order remained in dispute, the question was submitted to the Congress of Cambrai in 1724, but no decision was reached. All efforts to bring about a solution under international law having remained without effect, the two Houses tacitly agreed to confer the Order independently.

No mention was made of the Order at the signing of the Treaty of Campoformio in 1797, following Napoleon's first Italian campaign, in force of which Austria renounced its domination over the Low Countries. This was due to the non-territorial character of the sovereignty of the Order, which implied that it had remained the property of the heir of the House of Burgundy, founder of the Order.

The Spanish Branch

The Spanish branch of the Order continued to subsist through ten successive Sovereign Masters, of whom a female Sovereign, Isabella II, Queen of Spain and Head and Sovereign of the House of Bourbon (1833–1868) and during the provisional Government of the Nation under President Joaquin Marie Lopez (1843). The Order was unlawfully suppressed by the Spanish Republic (1931–1941). King Alfonso XIII, King of Spain and ninth Head and Sovereign of the House of Bourbon (1886–1941), without renouncing his Sovereign Mastership, preferred to make no nominations to the Order during his exile. Generalissimo Franco (1892–1975), respecting the dynastic character of the Order, chose to leave the Sovereign Mastership to the Head of the House of Bourbon, though he did assume the Grand Mastership of the Order of Carlos III. After King Alfonso's renunciation shortly before his death, the Sovereign Mastership of the Order went to the Infant of Spain, Don Juan de Bourbon y Battenberg, Count of Barcelona and Head of the Royal (Spanish) House of Bourbon (1941), who renounced the Sovereign Mastership in 1977.

Since then the Head and Sovereign of the Spanish branch of the Order of the Golden Fleece is a reigning Monarch, Juan Carlos I, King of Spain, born in 1938. Since 1941 he was a member of the Order as Infant of Spain and Prince of the Asturias.

The membership of the Order includes only eleven Knights at present, among whom, besides King Juan Carlos, are Leopold III, ex-King of the Belgians; Umberto II, ex-King of Italy; Hiro-Hito, Emperor of Japan,

H.M. King Juan Carlos I of Spain
Head and Sovereign of the Spanish branch of the Noble Order of the Golden Fleece.

Painted by Juan Antonio Morales, Rome:
Courtesy: The Count de Sierragorda

Baudouin I, King of the Belgians; and Constantine, ex-King of the Hellenes.

The Spanish branch adopted a slightly different badge from the traditional one, without the motto, and developed its own practice of bestowal. It no longer possesses an aristocratic and religious character, but is more of a Royal Order with a civil character, remaining however, in the dynastic category. Nominations are made with the previous agreement of the Spanish Council of Ministers; it is therefore no longer subject to the exclusive authority of the Sovereign. Non-Catholics and even non-Christians have been awarded the Order since 1812 when the National Junta of Cádiz conferred it upon Arthur Wellesley, First Duke of Wellington and Duke of Ciudad Rodrigo, as a token of gratitude for the help Spain had received from him during her struggle with Napoleon. The bestowal was confirmed by Ferdinand VII, King of Spain and sixth Head and Sovereign of the House of Bourbon (1784–1833) who, among many others, made George Frederick, Prince of Wales, Regent of the United Kingdom of Great Britain and later King George IV (1762–1830), a member of the Order. Furthermore, female Sovereigns starting with Isabella II, were henceforth allowed to assume the Sovereign Mastership as also a foreign Sovereign, duly elected by the Cortes, the Italian King Amadeo of Savoy in 1870 during an interregnum (1870–1873).

The Austrian branch of the Order of the Golden Fleece is described under section IV: Catholic Dynastic Orders of Knighthood bestowed by a legitimate successor of a Sovereign in exile and Head of a Royal Family.

THE ROYAL ORDER OF MARIA LUISA

Spain

This is another example of a Dynastic Order given by a reigning Sovereign, King Juan Carlos. During his rule, Generalissimo Franco never conferred the Order because he respected its dynastic character. The Order was founded by Carlos IV, King of Spain (1788–1808) in 1792, so as to furnish his wife, Queen Maria Luisa of Parma, with the means to honour noble ladies for outstanding deeds of charity. The image of St. Ferdinand, an ancestor of the Royal Family, is portrayed on the centre medallion of the badge as the Patron of the Order, whose recipients were expected to show their devotion to him by their dedication to works of mercy. The badge itself consists of a Maltese gold-rimmed, violet and white enamel cross.

The Royal Order of Maria Luisa

III

CATHOLIC DYNASTIC ORDERS BESTOWED BY A SOVEREIGN IN EXILE

Two examples of Catholic Dynastic Orders conferred by a Sovereign in exile are "The Supreme Order of the Most Holy Annunciation" and the "Order of SS. Maurice and Lazarus", both belonging to the Royal House of Savoy and taken by ex-King Umberto of Italy into exile (1946).

THE SUPREME ORDER OF THE MOST HOLY ANNUNCIATION

Ordine Supremo della SS. Annunziata

This was the highest ranking Order of Knighthood of the Italian Kingdom. The recipients of the Order were considered cousins of the Sovereign and enjoyed precedence over all other officials of State. When Italy became a Presidential Republic, King Umberto II went into exile taking the Order with him. He continued to bestow it on distinguished personages, such as the King of the Belgians, Baudouin I, and the ex-King Constantine of the Hellenes.

Meanwhile the Italian Republic, by Law no. 178 of 30 March 1951, declared that "the Order of the *SS. Annuziata* and its decorations are suppressed." Many jurists believe that the law was based on a grave historical error, since the Order was dynastic and the Italian Republic had therefore no right to suppress it.

THE SUPREME ORDER OF THE MOST HOLY ANNUNCIATION was instituted in 1362 by Amadeus VI, Count of Savoy (1343–1383), under the title of the Order of the Collar. Its origin has clearly religious connotations. As the name given to it at a later date implies, it was founded in honour of the Blessed Virgin Mary, Our Lady of the Annunciation, portrayed on the gold medallion, which is suspended from a gold chain made up of love-knots and roses in memory of the fifteen mysteries in the life of Our Lady, with the letters F.E.R.T. interwoven, referring probably to the victory at Rhodes by Count Amadeus V in 1310. The letters F.E.R.T. have been interpreted as the initials of *Fortitudo Eius Rhodum Tulit* (by his bravery he conquered Rhodes), an allusion to the help Savoy rendered to Rhodes in 1310, or simply standing for the third person singular of the present indicative tense of the Latin verb *ferre*. In this case it would imply that the member of the Order is borne by the bond of faith he swore to Mary, or even that he puts up with all for the love of Mary.

Badge

Star

There is a popular and more profane interpretation of the letters F.E.R.T.: *Frappez, Entrez, Rompez Tout* (Knock, enter, break everything!). The letters may also refer to the motto *Foedere Et Religione Tenemur* (We are held by pact and religion) found on the gold doubloon of Victor Amadeus I (1718–1730), or be the initials of *Fortitudo Eius Republicam Tenet* (his strength defends the State).

The number fifteen became symbolic of the number of Knights forming the Order, that of the Chaplains celebrating fifteen masses each day, and that of the clauses of the original statute which under Amadeus VIII (1391–1451) was raised from fifteen to twenty in 1434. It was given its present name by Duke Charles III (1504–1553) in 1518, when the image of Our Lady of the Annunciation and the Angel, surmounted by the Holy Spirit, was represented on the medallion. The Order, which has only one class, enjoyed the greatest repute, ranking with the Order of the Golden Fleece and of the Garter. Though open mainly to Catholics who had rendered outstanding services, non-Catholics were admitted as honorary members, such as the Duke of Wellington in 1815 and Edward, Prince of Wales, in 1915. Recipients of this Order are required to have already been awarded the Order of S.S. Maurice and Lazarus.

THE ORDER OF SS. MAURICE AND LAZARUS

The Order of SS. Maurice and Lazarus emerged from the fusion of the Order of St. Maurice, founded under Amadeus VIII, first Duke of Savoy, in 1434 and the Order of Lazarus, founded in Palestine, probably around the year 1060, before the first Crusade. Shortly after, Amadeus VIII was elected anti-pope by the Fathers of the Council of Basel in 1439 and took the name of Felix V. He abdicated in 1449 after recognising the true Pope Nicholas V (1447–1455).

The aims of the Order of St. Maurice were to serve God, leading a monastic life, and to assist the State in its needs. The choice of its members was very meticulous: they had to be irreproachable in every aspect. Having remained dormant for a long time, Gregory XIII recognised it as a military-religious Order in 1572 and in the following year he authorised the fusion of the Order of St. Lazaraus with it under the rule of St. Augustine, already adopted by the Order of St. Maurice.

The specific object of the Order of St. Lazarus was to assist the lepers in the Holy Land wherever there was a particular need of such an apostolate. Its Master was himself always a leper, and many of the Knights suffered from the same disease. The Order enjoyed the protection and help of many Sovereigns and especially Popes, most of all of Clement IV (1265–1268).

Compelled to leave the Holy Land in 1291, the Order repaired to the Kingdoms of Naples and Sicily, and of France. Its main seat was the famous St. Lazarus hospital for lepers near Capua from the fifteenth to the sixteenth century. The decline began with the struggle for the Grand Mastership of the Order and the loss of many of its estates. To save the Order from total collapse, Pius II (1458–1464) tried to unite it with other Orders in 1459 so as to form the Militia of St. Mary of Bethlehem, but without success. Sixtus IV (1471–1484) also tried to fuse it with the Order of St. John at Jerusalem, but likewise in vain. Finally united with the Order of St. Maurice with the full support of the papacy, it assumed a hospitaller and military character adding to its original aim, that of the defence of the Holy See. All attempts to persuade the French branch of the Order of St. Lazarus to join in the fusion having failed, this branch was finally united with the Order of Our Lady of Mount Carmel as described in Chapter Nine.

Badge for Order I – IV class

Badge of Knights

The French branch of the Order of St. Lazarus was introduced into Britain by Roger de Mowbray, who was created the First Baron Mowbray in 1283 and who founded a St. Lazarus Hospital for Lepers on his own land near Melton Mowbray. However, the Order of Our Lady of Mount Carmel and St. Lazarus (see Chapter Ten) was finally abolished in 1830, and the Holy See does not recognise any Orders operating under the name of St. Lazarus (see Chapter Eleven).

The Order of SS. Maurice and Lazarus prospered immensely from the fusion and the support it was given by the House of Savoy and the Papacy. It thus became so famous that many European Sovereigns would recommend their most illustrious Knights for admission to it. Over the centuries it continued to progress in many areas for the good of mankind and

Star of Grand Officer

became powerful and very rich. In 1860 King Victor Emmanuel II of Italy (1861–1878) assigned to it the estates belonging to the Sacred and Military Constantinian Order of St. George, which had been suppressed following the annexation of Parma to the Italian Kingdom. In 1868 he reformed it more on the lines of an Order of Merit without diminishing its prestige. It underwent several other reforms until, having lost his Kingdom, ex-King Umberto II of Italy took the Order of SS. Maurice and Lazarus with him into exile where he still confers it.*

Composed of five classes, the Order's badge consists of its original white enamel cross *botonnée* combined with the green cross *potence* of St. Lazarus, and surmounted by a gold crown.

* On 3 March 1951, the President of the Italian Republic instituted the Order *Al Merito della Repubblica Italiana* to take the place of the Order of SS. Maurice and Lazarus which had been officially abolished by the legislature and the executive of the Republic. The accepting and wearing of the decorations of the Order of SS. Maurice and Lazarus was outlawed. The Republic of Italy considered the Order as belonging to the former Crown of Italy and therefore to the State and felt justified in abolishing it and substituting it with another Order. Ex-King Umberto, however, insisted on the dynastic character of the Order, and, as we have already said, when the reign of the House of Savoy ended in 1946 and he went into exile after less than one month as King of Italy, he took the Order of SS. Maurice and Lazarus with him and continued to bestow it abroad. The Holy See never ceased to recognise the ex-King's Grand Mastership of the Order because of its dynastic nature and historic development.

In stark contrast to the uncompromising stand taken by the Republic of Italy with regard to ex-King Umberto and his claim to the Order of SS. Maurice and Lazarus, the Sacred and Military Constantinian Order of St. George of the Royal House of Bourbon of the Two Sicilies, as we shall say later on, was fully recognised as a Royal Dynastic Order by Presidential Decree of the Italian Republic, and Italian citizens are allowed to accept and wear the chivalric insignia bestowed upon them by the Grand Master of the Order, who is the Head of the House.

IV

Catholic Dynastic Orders of Knighthood Bestowed by a Legitimate Successor of a Sovereign in Exile and Head of a Royal Family

There are several Catholic Dynastic Orders of Knighthood which are still being bestowed by a legitimate successor of a Sovereign in Exile and Head of a Royal Family. Among these, the two most important are the Most Noble Order of the Golden Fleece of the Austrian branch and the Sacred Military Constantinian Order of St. George of the House of Bourbon of Naples and the Kingdom of the Two Sicilies.

THE NOBLE ORDER OF THE GOLDEN FLEECE

The Austrian Branch

We have already traced the early history of the Noble Order of the Golden Fleece from its beginning to its separation into two branches.

Emperor Charles VI, first Sovereign Master of the Austrian branch of the Order after its separation, was succeeded by Emperor Francis I (1708–1765) who in 1740 became the ninth Head and Sovereign of the House of Habsburg – Lorraine. He was followed by the successive Emperors Joseph II (1741–1790), Leopold II (1747–1792), Francis II (1768–1835), Ferdinand I (1793–1875), Francis-Joseph I (1830–1916), Charles I (1887–1922). The present Sovereign Master is Archduke Otto, sixteenth Head and Sovereign of the House of Habsburg-Lorraine, who was born in 1912. He is the legitimate successor of a Sovereign who died in exile, being the firstborn son of Emperor Charles I who had been compelled to abandon his throne of Austria after the proclamation of the Republic of Austria on 2 November 1918.

Following the abdication of Emperor Charles I, a group of notable Belgians attempted to persuade the Belgian Government to secure the inclusion of a special section in the Treaty of Versailles (1919), prescribing the return of the treasure of the Order of the Golden Fleece to Belgium. They also endeavoured to persuade King Albert of the Belgians to claim the Sovereign Mastership of the Order on the basis that it was founded in what is now the Kingdom of Belgium and had always been headed by a ruling Sovereign. King Albert refused to do so, considering

H.I. and R.H. Archduke Otto von Habsburg
Head of the Imperial and Royal House of Habsburg Lorraine and Sovereign of the Austrian branch of the Noble Order of the Golden Fleece.

Courtesy: Archduke Otto von Habsburg

such an initiative offensive to the House of Habsburg-Lorraine with whom his own House had always maintained friendly relations, and also contrary to his own plainness of life. Furthermore the Belgian Government rejected the proposal submitted to it because the treasure had been transferred to Vienna between 1794 and 1797 by the House of Habsburg-Lorraine itself under the sovereign Mastership of Emperor Francis II. There was therefore no question of returning the treasure on the grounds that it had been looted by the enemy during the 1914–1918 war.

The sovereignty of the Austrian branch of the Order in the hands of the Head of the House of Habsburg-Lorraine was acknowledged by the Republic of Austria, which in a special decree dated 16 September 1953 recognised its independent juridical personality under international law (. . . *als Rechtspersönlichkeit Ausländischen Rechtes*), as belongong to the House of Habsburg-Lorraine. This included the recognition of the property rights of the Order over its own archives and treasures which had been transferred from Brussels to Vienna while the Napoleonic revolutionary army advanced in Belgium after its victory at Fleurus in 1794. The Austrian Government has assumed the custody of these archives and treasures which are kept at the Weltliche Schatzkammer and the Geistliche Schatzkammer (i.e. two treasuries, one temporal, the other ecclesiastical) at Hofburg, and allows the Order to dispose of them freely for ceremonial and cultural purposes.

The badge of the Order consists of a golden sheepskin with head and feet attached to a blue enamel white dotted flintstone and emerging gold-rimmed red flame, all hanging from a gold crown-shaped plaque

Golden Fleece pending from Chain

bearing the image of Jason slaying the dragon and the motto: *Pretium laborum non vile* (The reward of labour is not of little worth), and on the reverse: *Non Aliud* (No other), referring to the primacy of the Order among all other Knighthoods. The badge is suspended from a gold chain, which is indeed the most important part of the insignia, composed of interlinking plaquettes representing a rifle and a flintstone in the form of the letter "B", standing for Burgundy. The chain may be replaced by a ribbon of crimson moiré for practical reasons.

The rifle and the flintstone are reminiscent of the motto of the Duchy of Burgundy: *Ante ferit quam flamma micet* (It hits before the flame blazes), probably inspired by the invention of firearms in the fifteenth century.

The Fleece recalls the Greek legend of the Golden Fleece captured by Jason from the dragon, thus symbolising Jerusalem which, in its original Crusader spirit, the Order was to win back to Christendom from the Muslims. It may be a reminder of the fleece of wool with which Gideon tested God's will (*cf.* Book of Judges, 6:33–40) and which was to be interpreted as representing the Immaculate Virgin Mary, Patron of the Order. In a more worldly context some believe that it may have been chosen as a token of the manufacture of wool, the staple industry of Bruges and the Lowlands.

In fact, since the reign of Philip the Handsome, no one thought of Jason anymore because of the pagan connotation. Bishop Guillaume Filastre, Chancellor of the Order, gave six references for the symbolic use of the fleece: Jason, Gideon, Jacob, Mesa, Job and David. Each one of the fleeces referring to these personages represented one of the virtues with which a true knight should be adorned: magnanimity, justice, prudence, loyalty, patience and clemency.

The Austrian branch of the Order of the Golden Fleece has preserved its original aristocratic and religious character. It is therefore granted only to members of Royal Families and the Nobility who profess the Catholic faith.

Among the Knights of the Order, besides the leading members of the Imperial and Royal House of Austria, we find the following: Jean, Grand Duke of Luxembourg; Albert, Prince of Liège and of Belgium; François-Joseph II, Prince Sovereign of Liechtenstein; Jean-Adam, Crown Prince of Liechtenstein; Frà Angelo de Mojana di Cologna, Prince and Grand Master of the Sovereign Order of Malta; the Heads of the leading German Houses, such as Karl, Duke of Würtemberg; Marie Emmanuel, Margrave of Meissen, Duke of Saxe; Albert, Duke of Bavaria (House of Wittelsbach).

COROLLARY

This brief note on the Order of the Golden Fleece would be incomplete if mention were not made of THE MILITARY IMPERIAL ORDER OF THE THREE GOLDEN FLEECES, founded by Napoleon at the imperial headquarters of Schönbrunn. This Order had no religious reference whatsoever nor was it a Dynastic Order.

Napoleon says in the relevant decree of 15 August 1809: "*My eagles have vanquished the Golden Fleece of the Kings of Spain and the Golden Fleece of the emperors of Germany. It is my wish to create, for the French Empire, an Imperial Order of the Three Golden Fleeces. Its emblem will consist of my own eagle with outspread wings, holding in each of its talons one of the princely Fleeces which it has vanquished, and it will proudly display, hanging from its beak, the Fleece that I have founded.*"

Prototype: Eagle holding three fleeces

The appropriate badge of the Order, weighing some nine ounces, consists of a large, gilt brass crowned French Imperial Eagle with a firestone resembling that of the original Order, to which three brass sheepskins are attached. This "precious" emblem can be seen at the *Musée National de la Légion d'Honneur et des Ordres de Chevalerie* in Paris.

Because of the vigorous protests of the recipients of the *Légion d'Honneur*, who resented being degraded by the new Order, Napoleon's decree was never executed.

THE SACRED AND MILITARY CONSTANTINIAN ORDER OF ST. GEORGE

Sacro Militare Ordine Constantiniano di San Giorgio

There are several other examples of Dynastic Orders conferred by the legitimate successor of a Sovereign in exile and Head of a Royal House, even after a considerable lapse of time. Among these the most important Order is The Sacred and Military Constantinian Order of St. George.

THE SACRED AND MILITARY CONSTANTINIAN ORDER OF ST. GEORGE is believed to be derived from the Order of the Angelical Knights, also known as the Order of the Golden Knights, founded in 1190 by Isaac II Angel Comnenus, Byzantine Emperor. The Byzantine origin of the Order explains why it is dedicated to St. George, whose cult is very widely spread in the Near East. The title of Constantinian indicates the traditional belief that the Order goes back as far as Emperor Constantine the Great as its founder. It was, however, transferred to Italy by the Comnenus Imperial Family when Constantinople fell into the hands of the Turkish Sultan Mohamed II (1451–1481). It was recognised by the Republic of Venice as a Dynastic Order, and approved by the Holy See towards the middle of the fifteen-hundreds, when Julius III, on 17 July 1555, confirmed the Grand Mastership of Andrew and Jerome, Princes of Thessaly. The first official document relating to the Order is its statute of 1522. In 1623 the Grand Mastership of the Order was handed over to Marino Caracciolo, Prince of Avellino, with the subsequent approval of Urban VIII. When the Prince died, the Grand Mastership was returned to John Andrew of Drivastus. A descendant of John Andrew of Drivastus transferred the Order to the first Duke of Parma and Piacenza, Francis Farnese and his successors, in 1697. This act was approved by Innocent XII on 29 October 1699. The Order having won the highest esteem in European countries, Clement XI (1700–1721) approved it once again on 6 June 1718 and made it directly dependent on the Holy See, enriching it with many privileges.

In 1727 Prince Antonio Farnese* decided to ensure the future of the Order by giving it to Don Carlos of Bourbon (1716–1788), son of Philip V, King of Spain (1700–1746). When Carlos became King of Naples in 1734, he retained the Grand Mastership of the Order until he became King of Spain in 1759. By the official statement known as *Prammatica*, he renounced all his rights to the throne of the Two Sicilies including his right to the Grand Mastership of the Sacred and Military Constantinian

Duke Antonio's decision was based on the fact that his heiress to the Farnese States was the second wife of Philip V of Spain and the mother of Don Carlos.

Order of St. George, which he left to his son Ferdinand, who succeeded him as King of Naples, thus becoming the fourth Grand Master.* The Spanish branch of the House of Bourbon, however, did not agree with this point of view. It maintained in fact that Carlos could not give up the Grand Mastership of the Order when be became King of Spain in 1759 because this would have been against rulings of international law under which a pure and simple renunciation of all dynastic rights is not possible.

The Grand Mastership of a Dynastic and Family Order is a right which is attached to the person and not to the throne of the Sovereign. Carlos III of Spain indeed handed the Grand Mastership over to his son Ferdinand, but that was at a later date and separately from his renunciation of the throne of the Two Sicilies. At any rate, the Order returned to Naples with King Ferdinand, who was its Grand Master until 1825. The Popes continued to approve and recommend it, as did Clement XIII in 1763 and Pius VI in 1777.

In 1816 Maria Luisa, Duchess of Parma,† established a Constantinian Order of St. George for the Duchies of Parma and Piacenza, and she

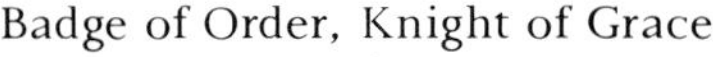
Badge of Order, Knight of Grace

Grand Cross, also Knights of Grace

* The *Prammatica* of 1759 stated that the Royal Houses of Spain and of the Two Sicilies were separated and the two Crowns could never be united.

† Maria Luisa, wife of Napoleon I, in exile received under the treaty of Vienna, 1815, for life the sovereignty of the Duchies of Parma, Piacenza and Guastalla, which after her death were to be returned to the previously reigning House of Bourbon of Parma.

Badge of a Knight
di Merito and *di Ufficio*

ssumed its Grand Mastership. A dispute arose between the Bourbons of Naples and those of the Parma branch over the possession of the original Order. Finally, to avoid an open conflict, the two branches of the Royal amily agreed tacitly to confer the Order independently, which their Heads did, as reigning Sovereigns, until the annexation of both Parma 1859) and Naples (1860) to the newly founded Kingdom of Italy. Both overeigns in exile subsequently continued to confer the Order, but the Holy See gave its support only to the House of the Two Sicilies, which ever ceased to bestow it as a legitimate Dynastic Order.

In 1861, as we have said earlier, the government of the Kingdom of taly sequestered the property of the Order to the advantage of the Order f SS. Maurice and Lazarus, but made it clear that the Sacred and Military Constantinian Order of St. George was not thereby abolished.

A new dispute arose between the Naples branch and the Spanish ranch of the Royal House of Bourbon following a statement issued at Cannes in 1900 by Carlos, Infant of Spain, who was the second son of Alfonso, Count of Caserta and eighth Grand Master of the Order until 934. Imitating his ancestor Carlos III, he had renounced his right of uccession to the throne of the Two Sicilies, including his right to assume the Grand Mastership in view of his forthcoming marriage to Maria Mercedes, Princess of the Asturias and Infanta of Spain. When Alfonso died in 1934, he was succeeded by his eldest son, Prince Ferdinand, who was Grand Master until 1960. He in turn was succeeded by the younger brother, Prince Ranieri, who assumed the title Duke of Castro and the Grand Mastership of the Order, which he exercised until 1966 when he ransferred it to his son, Prince Ferdinand, Duke of Calabria, who in 1973 on the death of his father became Duke of Castro and succeeded as Head of the Royal House. Carlos's son Alfonso (of the Spanish branch), who had assumed the title of Duke of Calabria, protested very strongly and he even endeavoured twice to secure the support of John XXIII on his behalf basing his claim to the Grand Mastership on the successional laws of the Royal House of the Kingdom of the Two Sicilies.

The policy of the Holy See has always been one of non-involvement in the legal disputes between the two branches of the House of Bourbon Until 1924 the Holy See had appointed a Cardinal Patron to the Order but ceased to do so when, following a protest from the Order of SS Maurice and Lazarus, supported by the Italian Crown, it decided to hold in abeyance the appointment of a new Cardinal Patron, pending the solution of the dispute the Order had with the Italian Government and, indeed, within its own Family.

The dispute of the Sacred and Military Constantinian Order of St George of the Royal House of Bourbon of the Two Sicilies with the Government of the Italian Republic was solved when the Presidency of the Republic, after consulting the competent governmental ministries on 20 July 1963 officially declared that:

> "The National Association of the Knights of the Sacred and Military Constantinian Order of St. George is a moral person recognised and authorised in Italy as a legitimate Dynastic Order of the Royal House of Bourbon of the Two Sicilies, of which the Head now is H.R.H. the Prince Ranieri Maria of Bourbon Duke of Castro."*

Italian citizens were henceforth permitted to accept and wear the decorations of the Order after obtaining the licence to do so normally required for this purpose. The Sacred and Military Constantinian Order of St. George was subsequently recognised by the Sovereign Military Order of Malta, with which it is associated in several relief projects.

Now that the dispute between the S.M. Constantinian Order and the Government of the Italian Republic has been solved with a favourable decision on the part of the Italian Government, the Order hopes that the way may also be open for the Holy See to review its own position and modify its hitherto restrained attitude. If this were to happen, it would not mean that the Holy See would give the Order special preferential treatment or would be involved in its life any more than it is in that of other Catholic Orders not under its protection. When early in 1981 the Duke of Castro asked the Holy See to appoint a Chaplain General for the

* The President of the Italian Republic confirmed the 1963 decision in 1981 appertaining to all members of the Orde he also confirmed that the Headship of the Royal House and the Grand Mastership of the Order belonged to Princ Ferdinand Duke of Castro.

Vestments and insignia of the Grand Prior of the Sacred and Military Constantinian Order of St. George, sacred vessels and silverplate used during religious services, all dating from the nineteenth century.

Courtesy: The Grand Chancellor of the S.M. Constantian Order of St. George

Order, the Holy See advised him to direct his request to His Eminence th Cardinal Archbishop of Naples where the Order's headquarters are situ ated. This was immediately done and the Cardinal Archbisho appointed a Chaplain General and Spiritual Adviser to the Order. He act on behalf of the Cardinal Archbishop of Naples and not of the Holy See.

The badge of the Order is suspended from a gold crown pending from sky-blue moiré ribbon and consists of a red enameled, gold-rimmed cros *fleury*, the arms of which bear the letters I. H. S. V. *In Hoc Signo Vince* (You will conquer by this sign) which recalls the vision the Empero Constantine had in his sleep the night before the battle of Saxa Rubr (312), showing a luminous cross in the sky with this motto, and com manding him to inscribe the cross and the motto on the shields of hi soldiers. This he did and won the battle. The Greek letter *Chi (X)* wit the letter *Rho (P)* behind it, is superimposed on the cross, forming th mysterious monogram for *Christos*, inscribed by Constantine on th labarum. The *Alpha* and *Omega* $(A - \Omega)$ appear on the horizontal arm of the cross to symbolise that Christ is the beginning and end of all (*cf* Ap.: 1,8). At the base of the cross on the Grand Master's Chain and th insignia of the Bailiffs of Justice hangs the figure of St. George slaying th dragon.

Grand Cross, Ecclesiastical Knights

The Grand Cross is an eight-pointed star which has the gold-rimme red cross *fleury* and the letters in gold superimposed on it. Ecclesiastica Knights wear a four-pointed star with the cross superimposed on it.

The Order's patronal feastday is St. George's Day, 23 April.

THERE ARE SEVERAL OTHER, THOUGH NOT AS EXALTED CATHOLIC DYNASTIC ORDERS WHICH ARE STILL BEING CONFERRED BY LEGITIMATE SUCCESSORS OF FORMER RULERS AND HEADS OF A ROYAL FAMILY. AMONG THEM WE SHALL MENTION THE FOLLOWING ACCORDING TO THE DIFFERENT CATHOLIC HOUSES

THE ROYAL HOUSE OF BOURBON OF THE TWO SICILIES

THE ROYAL AND ILLUSTRIOUS ORDER OF ST. JANUARIUS

This illustrious and esteemed Order was also founded as a Dynastic Order in 1738 by Carlos, Infant of Spain, ninth Duke of Parma, King of Naples and of Sicily, before he became King Carlos III of Spain. His aims were to honour St. Januarius, Patron of Naples, who suffered martyrdom in the year 305, and to mark his marriage to Princess Amalia Walburga of Saxony, daughter of Augustus III, King of Poland and Elector of Saxony. The Order, which received the approval of Benedict XIV in 1741, was soon held in high regard. Carlos took the Order with him when he became King of Spain in 1759. He retained its Grand Mastership until 1766 when he handed it over to his son Ferdinand IV, King of Naples, who meanwhile had come of age. Ferdinand was already a Knight of the Order before becoming its Grand Master (1759–1766). In 1771 Carlos III took the statutes of the Order of St. Januarius as a basis when he founded the Most Distinguished Order of Carlos III, to this date Spain's leading State Order of Knighthood, to thank God for having answered his prayers in giving him a grandchild and successor on the Feastday of St. Januarius (19 September).

The Order of St. Januarius prospered so well that even after the fall of the Sicilian Monarchy in 1860, King Francis II (1859–1860) and his successors continued to bestow it as a Dynastic-Family Order. For reasons similar to those of the Sacred and Military Constantinian Order of St. George, pertaining to the dispute of succession between two different branches of the Family, the Royal and Illustrious Order of St. Januarius is contended by both.

The badge of the Order of Januarius consists of an eight-pointed, red enamel cross, rimmed in gold and bordered in white with a gold *fleur-de-lis* between each arm. The red robed and mitred figure of St. Januarius,

Star

Ceremonial Chain

bishop and martyr, holding two vials filled with his miraculous blood i his left hand, and giving his blessing with the right hand, is portrayed i the centre. The badge bears the motto *In Sanguine Foedus* (the covenan is sealed by the blood), and the ribbon of the Order is red.

Silver bust of St. Januarius in the Cappella del Tesoro, Naples, ceremonially dressed on high feastdays in ancient vestments.

A similar bust dating from ca. 164((1.18 m. high), also from Italy, an used for over three centuries as a reli quary.

Private Collecti

THE ROYAL HOUSE OF BAVARIA (WITTELSBACH)

THE ORDER OF ST. GEORGE, DEFENDER OF THE FAITH IN THE IMMACULATE CONCEPTION

Founded during the Crusades, according to a traditional belief, it was re-established in 1729 by Maximilian Emmanuel Elector of Bavaria, to reward exceptionally meritorious services rendered to the State by Catholic members of the Nobility. It was Bavaria's second highest Order.

Commander's Cross — Grand Cross, Star — Grand Cross

The Immaculate Conception is portrayed on the obverse of the centre medallion with St. George slaying the dragon on the reverse side of the medallion. The inscription reads: *V(irgini) I(mmaculatae) B(avaria) I(mmaculata)*: "to the Immaculate Virgin by Immaculate Bavaria".

THE ORDER OF ST. HUBERT

It was founded in 1444 by Gerhard V, Duke of Jülich-Berg (Bavaria) to commemorate the victory of the Bavarian Army over Arnold of Egmont at Ravensburg on St. Hubert's Day. It is also known as the ORDER OF THE HORN because of the little hunter's horns forming the chain. The Order became extinct towards the end of the fifteenth century and it was revived by Elector Johannes Wilhelm, Duke of Neuburg, and definitively confirmed in 1800 by Elector Maximilian Joseph, later King of Bavaria, who made it the highest ranking Order of the Bavarian Crown and reserved it for members of the Royal Family, a few foreign princes and

Badge

Star

twelve counts and barons. The legend of St. Hubert is portrayed on the badge, which consists of an eight-pointed cross, gold-rimmed and flecked. The motto is IN TRAU VAST (firm in loyalty).

THE ROYAL HOUSE OF BOURBON-ORLÉANS*

THE ORDER OF THE HOLY GHOST

The Order was founded in 1578 by Henry III, King of France (1574–1589) to mark his election to the Crown of Poland and elevation to the throne of France. The aim of the Order was to defend the Catholic Religion and to uphold the dignity of the Catholic nobility. Because of the exclusive character of this highly regarded Order, its membership was restricted to one hundred knights.

Star

Ceremonial Chain

* These French Orders are not conferred at present since H.R.H. Prince Henri, Count of Paris and Head of the House of Bourbon-Orléans is of the opinion that Dynastic Orders should be bestowed only by ruling Sovereigns.

In abeyance from 1791 to 1813 because of the French Revolution, the Order was re-established by Louis XVIII (1814–1815 and 1815–1824) and made to rank in France with the English Order of the Garter and that of the Golden Fleece. The Order has one class; its badge consists of an eight-pointed, gold, green and white enamel cross, with a white enamel dove (representing the Holy Ghost) in the centre and the figure of St. Michael slaying the dragon on the reverse of the cross. The motto is *Duce et Auspice* (led and inspired – i.e. by the Holy Ghost).

Among the politically planned Orders, this was the first one to adopt a cross as its badge instead of the emblematic figure of the Order. The image of St. Michael on the reverse of the badge recalls the merger of the Order of St. Michael with that of the Holy Ghost, brought about by King Henry III in 1578.

THE ROYAL AND MILITARY ORDER OF ST. LOUIS

Founded by Louis XIV, King of France (1643–1715), in 1693 as a military and civil award for Catholics who had rendered at least twenty-eight years of distinguished service, it was confirmed by King Louis XV, suppressed during the Revolution (1789) and finally revived again by Louis XVIII in 1816. St. Louis is portrayed on the centre medallion of the badge, which consists of an eight-pointed, gold-rimmed, white enamel cross. On the reverse are the words: *Bell(icae) Virtutis Praem(ium)* (a reward for military valour).

The Order comes in three classes: Grand Cross, Commander and Knights. A neutral Military Order of Merit was founded to complement it in 1759, open to well-deserving Protestants.

Badge

Star

THE ORDER OF ST. MICHAEL OF FRANCE

This Order was instituted in 1428 by Louis XI, King of France, (1461–1483), following an alleged apparition of the Archangel at the siege of Orléans. Being one of France's most esteemed Orders, it eventually suffered because of its lavish bestowal. Subsequently united with THE ORDER OF THE HOLY GHOST in 1578, it was radically reformed by

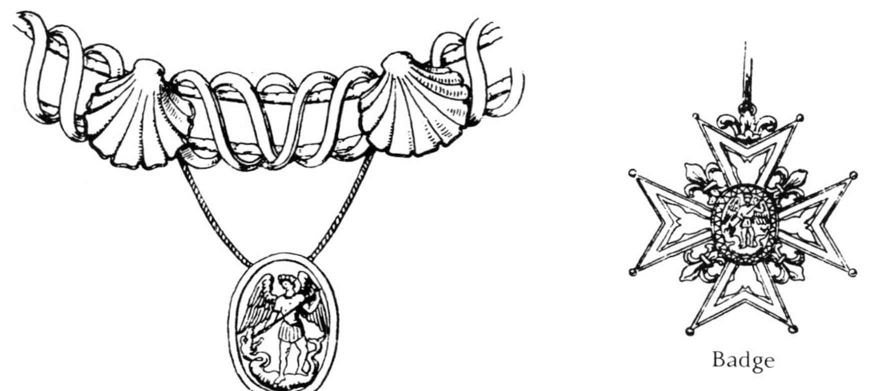

Plaque and Ceremonial Chain

Badge

Louis XIV (1661–1665). Having been suspended at the beginning of the Revolution in 1789, Louis XVIII re-established it in 1816, limiting its membership to one-hundred Knights in one class, of Catholic and of noble birth. The badge is an eight-pointed, ball-tipped cross with *fleurs-de-lis* between the arms and St. Michael slaying the dragon on an oval central medallion.

THE IMPERIAL AND ROYAL HOUSE OF HABSBURG–LORRAINE

ORDER OF THE DAMES OF THE STARRY CROSS

This Order was instituted by the Empress Eleanor Gonzaga, mother of the Emperor Leopold I (1657–1705) in 1668, in only one class, to honour Catholic ladies of the high nobility, committed to works of Christian charity. The Order was approved by Clement IX. Its aim was to commemorate the finding of a crucifix made from the wood of the True Cross which had been feared lost in a fire. The badge consists of a gold-rimmed, red enamel cross, placed in a double-headed gold and black enameled

Badge

eagle, with the inscription *Salus et Gloria* (Salvation and Glory). The Order is bestowed by His Imperial and Royal Highness Archduke Otto of Austria.

THE ORDER OF ST. JOSEPH

Established in 1514 to reward exceptionally meritorious military, civil and spiritual deeds, it remained inactive until Ferdinand III, Grand Duke of Würzburg, revived it when he became Grand Duke of Tuscany in 1807. Its members were once all of the Catholic faith. The image of St. Joseph appears on an oval medallion in the centre of a twelve-pointed, gold-rimmed white enamel star, hanging from a golden crown. The motto is *Ubique Similis* (everywhere the same). The Order is bestowed by H.I. and R.H. Godfrey, Archduke of Austria, Grand Duke of Tuscany.

Grand Cross

THE ORDER OF ST. STEPHEN

This was one of the most illustrious military Orders, founded b Cosimo de'Medici, Duke of Florence, in 1562. Its members were of noble Catholic birth, committed to fighting pirates, defending the Catholi faith, and liberating Christian slaves. The Order fought the Turks suc cessfully. After being abolished by the French Revolution, it was Fer dinand III, Grand Duke of Tuscany, in 1817 who revived the Order. It badge consists of a gold-rimmed red enameled Maltese Cross, with gol *fleurs-de-lis* between the arms and suspended from a golden crown. Th Order is bestowed by H.I. and R.H. Godfrey, Archduke of Austria, Gran Duke of Tuscany.

The red cross on a white ground in the battle-flag of the Grand Duch of Tuscany is emblematic of the Order, which won many battles, as i witnessed by the collection of numerous flags conquered by it from enemy ships and displayed in the Church of St. Stephen in Pisa. Th Order was abolished in 1866 when the Grand Duchy was annexed to th Italian Kingdom but the Archduke of Austria of the Tuscany line con tinued to award it because of its dynastic character.

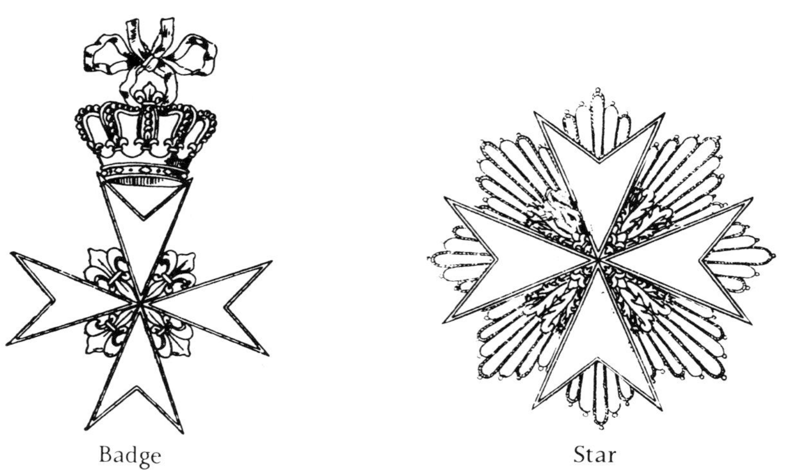

Badge

Star

Chapter Eight

STATE-FOUNDED CATHOLIC ORDERS STILL EXISTING AND THE HOLY SEE

It is quite clear from what we have already said, that the presence of the Holy See in the field of chivalry has always been a very active one. The question may be asked however: why is it that although the Papacy was always ready to approve Orders of Knighthood in good standing founded by others, it was rather slow and wary in establishing Orders of its own? Apart from the ORDER OF CHRIST, which in its earliest stage could be placed in the same category as other monastic-military Orders then in existence, most of the other Orders directly founded by the Holy See belong rather to the category of Honorary Orders and, later on, Orders of Merit, even before such Orders became a common feature of the modern State.

The reason for such cautious procedure is two-fold. On the one hand, the Holy See did not desire to become involved in all the complexities of military aspects of institutions as they were constituted in the Middle Ages. On the other hand, it felt no special need to establish Orders directly depending on itself, and only intervened in the life of Orders established by others, when it came to approving or disapproving the religious aspect. In fact the object of the majority of these Orders was the defence of Catholic beliefs and ideals, which were the universal heritage of all the members of the *Res Publica Christiana*. The Holy See could rely entirely on the loyalty of Catholics in the chivalrous society of Western Europe when it proved necessary to defend these ideals and beliefs even when the founding Rulers were moved also by political aims. Thus several Orders of Knighthood were established in the Iberian peninsula on the model of the early monastic-military Orders during the thirteenth and fourteenth centuries. Their main objective was to drive out the Muslims who were putting Spain and Portugal to a very difficult test in a rugged struggle which lasted several centuries. The repulse of the Muslims in such circumstances also meant the restitution of full religious freedom to the lands which had been invaded.

Such a society however was subject to the odds of historical evolution. Three factors intervened eventually to hasten its transformation. They were the rise of absolute monarchy claiming the undivided allegiance of its subjects, the decline of the feudal nobility forming a military aristocracy over which the Church had exercised a particular influence, and at a later date the upsurge of secular political republicanism, severing all links with religious institutions of any kind.

Nevertheless the spirit of chivalry continued to subsist even when the deliverance of the Holy Places was no longer a determining factor of Catholic Knighthood, and when the unity of the *Res Publica Christiana* was broken up by the all-pervading principles of Protestantism, and when secularism became more and more the basis of the whole social structure.

Catholic Sovereigns appreciated the importance of the spirit of chivalry for the cohesion of the social body and the defence of the State against the invasion of Europe by Muslim armies from the East and the South on the more exposed Mediterranean countries. This explains why the majority of the Orders of Chivalry, which appeared on the European scene after the loss of the Holy Places, was founded in Italy, Spain and Portugal.

Some of these Orders of Chivalry are still in existence and we shall deal with them briefly in this chapter, as we shall also deal with some Honorary Orders and Orders of Merit, founded at a later date by Catholic Sovereigns, who gave the Orders a clearly Catholic character by basing their statutes on Catholic principles and placing the Orders under the protection of a popular Catholic Saint. Many other Orders established by Catholic Sovereigns have become extinct; they will be the subject of the following chapter.

Monastic-Military Orders

The four Spanish Orders of Knighthood in this category, the Military Orders of Alcantara, Calatrava, Montesa and Santiago are among the most ancient and noble Catholic Orders of Knighthood. Though suppressed by the Spanish Republic in 1931, they continue to exist to the present day and enjoy the highest esteem in all quarters.

THE MILITARY ORDER OF ALCANTARA

SPAIN

This Order first existed as a confraternity, formed by Don Suero and Don Gómez Fernandez Barrientos in 1156. It was established as an Order of Knighthood by Ferdinand II, King of León and Galicia (1157–1188) in 1175, under the name of the Knights of St. Julian of Pereiro. The Order's aim was to drive the invading Moors back to Africa. It was approved by Alexander III (1159–1181) in 1177 under the rule of St. Benedict, and received the subsequent support of many other Popes.

Star

The Order assumed the title of ALCANTARA in 1212. Its members continued to follow the rule of St. Benedict, took vows of chastity and swore to defend the Catholic faith and in particular the belief in the Immaculate Conception of the Virgin.

The badge of the Order consists of a rhomb-shaped, white enameled gold-rimmed medallion, bearing four *fleurs-de-lis* in the form of a cross (green). A plumed helmet and trophy of flags serve as its support. The badge is similar to that of the Order of Calatrava, with which it was closely connected.

THE MILITARY ORDER OF CALATRAVA

SPAIN

This Order was founded by Don Sancho III, King of Castile (1157–1158), in 1158 under the rule of St. Benedict and the constitution of St. Bernard. It was approved by Alexander III in 1164 and by many subsequent Popes. Adrian VI (1522–1523) gave its Grand Mastership to the King of Spain, Charles V. Its aim was to defend the faith and the kingdom by fighting the Moors. Membership was restricted to Catholic noblemen with no Moorish or Jewish ancestry. Doña Gazelas Maria Yonnes founded a parallel Order of Calatrava for ladies in 1219.

Badge

The badge of the Order of Calatrava is very similar to the badge of the Order of Alcantara, the only difference being the colour of the cross which is red.

THE MILITARY ORDER OF MONTESA

SPAIN

This Order was instituted by James II, King of Aragon (1291–1327), and approved by John XXII (1316–1334) in 1317, in honour of Our Lady of Montesa and St. Peter, and also to replace the Order of the Knights Templars who had been suppressed by Clement V (1305–1314) in 1312.

The aim of the Order was to defend Spain against the Moors. Its membership was restricted to the Catholic nobility. In 1399, the Aragonese anti-pope Benedict XIII (ca. 1394–1423) united the monastic and military Order of St. George of Alfama with that of Montesa, since their aims were identical.

The badge of the Order is similar to that of the Order of Calatrava, but with a red Greek cross in the centre.

Badge

THE MILITARY ORDER OF SANTIAGO
(or OF ST. JAMES OF THE SWORD)
SPAIN

This Order may trace its origin back to a confraternity existing since 1030, but it was founded as an Order by Ferdinand II, King of León and Galicia, in 1170. It was approved by Alexander III (1159–1181) in 1175 and confirmed by Innocent III and the Fourth Lateran Council in 1215. Its early object was to defend the roads leading to the famous shrine of St. James of Compostela, and to protect the pilgrims. The members of the Order shared community life with the canons of the church of St. Eligius at Lerio, near the shrine, under the rule of St. Augustine. It was composed of Knights of fully noble birth, canons and nuns. All took the vows of poverty, obedience and chastity at the beginning, but Alexander III dispensed the Knights who wished to marry from their vow of chastity. The same dispensation did not extend to the Dames who had come to join the Order. Eventually the Knights became so wealthy and powerful that their Grand Master, who had been given episcopal dignity and authority over the Order, ranked second after the King. In 1499, Alexander VI (1254–1261) transferred the Office of Grand Master, vacant since 1493, to the Crown of Castile, in the reign of Ferdinand II the Catholic (1479–1516). Adrian VI made the King of Spain, who was then the Emperor Charles V, Perpetual Administrator of the Order. The Order remains under the protection of the Crown to this day. Since 1655 the Order's objects include the defence of the belief in the Immaculate Conception.

The badge of the Order is similar to that of the Order of Calatrava, except that the gold-rimmed, red enamel cross *fleury* has a longer lower arm, while the upper arm ends in the shape of an overturned heart,

Knight's Cross

Badge

suspended from a trophy of flags and a plumed hat. The star consists of the red cross of the badge; the ribbon is red moiré.

There exists an independent secularised Portuguese branch of the Order, with which we shall deal in Chapter Ten.

Orders of Merit

THE MOST DISTINGUISHED ORDER OF CARLOS III

Spain

Established in 1771 by Carlos III of Bourbon, King of Spain and the Indies (1779–1788), as a token of thanks to God for giving him a grandson for his succession, the Order was approved and granted special privileges by Clement XIV (1769–1774) in 1772 and by Pius VI (1775–1799) in 1783. The Order was placed under the protection of the Immaculate Conception of the Virgin, proclaimed the Patron of Spain during the reign of Carlos III. Its statutes are based on those of the Order of St. Januarius of the Two Sicilies.

The aim of the Order was to defend the Catholic religion and the mystery of the Immaculate Conception, and to serve the Kingdom faithfully. The Patriarch of the Indies was the Chancellor of the Order.

Suppressed during the Napoleonic occupation in 1808, the Order was re-established in 1814 by King Ferdinand VII (1784–1808 and 1814–1833). Once again abolished by the Spanish Republic, it was revived by Generalissimo Franco in 1942. It is now the highest ranking Spanish Order of Merit.

Knights Grand Cross

The badge of the Order is suspended from a golden laurel wreath and consists of a gold-rimmed, white and blue enameled Maltese cross with gold *fleurs-de-lis* between its arms and the figure of the Immaculate Conception (from Murillo's painting of the Virgin Mary) on the centre medallion. The inscription reads: *Virtuti et Merito* (for bravery and merit).

THE ORDER OF CISNEROS

Spain

This Order was founded by Generalissimo Franco in 1944 in honour of Cardinal Francisco Jiménez Cisneros, a Spanish Prelate and Royal Adviser (1456–1517) to stress that the new Government of Spain must rest on a solid basis and serve the Christian cause.

The badge consists of a gold-rimmed, red enameled Maltese cross, with a gold ball on each tip and a black eagle in its centre, superimposed on a gold star with ten gold arrows as rays.

THE EQUESTRIAN ORDER OF ST. AGATHA

Republic of San Marino

This Order was founded in 1923 by the Regent Captains of the Most Serene Republic of San Marino, as a mark of gratitude to St. Agatha for having, as co-Patron of the Republic, protected it against the many attempts of invading armies to deprive Mount Titano, on which the

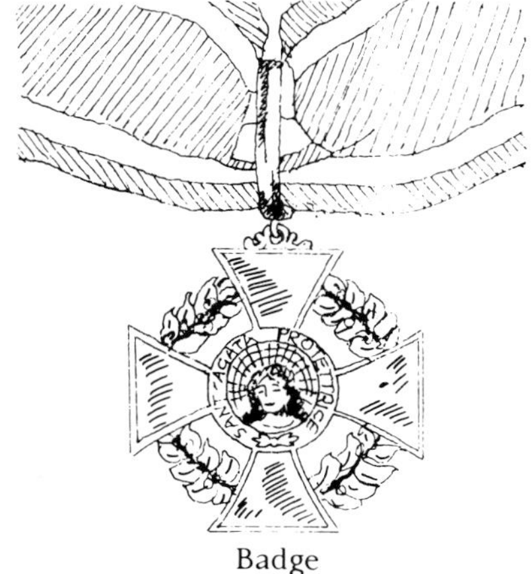

Badge

Republic is situated, of its independence and sovereignty. This was recognised by Nicholas IV (1288–1292) as early as 1291, and repeatedly by subsequent Pontiffs, who disapproved of the endeavours of certain Papal Legates to submit the Republic to the Papal States. The Order has five ranks. Its badge consists of a gold-rimmed, white enamel cross *pattée*, with a gold and green wreath between each arm. The figure of St. Agatha is portrayed on the centre medallion with the inscription: *S. Agatha Protectrice* (St. Agatha Protectress). The coat of arms of the Republic is on the reverse with the inscription: *Bene Merenti* (To one who has well deserved). The star is an eight-pointed gold and silver multirayed plaque, bearing the obverse of the badge.

THE ORDER OF ST. CHARLES

Principality of Monaco

This Order was founded in 1858 by Prince Charles III of the Principality of Monaco, in honour of his Patron Saint and as an award, in five classes, for outstanding service rendered to the Prince and the State.

The badge consists of an eight-pointed, ball-tipped cross, gold-rimmed and red-bordered, surrounded by a gold and green laurel wreath, suspended from a crown. Inscribed in gold on a white enamel band around the centre are the words *Princeps et Patria* (Prince and Country). The coat of arms of the Grimaldi family, the reigning House of Monaco, is on the reverse, which is red and white enamel bearing the inscription *Deo Iuvante* (With God's help).

Badge

Grand Cross

heir Most Serene Highnesses Rainier, Prince Sovereign of the Principality of Monaco and Princess Grace of Monaco wearing the Order of St. Charles of the Principality of Monaco.

Courtesy: The Embassy of the Principality of Monaco in Brussels

The star consists of the obverse of the badge, without the crown, an superimposed on an eight-pointed silver plaque. The ribbon is whit edged and has equal stripes of red, white, red, the colours of Monaco

THE MILITARY ORDER OF ST. FERDINAND

Spain

Founded in 1811 by General Cortes of the Kingdom of Spain, it wa confirmed by Ferdinand, King of Spain, in 1815. Its object is to honour th saintly King Ferdinand III of Castile and León (1199–1252), whose bod lies in the royal chapel of the Cathedral of Seville, and to rewar meritorious service in the Army and Navy. Re-confirmed by King Alfons XIII in 1920 and then suppressed by the Spanish Republic in 1931, it wa finally revived by Generalissimo Franco in 1940.

The badge of the Order is a Maltese, ball-pointed, white enamele gold-rimmed cross, with the figure of St. Ferdinand in regal robes po trayed on the centre medallion, surmounted on a green and gold laur wreath and suspended from a smaller gold and green wreath.

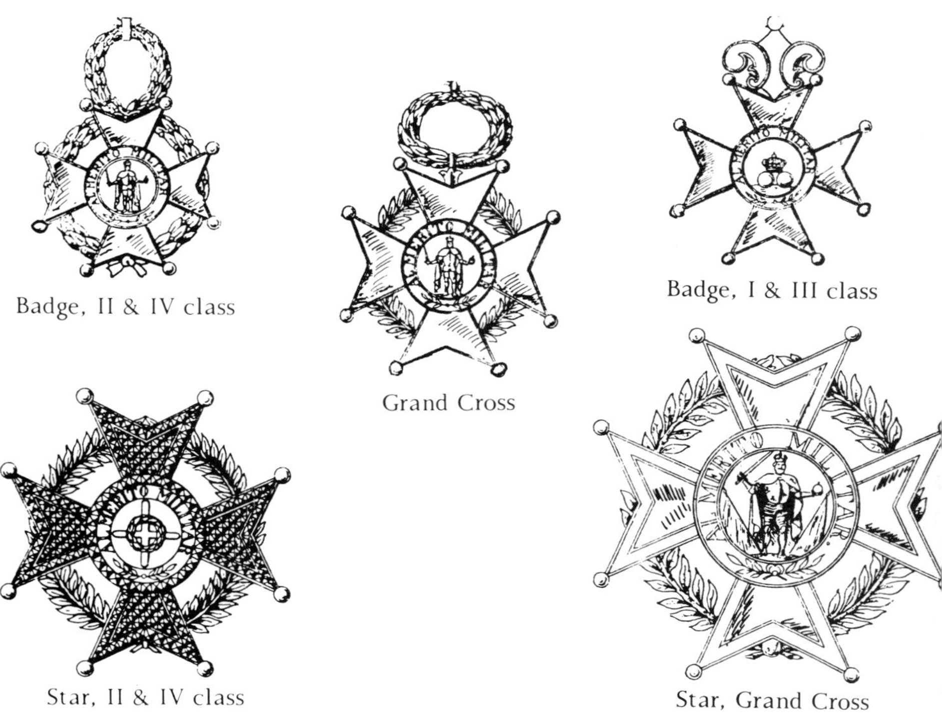

Badge, II & IV class

Grand Cross

Badge, I & III class

Star, II & IV class

Star, Grand Cross

'HE ROYAL AND MILITARY ORDER OF ST. HERMENEGILDUS

SPAIN

Founded in 1814 by Ferdinand VII, King of Spain (1808 and 1814–1833), was dedicated to St. Hermenegildus, who, taken prisoner as he led a ıilitary insurrection, suffered martyrdom rather than abjure his ;atholic faith at Tarragona, in the year 585. His public cult was author- ;ed by Sixtus V in 1585. Abolished during the Spanish Republic in 1931, it 'as revived by Generalissimo Franco in 1951 to reward outstanding ervice of members of the Spanish Army and Navy.

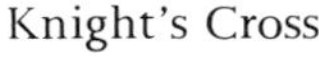

Knight's Cross

Star, Knights Grand Cross

The badge consists of a gold-rimmed, white enameled Maltese cross, ith the golden figure of St. Hermenegildus on horseback on the centre ıedallion.

THE ORDER OF ISABELLA THE CATHOLIC

SPAIN

This Order was established by Ferdinand VII, King of Spain (1808 and 814–1833) in 1815 to honour the memory of Isabella, Queen of Castile nd wife of Ferdinand of Aragon (1451–1504), with whose support Col- mbus was able to undertake his enterprise which led to the discovery of he Americas. The Order was approved by Pius VII in 1816. Once awarded or services rendered in the Spanish-American colonies, it is now granted s a reward for distinguished diplomatic, civil and military merit. It has ad a rather chequered history and undergone various reforms. bolished in 1873 by the first Spanish Republic, it was re-established shortly after when the King returned to power. The second Spanisl Republic allowed it to subsist. In 1938 Generalissimo Franco restored th(Order to its primitive splendour and status, making it Spain's seconc highest ranking Order of Merit. The Decree of that year confirms th(object of its original foundation: to honour the Queen Isabella "whc opened the gates of the Catholicity of an Empire with a never settin; sun."

The Order has five classes; the highest class, that of "Knight of th(Collar", was instituted by King Alfonso XIII (1886–1931) in 1927. I consists of twenty-five Knights, whose emblem is a beautiful golder chain, made up of seven plaquettes reproducing the badge of the Orde interlocked with the initials F (Ferdinand) and Y (Isabella), with in th(centre on one side a trophy of the arms of the House of Aragon and th(cross of the Order suspended from a wreath hanging from the chain on th(other side.

Grand Cross

Star, Knights and Dames Grand Cross

The badge, attached to a green laurel wreath, is a gold-rimmed, rec enameled, ball-pointed Maltese Cross with gold rays between its arm: and the gold "Pillars of Hercules" with a white banner bearing the inscription *Plus Ultra* (Still farther) portrayed on the centre medallion. Two blue world globes capped by a gold crown appear next to the Pillars. The medallion is surrounded by a white enamel band with the inscription *A La Lealtad Acrisolada* (To well tested loyalty) and *Por Isabel la Catolica*.

The star is similar to the badge for the first class but somewhat larger. A laurel wreath surrounds the medallion. The ribbon is of yellow moiré with white stripes.

In 1927 King Alfonso XIII decreed that ladies should be honoured by he Order with two different awards: the *lazo* (the Order's ribbon tied in bow) and, in exceptional cases, the *banda* (a riband) to both of which s appended the star of the Order as described above.

THE CIVIL AND MILITARY ORDER OF SAN MARINO

Republic of San Marino

This Order was established in 1859 by the Grand and General Council f the Republic of San Marino, as its statutes say "as a sign of gratitude owards Divine Providence and the creator of the Republic, Marino". In act, the founder of this Republic, the most ancient in the world, was a ertain Marino, a stone-cutter from the island of Arbe, who fleeing from he persecution of the Emperor Diocletian (284–305), took refuge with is associate, Leo, on Mount Titano, given to him by a noble lady of imini whom he had converted to Catholicism. He is celebrated as a ational Patron Saint on the fifth Sunday after Easter. This Order is the nain Knighthood of the Republic. It has five classes of which the first lass, Knight Grand Cross, is reserved for Heads of State, members of eigning Royal Families, high State Officials and very meritorious perons.

Badge

The badge is a gold-rimmed, white enamel cross, suspended from a crown (though San Marino was always a Republic), with birostrated arms and a gold ball in the middle of each and a gold tower between each arm. The portrait of St. Marinus encircled by a gold-rimmed blue band bearing the inscription *San Marino Protettore* (St. Marinus Protector) is on the centre medallion. The coat of arms of the Republic appears on the reverse, surrounded by a gold and blue band with the inscription *Merito Civile e Militare* (Civil and Military Merit). The star consists of a gold-rimmed, white enamel multirayed cross with a green and gold wreath between its arms and the inscription *Relinquo Vos Liberos Ab Utroque Homine* (I leave you free from both men) – clearly referring to early attempts of submission by external Powers, both temporal and spiritual.

THE ORDER OF THE CROSS OF ST. RAYMOND OF PEÑAFORT

SPAIN

This Order was instituted by Generalissimo Franco in 1945, under the protection of the great Spanish canonist whose name it bears, and who is the Catholic Patron of lawyers. The object of the Order is to honour outstanding jurists and canonists of both sexes.

The badge consists of a ball-pointed, gold-rimmed, white enamel cross, surrounded by a golden laurel wreath, with the figure of St. Raymond de Peñafort on the centre medallion and the inscription *In Iure Merita* (to honour legal merit). To the Order belongs the Peñafort Medal which is awarded in four classes and suspended from a red ribbon with narrow blue borders; it is an eight-pointed medallion.

Star, Knights Commander

CHAPTER NINE

EXTINCT CATHOLIC ORDERS OF KNIGHTHOOD AND THE HOLY SEE

When we speak of "extinct" Catholic Orders of Knighthood we intend o deal with those preponderantly but not exclusively mediaeval Orders vhich owe their existence to a Catholic initiative, were recognised and ven approved by the Holy See, but have ceased to exist. Attempts have een made from time to time to resurrect these Orders, but without uccess, especially because they had fulfilled the purpose for which they ad been established and found it difficult to survive in a new political nd social context.

Many of the "autonomous" or in some case "self-styled" Orders with vhich we shall deal in Chapter Eleven, have called themselves after hese ancient Orders but, as we shall see, they are not recognised by the Ioly See nor by public law for that matter, because their attempted 're-establishment" is due to the efforts of private individuals or bodies nd not to the initiative of a Sovereign Power, who is the *fons honorum* the source of honours).

In the beginning, Orders of Knighthood of a religious and military haracter were indeed the result of private endeavours. Once their value nd credibility were established, they were taken under the patronage of he Papacy or a State. It was only after the thirteenth century that these)rders became institutionalised so as to require a formal act of establ-shment emanating from a Sovereign Power, be it the Holy See or a State. uch a measure was the natural outcome of the evolution of political and ocial organisation, but it was especially required to contain excesses nd to suppress abuses.

In conformity with the social pattern of the times and also because of he hardships involved in the enterprise, only men were admitted as full nembers to the ancient Orders.

Women were often present in the life of the Orders, rendering precious ervice in the various works of mercy allocated to them.

The Order of the Hatchet had as members a group of women, who were iven the title "Dames of the Hatchet" as a reward for their brave ehaviour during the siege of Tortosa in Catalonia in 1149. As we have lready seen, women were admitted to the Military Order of Santiago as arly as 1175. The Order of the glorious St. Mary, founded by Loderigo l'Andalò, a nobleman of Bologna, and approved by Alexander IV in

1261, was the first religious Order of Knighthood to grant the rank o *militissa* to women. This Order was suppressed by Sixtus V in 1558.

At the initiative of Catharine Baw in 1441, and ten years later o Elizabeth, Mary and Isabella of the House of Hornes, Orders were founded which were open exclusively to women of noble birth, who received the French title of *chevalière* (lady knight) or the Latin title *equitissa*.

Nobility was a common requirement for admission to an Order o Knighthood. Members of the upper classes who were not nobles, were ennobled upon entrance into the Order. This was due to the fact that on the one hand equality had not as yet been introduced as a governing principle in the society of the times, and also that only nobles and their liegemen were considered fully reliable to fight for their Prince. On the other hand, when the Crusades began and the first Orders of Knighthood were founded, the feudal nobility, who had attained the summit of their power, were the main instrument of the Papacy in the struggle for the deliverance of the Holy Land.

Loyal supporters of the Throne, who were not of noble birth, were named "companions". They were not enrolled among the members of the Order as such, but wore badges resembling its insignia and did not have the same obligations.

The Christian concept of knighthood was served a severe blow first with the advance of absolutism, especially starting from the sixteenth

Cross of the Militia of Our Lady

century onwards when according to the formula *cuius regio illius et religio*, the custom was that the ruler's religion was to be imposed upon his subjects as the State religion. From then on Orders of Chivalry became more and more an instrument of political propaganda.

Absolutism among the Princes thus set one nation against the other and stultified any international effort to bring peoples together such as that which had been produced by the early Orders of Knighthood. The situation grew even worse when the king identified the State with himself (*l'état c'est moi*) in the seventeenth century. But it was the secular State in the eighteen-hundreds which finally took upon itself to rid society and all civil institutions of every religious influence and character. The ancient Orders of Knighthood were consequently replaced, in most cases, by Orders of Merit newly instituted by the State, generally following the pattern of the *Légion d'Honneur* founded by the French Republic in 1802. In truth, it was a normal development since the feudal loyalty demanded by the original chivalric system was no longer consistent with the tenets of modern society. The principle of equality finally introduced in human relations, was also applied to Orders of Knighthood, often at the expense of the nobility. The commendable rule was thus established that highminded standards and noble actions are the monopoly of no particular social class, but the heritage and duty of all free men and women alike. The Orders opened their doors thus to women as well.

It must be said, however, that despite all efforts of secularisation, the basic principle of altruistic and gentlemanly behaviour inspiring Orders of Knighthood remained unchanged, even in the Orders of Merit. In fact they were instituted to reward men and women who had performed meritorious deeds and to set them as an example capable to stimulate their fellowmen to follow in their path. Furthermore, even in our day of almost universal secularising tendencies in the Western world, Orders of Merit continue to follow the structural model of the ancient knighthoods as emblems, titles and ranks are concerned, and have no qualms about their use, though their origin is distinctly Catholic, such as Grand Cross, Cross, and even Commander and Knight forming the traditional three classes. The division in five classes was introduced by the French Republic when it suppressed the French Military Orders of the previous régime and replaced them with the *Légion d'Honneur*. The relationship between the members of these Orders of Merit is, however, very superficial or even non existent, as are also, generally speaking, the obligations of the same towards the Orders themselves.

One could carry these reflections further by observing that even the Communist States have imitated the general concept and pattern of the ancient knighthoods, albeit replacing the cross by the star or other emblems acceptable to their philosophy and excluding every reference implying an ethico-religious or chilvalric connotation. Thus in H.V Krantz's *Handbuch Europäischer Orden in Farben*, published in Berlin in 1966, we find the U.S.S.R. with fourteen Orders of Knighthood, and many other Communist States, such as Hungary with eight, and Bulgaria with six, Orders of Knighthood, etc. It was only after the second World War that the Soviet Union began to adopt the general rule of dividing Orders into different classes.

One might also add that notwithstanding the essential historical link with the exploits of the Crusaders and the typical Western character of the very institution of Knighthood, even Muslim States have imitated the Christian West in establishing Orders of Knighthood. It is obvious that they too would reject all Christian emblems from their armorial and insignia and replace them with a star, the sun, a crescent, a flower or the like. They do however retain the titles and ranks of Commander and Knight which are so markedly reminiscent of an era when Muslims and Christians were fighting one another.

It is absolutely impossible to draw up a complete list of the Catholic Orders which have existed over the centuries throughout the Middle Ages and modern times. Their name is indeed legion and this is largely due to the fact that their existence and reason for establishment was not restricted to military exploits. They were likewise intended to provide Western society, whose mediaeval texture was officially Catholic, with pious organisations of laymen, placed under the patronage of some favourite Saint, in which and through which layfolk could attend to their own spiritual progress, mindful of the words of St. Paul: "Let us . . . throw off the deeds of darkness and put on our armour as soldiers of the light. Let us behave with decency as befits the day: no revelling or drunkenness, no debauchery or vice, no quarrels or jealousies! Let Christ himself be the armour that you wear!" (Rom. 13, 12–14). These words were taken literally for all they meant in the age of faith. Furthermore, these Orders, besides offering the spiritual advantages of monasticism, enabled their members to be of social service. They were, in fact, the ancestor of social organisations so fully developed in our day, totally committed to the care of the sick and, in general, to the practice of all the beatitudes given by Jesus to his disciples in the Sermon on the Mount as a code for perfect Christian behaviour (Matth.5, 1–15). Their diversified activity was all the more welcome because the State and society were not yet organised in such a way as to be able to attend to works of mercy and social welfare. This, as we have already said, the State began to do towards the end of the eighteenth century. The Orders of Merit which then took the place of the ancient monastic-military Orders were not invested with any special social activity, since the modern State gradually claimed for itself the right and duty of organising social welfare.

In a general way, Catholic Orders of Knighthood may be divided into *ephemeral* or short-lived Orders and *longevous* or long-lived Orders. We shall do no more than mention a very few of the *ephemeral* Orders. Despite their short existence they are of interest in that they demonstrate the different facets of the spirit of chivalry and often provide the name and structure for many "autonomous" or "self-styled" Orders.

I

SHORT-LIVED ORDERS OF KNIGHTHOOD

The Order of St. Mark (early Middle Ages; no precise date available);
The Order of St. Anthony of Vienna (1005);
The Order of SS. John and Thomas (1205);

Insignia of the Order SS. John and Thomas

The Order of the Militia of Jesus Christ, or of St. Dominic (1216);
The Order of Mercy (1218);
The Order of the Glorious St. Mary (1261);
The Order of St. James, or of the Shell (1290);
The Order of the Dove (1379);
The Order of St. Anthony of Hainault (1382);
The Order of St. John Lateran (1560);

The Order of Our Lady of Loreto (1587);
The Order of Jesus and Mary (1615);
The Order of the Immaculate Conception (1617);
The Order of the Celestial Collar of the Holy Rosary (1645);
The Order of Brotherly Love (1708);
The Order of St. Bridget of Sweden (1814).

II

LONG-LIVED ORDERS OF KNIGHTHOOD

Longevous or long-lived Orders of Knighthood are of greater interest because of the important part they played in the religious, military and civil history of a country. They may be divided chronologically into two broad categories: the ancient Orders, which were more of a monastic military nature, and existed throughout the Middle Ages up to the sixteenth century; and the modern Orders, which were more of an honorary and meritorious character and appeared between the sixteenth and the eighteenth centuries. We shall again recall only the more significant among these Orders, arranging them alphabetically and adding a brief note about their origin, character and history.

Because of its extraordinary importance in the history of Orders of Knighthoods, we shall, however, begin with the Order of the Knights Templars and deal with this Order at greater length.

Mediaeval Period

THE ORDER OF THE KNIGHTS TEMPLARS

Also known as the Order of the Poor Knights (or Soldiers) of Christ and of the Temple of Solomon, it is generally accepted that the Order of the Knights Templars was founded in 1119, by Hugues de Payens, a Knight of Champagne, as a religious community, whose aims were to fight with a pure mind for the supreme and true King, "living in chastity, obedience and poverty, according to the rule of St. Benedict", to forsake that form of chivalry "of which human favour and not Jesus Christ was the cause", to protect the Holy Sepulchre and the pilgrims flocking to the Holy Land after the first Crusade, and finally to guard the public roads leading there. St. Bernard was the Order's spiritual adviser. The King of

Jerusalem, Baldwin II, accommodated the newly founded community in a part of his royal palace near the site of the Temple of Solomon, whence the name Templars or *pauvres chevaliers du temple* (poor knights of the Temple).

The rule of the Order was sanctioned by the Council of Troyes in 1128 and approved by Innocent II in 1139. Its members, consisting of Knights, Chaplains and Men-at-arms, owed obedience to their Grand Master and to the Pope, and enjoyed absolute exemption from all other ecclesiastical jurisdiction. They wore a long white cloak, to which a red cross at the left shoulder was added at a later date. The Order's seal depicted two Knights riding together on one horse, thus recalling that the first Master was so poor that he had to share a horse with another Knight.

The Order's banner was charged with a red cross and striped black and white. Hence their war-cry *Bauçant*, which in Old French meant an animal with white spots on a black or bay ground.

Establishments of the Order multiplied in the Christian West, enriched with spiritual favours and material possessions. Its first house in England was built near Holborn Bars, London, as early as 1121. It settled later in a building it was offered between Fleet Street and the Thames in 1162. The two famous Inns of Court, known as the Inner and the Middle Temple, stand on the site once occupied by the Templars and where the Temple Church, dating from 1183, alone remains.

Seal of the Knights Templar

The seal of the Order portraying a horse carrying two knights is reproduced on one of the windows of the Temple Church. The seal itself was discovered in the sixteenth century in a very poor state of preservation. The antiquaries and notaries of that time misinterpreted the seal, mistaking the two knights for two wings. This explains why, since the sixteenth century, the Inner Temple has, as its official seal a "corruption" of the true seal, representing a Pegasus, a mythological winged horse, sprung from Medusa at her death and who with a blow from his hoof caused Hippocrene, the fountain of the Muses, to spring from Mount

Helicon. The "corruption" was put right in the windows of the Temple Church, which were set in later.

Though powerful and wealthy, there do not appear to have been more than twenty of the total of one-hundred and forty-four Templars in the British Isles resident in the City of London.

Edward II (1307–1327) suppressed the Order's English branch and confiscated its possessions, assigning the Order's properties to the Knights Hospitallers, who in the reign of Edward III (1327–1377) granted these estates to the Students of the Common Law of England.

The Order was in its time greatly admired, feared and exploited by the political leaders of the West. Thanks to their immense wealth, the Knights were a most important factor of political influence in Europe. Their property consisted not only of territorial possessions but also, and especially, of a power to dispose of large sums of money, thanks to which they became the most important and greatest international financiers of the age. They had several Banks, the most important of which was the Paris Temple, the very centre of the world's money market. It was in this area that the Order acquired an autonomy which made it practically independent of temporal rulers, who only too often had recourse to the services of the Templars when in need of financial help. But the very riches and the wealth of the Order were to become the cause of its ruin. Its privileges, immunities and in particular its almost limitless wealth were eventually resented by the political leaders, and by none more than Philip the Fair, King of France (1285–1314), in whose kingdom the Order had constituted a State within a Sate.

King Philip set about perfidiously to suppress the power and wealth of the Templars, which he succeeded in doing in 1307 by ordering the arrest of all the Knights in his realm. There is no doubt that the Knights were arrested on false charges, and Philip called upon all other princes to imitate his example. He brought pressure to bear especially on the French Pope Clement V (1305–1314), who was extremely susceptible to French influence. After much hesitation, and quite unwillingly, Clement V surrendered to Philip's instigation and to the decision of the Council of Vienna (1311). He suppressed the Templars in 1312 and subsequently transferred their possessions to the Hospitallers.

The Templar's stronghold in Paris was taken over by the Knights of St. John in 1313. The old tower was later transformed into a prison, where the royal family of France was confined. It was demolished by Napoleon at the beginning of the Empire (1804).

Untold suffering was the lot of the Templars, upon whose tragic history

The Temple Church in the City of London, popularly known as the Round Church. It was consecrated in 1185 and the choir was added in 1240. In 1312 the property of the Knights Templar, including the church, passed to the Knights Hospitallers, who themselves were suppressed during the Reformation. The property passed to the Crown and in 1608 James I gave the freehold of the property of the Knights Templars to the Benchers of the Inner Temple and the Middle Temple, subject to the lawyers "maintaining the Temple Church and its services for ever". It has been their pride to do so until the present.

Courtesy: The Master of The Temple
Very Rev. Canon J. Robinson

silence fell heavily after the burning of the Grand Master Jacques de Moley in 1314 by King Philip the Fair of France.

The memory and the example of the Knights, however, continued to inspire various movements over the centuries, which endeavoured to perpetuate the system and organisation of the Knights Templars, and among such movements we even find Masonic societies in the United States of America. In more recent times a disturbing number of autonomous and self-styled Orders, all bearing the name "Templars" have appeared on the public scene. They pretend to be the legitimate successors of the Order of the Knights Templars, but such a claim obviously lacks any historical and juridical support. Some of them produce copies of ancient papal documents referring to the extinct Order as a proof of their legitimacy, which, of course, is not recognised by the Holy See. Others search permission – which is never granted – to use the Temple Church in the City of London in order to assert some connexion with the old Order and thereby attain a measure of credibility. This reprovable behaviour needs to be brought to the special attention of the public which must be warned against the abuses of these self-styled Templars.

THE ORDER OF THE ANCIENT NOBILITY OF THE FOUR EMPERORS

EMPIRE

Founded by Emperor Henry VII in 1308 under the Patronage of the Guardian Angel, it became extinct in the sixteenth century, was later revived and united with the Order of Merit of the Lion of Holstein-Limburg, under the patronage of St. Philip. Its object was the defence of the faith. It was reserved for members of the nobility and higher clergy, and was held in great esteem. The Order ceased to exist during the second half of the last century.

THE ORDER OF THE DEFEATED DRAGON

EMPIRE

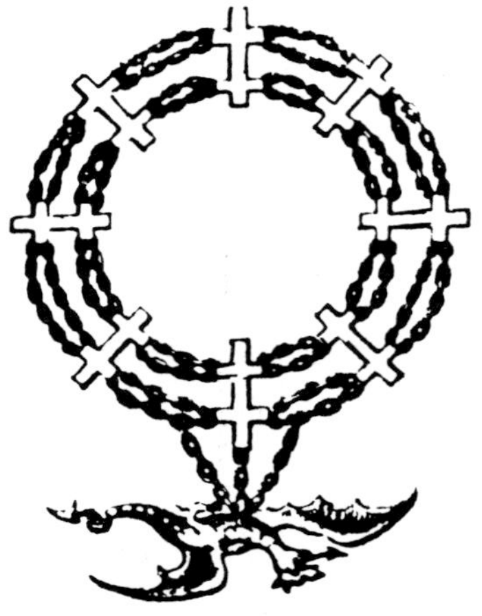

Collar of Knights

The Order was established in 1418 by Emperor Sigismund after the Council of Constance, to defend the Church against the heretics, especially the Hussites. The defeated dragon is a symbol of the destruction of heresy. The Order flourished in Germany and Italy.

THE ORDER OF THE FLEET

or

THE ORDER OF THE TWO MOONS

France

It was founded by St. Louis, King of France, in 1262. Its object was to encourage members of the nobility to go to the Middle East to fight the Muslims and defend the interests of the Church.

THE ORDER OF THE HACHA or HATCHET

Spain

This Order was founded in ca. 1149 by Raymond Berengarius, Count of Barcelona, as a female Order of Knighthood, to honour the women who fought for the liberation of Tortosa in Catalonia. The town was attacked by the Moors and the women helped in their defeat. The Dames admitted to the Order received many privileges and took precedence over men in public assemblies.

THE ORDER OF THE HOLY GHOST OF MONTPELLIER

France

Established in 1195 at Montpellier at a confraternity at the service of the Hospital, it was approved and transformed into a Religious, Hospitaller and Military Order in 1198. Its object was to care for the sick and to fight the Albigenses. Suppressed by Louis XIV (1643–1715) in 1672, and revived in 1693, it lost its military character in 1708 and in 1711 it was finally united with the ORDER OF OUR LADY OF MOUNT CARMEL AND ST. LAZARUS by Pope Clement XIII (1758–1769).

THE ORDER OF THE HOLY VIAL

France

Believed to be the most ancient of French Orders, founded, by Clovis I in 493, it was reserved exclusively for members of the nobility. Having

Insignia of the Order of the Holy Vial

disappeared in the course of centuries, an attempt was made to revive it in the eighteen-hundreds but without success.

THE ORDER OF THE MILITARY CINCTURE

Sicily

It was founded by Roger I Grand Count of Sicily (1072–1101), in the eleventh century to reward members of the highest ranking families of the kingdom for their services and their fidelity. The Knights of this Order were known as the *Torquati Aurati* or Aureate Knights because of the gold chain they carried around the neck.

THE ORDER OF MONTJOIE

Spain

Founded in Palestine in ca. 1180 for the protection of the pilgrims to the Holy Land, it took its name from Mount Joy, built by the Christians near Jerusalem. The Order was approved by Alexander III (1159–1181), who gave it the rule of St. Basil. After the loss of the Holy Land, the Order retired to Spain to fight the Moors, and it finally ceased to exist in 1221 after being divided into two different Orders, Montfrac and Truxillo; the members of the former eventually joined the Order of Calatrava, those of the latter the Order of Alcantara.

THE ORDER OF OUR LADY OF BETHLEHEM

PAPAL

This Order was founded by Pius II (1458–1464) in 1459 to defend the island of Lemnos against the Muslims. When the island fell, the Order collapsed and its estates were given to the Order of Malta by Innocent VIII (1484–1492) in 1484.

THE SACRED AND MILITARY ORDER OF OUR LADY OF MERCY

SPAIN

Founded in 1218 by St. Peter Nolascus under the rule of St. Augustine for the ransom of Christians captured by the Muslims, it immediately obtained the support of King James I of Aragon (1213–1276) uncle of the founder, and the approval of Gregory IX (1227–1241) in 1235. During the first century of existence it was an exclusively military Order including priests among its members for spiritual administrations. The Order spread through Spain, Sicily and Southern France, and had a famous monastery in Paris. Its first eight Grand Masters were elected among the Knights, but since 1317 the Holy See decreed that the office should be held by a priest. The Knights protested, and John XXII (1316–1334) having decided to change it into a merely religious institution, the Knights joined the newly founded Order of Montesa. Attempts have been made to revive the Order as a Knighthood in the past few decades but they met with the Holy See's strong disapproval. The Knights wore a white mantle; their badge consisted of the arms of the House of Aragon surmounted by a cross.

The religious branch of this Order has survived under the name of the Order of the Blessed Virgin Mary of Mercy. Its headquarters are at present in Rome and it has, as its aims, the preservation and defence of the faith of those who are persecuted, the apostolate among prisoners and other parochial, educational and missionary activities.

THE ORDER OF ST. GEORGE OF ALFAMA

SPAIN

Established in 1201 by Peter II, King of Aragon (1196–1213) as a religious military Order in honour of St. Peter and to fight the Moors, it was united with the Monastic and Military Order of Montesa by the anti-pope Benedict XIII (1394–1423) in 1399.

THE ORDER OF ST. GEORGE OF BURGUNDY

Belgium

Also known as the Order of Belgium or the Order of Miolans, it was founded in 1390 by Philibert of Miolans in honour of St. George, whose relics he had brought to Belgium from the Holy Land. It began as a confraternity but became a religious-military Order in 1485 with its membership restricted to the French County and dedicated to defending the purity of the faith and observing obedience to the Sovereign. Having gone into abeyance, the Bourbons revived the Order, which remained dormant during the French Revolution but was finally abolished by Louis XVIII, King of France (1814–1815 and 1815–1824), in 1824.

THE ORDER OF ST. GEORGE IN CARINTHIA

Empire

This Order was established by Emperor designate Rudolph I of Habsburg (1273–1291) in 1273 to continue the ORDER OF ST. GEORGE OF AUSTRIA. It was re-established on Christmas night in Rome in the year 1468 by Emperor Frederick III (1452–1493) as a lay and religious, military and civil Dynastic Order. The Order was approved on 1 January 1469 by Paul II (1464–1471) and again in 1472 by Sixtus IV (1471–1484). It was amplified by Emperor Maximilian I (1493–1519) and approved by Alexander VI (1492–1503) in 1493 together with the Confraternity of St. George in Carinthia, to which he asked to be admitted as a member together with the Sacred College. In the fifteenth and sixteenth centuries the Order was described as one of the most important of the Holy Roman Empire. The badge consisted of a four-pointed star with a red enamel cross *botonné* in the centre, bearing the Carinthian crown of the Holy Roman Empire on the upper arm. The Order was finally abolished and suppressed in 1781 by Emperor Joseph II (1765–1790). This Order is now listed in Chapter Eleven among the self-styled Orders which are in no way approved or recognised by the Holy See. Any documents, pontifical and ecclesiastical, once granted for religious purposes to this Order are not acknowledged by the Holy See as applicable to this newly erected association.

THE ORDER OF ST. HUBERT OF LORRAINE
or
THE ORDER OF THE BAR
FRANCE

Founded in 1416 by Louis, Duke of Bar, it was placed under the patronage of St. Hubert. Its object was to reward members of the nobility for accomplishing acts of outstanding charity. King Louis XV of France

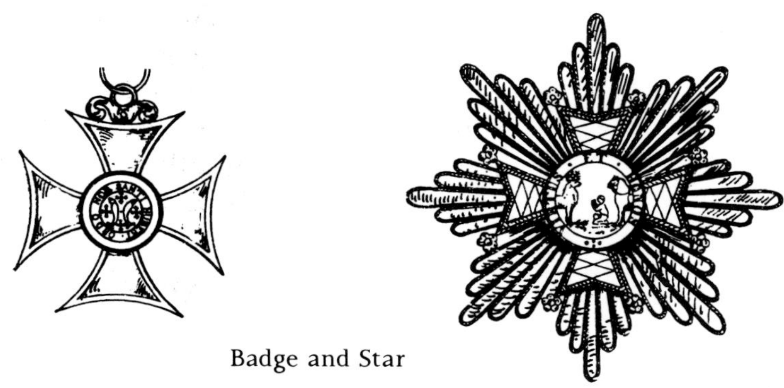

Badge and Star

(1715–1774) took the Order under his special protection. Suppressed by the French Revolution, the Order was revived by Louis XVIII in 1816 but finally abolished in 1824.

THE ORDER OF ST. JAMES OF ALTOPASCIO
TUSCANY

This Order was founded in Altopascio, Tuscany, in 952 with the object of helping pilgrims and defending the roads. Originally its members were religious brothers, who specialised in building bridges; hence the peculiar black mantle they wore with a red hood and figures of hammers on it. It had a Grand Master in Italy and a Commander General in France. In 1459 Pius II suppressed this Order and sent its members and applicants to the Order of Our Lady of Bethlehem, recently established by him. The Hospital of St. James near Lucca was assigned to the Order of St. Stephen. The French branch of the Order continued for at least another two centuries.

THE ORDER OF ST. MICHAEL'S WING

PORTUGAL

It was instituted by Alfonso I Enriquez, King of Portugal (1139–1185), in 1147 to celebrate his victory at Santarem on St. Michael's Day. The Order adopted the rule of St. Benedict.

THE ORDER OF THE SWAN

BRANDENBURG

Founded in 1440 by Frederick II, Elector of Brandenburg (1440–1470), the Order was placed under the protection of the Blessed Virgin Mary

Badge

whose image with the child Jesus was portrayed on the badge. The Order was bestowed regardless of sex or religion. Having remained dormant for a few centuries, King Frederick Wilhelm IV (1840–1861) revived it in 1843, but this revival was of short duration.

THE ORDER OF THE SWORD BEARERS

LITHUANIA

Instituted in 1202 by Albert of Apeldera, Bishop of Livonia, on the model of the Templars, and recognised by Innocent III (1198–1216), it was incorporated with the Teutonic Order by Gregory IX (1227–1241) in 1237. It was one of the most illustrious Northern Orders of the Baltic area;

Badge

Its object was to fight idolaters. The Order ceased to exist in 1562, after its Grand Master Gothard Kettler converted to Lutheranism in 1561. The Order was also known as 'Bretheren of the Militia of Christ', 'Knights of Livonia'. 'Knights of the Two Swords', 'Bretheren of the Sword' and 'Brothers of Christ'.

THE ORDER OF THE WHITE EAGLE

POLAND

Believed to have been established by Lech I, Prince of Poland in the sixth century, who named it after a nest of white eagles he found while

The Order of the White Eagle superimposed on the Russian Eagle after Russia annexed Poland but retained the Order which was raised to an Imperial and Royal Russian Order.

digging the foundations of Gnesen, its first statutes date back to 1325 when Casimir, the son of Wladislav I, King of Poland (1320–1323) of the Dynasty of Piast, married Anna, Princess of Lithuania. The Order remained dormant until Augustus II (1697–1704 and 1709–1733) revived it in 1704. After going into abeyance, following the defeat of the Polish Kingdom in 1795, Czar Nicholas I of Russia (1825–1855) incorporated it with Russian Orders until the Polish Republic revived it for the use o Poland (1921–1940). The Order was still conferred by the Polish Government in exile between 1940 and 1944. It was posthumously awarded to General Sikorski, Polish Prime Minister in exile, in 1943.

The medallion bore the figure of the White Eagle, emblem of Poland, with Our Lady and the Child Jesus on the obverse of the decoration, and the monogram of Mary on the reverse.

Modern Times

THE ORDER OF OUR LADY OF GUADALUPE

Mexico

This Order was founded in 1822 by Emperor Agustin de Iturbide o Mexico to honour the Patron of Mexico, Our Lady of Guadalupe. It became dormant after the Emperor's abdication in 1823 until Presiden Santa Anna revived the Order in 1853. Abolished once again in 1855 Emperor Maximilian I of Mexico re-established the Order in 1863. A gold figure of Our Lady of Guadalupe was portrayed on the medallion. The inscriptions read: *Religion, Independencia, Union* (Religion, Independence and Unity), and on the reverse: *Al Patriotismo Heroico* (For heroic patriotism).

Grand Cross

Star, Knights Grand Cross

THE ORDER OF OUR LADY OF MOUNT CARMEL and THE ORDER OF ST. LAZARUS OF JERUSALEM

FRANCE

The Order of Our Lady of Mount Carmel was founded by Henry IV, King of France (1589–1610) in 1607, to commemorate his conversion to the Catholic faith. The Order added the title of St. Lazarus to its name a year later, following the merger with the ancient Order of St. Lazarus of Jerusalem, which had been established in Jerusalem in 1060. After being confirmed by the King's successors, the Order was suppressed by the French Revolution in 1791 and revived temporarily by Louis XVIII in 1814. The Order of Our Lady of Mount Carmel and St. Lazarus was finally abolished in 1830. The Virgin and Child were portrayed on the badge.

The Cross of the combined Orders of Our Lady of Mount Carmel and Lazarus

Autonomous Orders now styled "of St. Lazarus", as listed in Chapter Eleven, are in no way approved or recognised by the Holy See.

Pontifical documents once granted for religious purposes to the ancient Order, are not applicable to the several newly founded Orders of St. Lazarus.

THE ORDER OF OUR LADY OF VILA VIÇOSA

PORTUGAL

Founded by John VI, King of Portugal and Brazil (1816–1826) in 1819 to honour Our Lady of the Conception, it was given as an award for outstanding civil and military merit to persons of Portuguese, Brazilian and foreign nationality. The initials *MA* (for Mary) are inscribed on the medallion with the words *Padroina do Reino* (Patroness of the Kingdom). The Order was suppressed by the newly installed Portuguese Republic.

Badge

Star

The gold crown from which the medallion was suspended is reminiscent of the crown of the Portuguese Kingdom which was placed on the effigy of Our Lady in 1646 by King John IV (1640–1656), who solemnly proclaimed Mary Patroness and Queen of Portugal. Since then the Portuguese Kings never again wore a crown. The Royal Chapel where the image is revered was built under the patronage of the Military Order of Avis and is the spiritual centre of Portuguese unity. It was visited by John Paul II (1978–) on 15 May 1982.

THE ORDER OF ST. ANNE (München)

Bavaria

Founded in 1784 by Anna Maria Sophia, widow of the Elector Maximilian IV, for noble Catholic ladies, its abbess was always a princess of the House of Bavaria. Its object was to encourage charitable deeds. The badge bore the figure of St. Anne.

THE ORDER OF ST. ANNE (Würzburg)

Bavaria

Established by the Countess Anna Maria von Dernbach in 1714 and approved by the Bishop of Würzburg, it was officially recognised by Ferdinand II, Grand Duke of Tuscany when he also became Grand Duke of Würzburg in 1811. It was reserved exclusively for ladies of the Bavarian nobility. Its object was to help needy young women.

THE ORDER OF ST. CHARLES

MEXICO

Emperor Maximilian of Mexico established this Order in 1865, two years before he was overthrown and executed, to honour St. Charles Borromeo and to reward ladies who had accomplished meritorious deeds of charity or civil service.

Knight's Cross

The decoration consists of a white enameled, gold-rimmed cross on which was superimposed a green enameled, gold-rimmed cross bearing on the obverse the words *San Carlo* and on the reverse *Humilitas*, which was the motto of St. Charles Borromeo, Cardinal Archbishop of Milan (1538 – 1563 – 1584). The Order came in two classes, the Grand Cross and the small Cross, and the ribbon was crimson moiré.

THE ORDER OF ST. ELIZABETH (Sultzbach)

BAVARIA

The Order was founded by Elizabeth Augusta, daughter of Joseph Charles, Count Palatine of Sultzbach and first wife of the Elector Charles Theodor, in 1766. It was reserved for noble Catholic ladies who had accomplished outstanding deeds of charity. The Order was confirmed by Clement XIII (1758–1769). Its badge portrayed the figure of St. Elizabeth being visited by Our Lady.

THE IMPERIAL ORDER OF ST. FAUSTIN

HAITI

This Order was established by Faustin I, Emperor of Haiti, in 1849 t honour his Patron Saint and to reward distinguished naval and militar service. It became extinct when the empire was overthrown in 1859.

The badge consisted of a gold ball-tipped, eight-rayed, double-pointe star, suspended from a golden crown. A crowned eagle adorned the blu enameled centre medallion with the inscription *Dieu, Ma Patrie et Mo Epée* (God, my Country and my Sword). The reverse bore a gold profile o the Emperor Faustin and the words *Faustin Empereur d'Haiti*.

The star was an eight-pointed silver plaque. The obverse of the badg was reproduced on the centre medallion. The ribbon was pale blu moiré.

THE ORDER OF ST. FERDINAND AND OF MERIT

NAPLES

Established by King Ferdinand IV of Naples in 1800 to reward militar and civil fidelity, the members of this Order were required to be Catholi and preferably belonging to the Sicilian nobility. St. Ferdinand wa portrayed on the centre gold medallion of the badge, superimposed upo a six-pointed gold star with a white enameled lily between each ray an the inscription *Fidei et Merito* (To loyalty and merit). The ribbon wa red with a dark blue edge.

Knights Grand Cross

THE ORDER OF ST. GEORGE OF RAVENNA

Papal

This was a military Order founded by Paul III (1534–1549) for Ravenna in 1534 to fight the Muslims off the Adriatic coast. The Order was suppressed by Gregory XIII (1572–1585) in 1574.

THE ORDER OF ST. GEORGE OF THE REUNION

Two Sicilies

Ferdinand I, King of the Two Sicilies (1816–1825), established this Order when he suppressed the Royal Order of the Two Sicilies which had been founded by Joseph Bonaparte, King of Naples (1806–1808), in 1808. His intention was to mark the reunion of Naples and Sicily (*i.e.* the Two Sicilies) and to reward persons who distinguished themselves for their loyalty and valour.

The Order came first in seven classes, then eight (1850). The badge of the Grand Cross had a pendant St. George. The badge consisted of a red enamel cross *fleury* superimposed on a green enamel laurel wreath with gold crossed swords between its arms. St. George slaying the dragon was portrayed in gold on the centre medallion, and the inscription was In *Hoc Signo Vinces* (You will conquer in this sign). The ribbon was sky blue with a yellow edge.

Because of its political connotations the Order became extinct in 1860 when the King of the Two Sicilies was expelled and his kingdom incorporated into the Italian Kingdom.

Knights Grand Cross

THE MILITARY ORDER OF ST. HENRY

POLAND – SAXONY

This Order was established in 1736 by Augustus III, King of Poland and Elector of Saxony (1733–1763), to mark his fortieth birthday and to honour the saintly Saxon Emperor Henry II. The Order was given for meritorious deeds, regardless of religion and class. The medallion bore the image of St. Henry in imperial robes; on the reverse of the Order were the arms of Saxony.

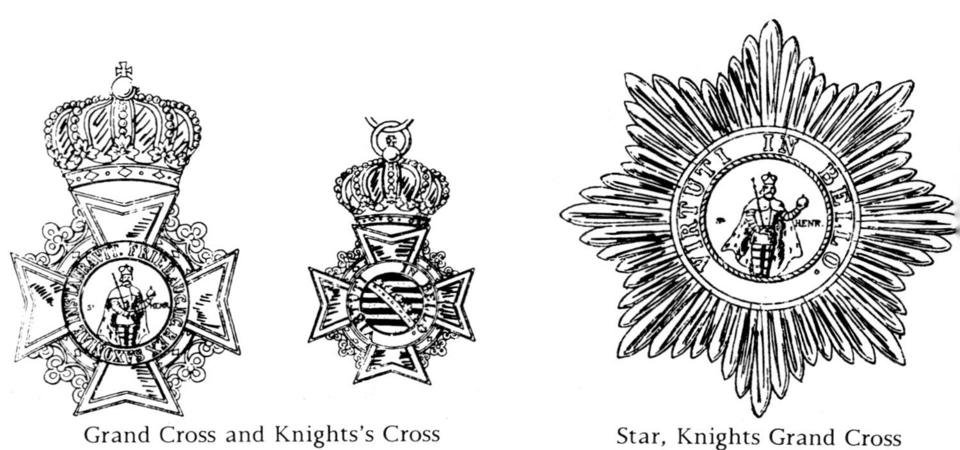

Grand Cross and Knights's Cross

Star, Knights Grand Cross

THE ROYAL MILITARY ORDER OF ST. HENRY

HAITI

Founded in 1811 by King Henry Christophe of Haiti to reward outstanding deeds of bravery of members of the Army, it was dedicated to St. Henry (the same as above) whose image was on the medallion.

THE ORDER OF ST. ISABELLA

PORTUGAL

It was established in 1801 by the Prince Regent John (1792–1816), the future King John VI of Portugal (1816–1826), inspired by his wife Princess Charlotte of Spain, as an award to Catholic ladies of the nobility for deeds of charity. It came in one class and was limited to twenty-six

Badge

members under the Grand Mastership of the Queen. The badge consisted of an oval, white enamel medallion portraying St. Isabella helping the poor, and a gold-winged angel, suspended from a gold crown. The inscription read *Pauperum Solatio* (Comfort of the Poor). The Order was suppressed by the Portuguese Republic in 1910.

THE ORDER OF ST. LOUIS

Parma

Founded in 1836 by Charles Louis of Bourbon, Duke of Lucca as the Order of St. Louis for civil merit, its name was changed by Charles III when it became an Order of the Duchy of Parma in 1849 and received new statutes. It was reserved for Catholics, with some exceptions. St. Louis was portrayed on the medallion with the words: *Deus et Dies* (God and Light).

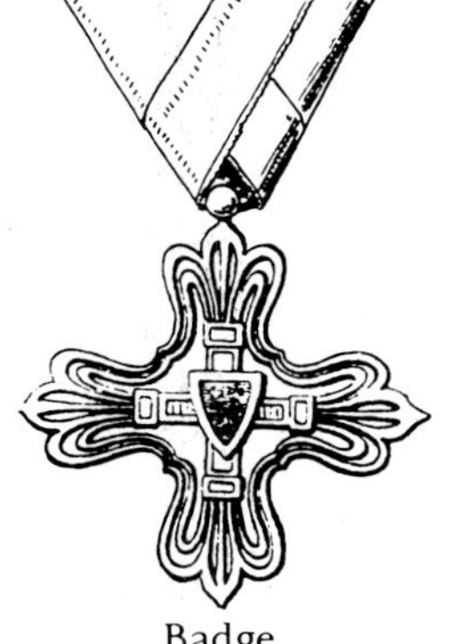
Badge

THE ORDER OF ST. MARGARET

FRANCE

Marie I, Queen of France, established this Order in 1888 to rewar meritorious military services.

The badge was a five-armed, double-pointed cross, ball-tipped an suspended from a royal crown. The Patron Saint was portrayed on th blue centre medallion with the inscription *Margarita Virgo* (Margare the Virgin). The blue moiré ribbon was gold-edged, except for the rank o Knight when it was silver-edged.

THE ORDER OF ST. MARY MAGDALENE

HAITI

Founded by Faustin I, Emperor of Haiti, in 1856, it disappeared thre years later when the empire was overthrown.

The badge was a six-rayed, double-pointed, gold ball-tipped star. A gold image of St. Mary Magdalene was portrayed on the green enamele centre medallion, surrounded by the inscription *Dieu seul* (Only God) The star was similar to the badge and the ribbon was white-edged, gree moiré.

THE ORDER OF ST. MICHAEL

BAVARIA

This Order was founded by James Clemens, Duke of Bavaria, Elector o Cologne, Bishop of Liege, Regensburg and Hildesheim, in 1693. Karl

Grand Cross

Star

Theodor, Palatine Elector, annexed it to the Bavarian Orders of Chivalry. Its original object was the defence of the Crown. In 1812 the Order was confirmed by King Maximilian Joseph, who added to the Order the aim of helping poor and sick soldiers. In 1837 and 1844 it was again confirmed by King Ludwig as an award for all meritorious deeds. St. Michael's Church in München, Bavaria, became the chapel of the Order. The medallion bore the figure of St. Michael and the inscription Quis ut Deus (*Who is like God*?).

THE ORDER OF ST. ROSE AND CIVILISATION

HONDURAS

Established in 1868 by the President of Honduras, Don José Maria Medina, its object was to reward outstanding civil, military and religious merit, and good deeds in general. The inscription changed according to the purpose of the bestowal. When granted for religious merit, it read: *Dios Honor Patria* (God, Honour and Country). The Order was suppressed in 1901.

Star, I and II class

THE ROYAL HUNGARIAN ORDER OF ST. STEPHEN

EMPIRE

This Order was founded by the Empress Maria Theresa of Austria-Hungary in 1764 as an award for extraordinary civil merit. It was placed under the patronage of St. Stephen, King of Hungary (969 – 1038), to whom Hungary owes its Christianity. It was the second highest ranking Order of the House of Habsburg, and open exclusively to members of the nobility.

Grand Cross

Star, Knights Grand Cross

Ceremonial Chain

THE ORDER OF THE SLAVES OF VIRTUE

EMPIRE

Founded in 1662 by Eleanor Gonzaga, Empress of Germany and widow of Emperor Ferdinand III (1637–1657), its purpose was to promote piety and virtue at the imperial court. It was reserved for Dames of noble birth. The Order was united with that of the DAMES OF THE STARRY CROSS in 1668.

Chapter Ten

ORIGINALLY CATHOLIC ORDERS OF KNIGHTHOOD STILL BESTOWED AS SECULAR ORDERS OF KNIGHTHOOD BY SOVEREIGN STATES

A number of Orders of Knighthood which were once Catholic but eventually lost their Catholic character are still bestowed by Sovereigns and Heads of State in several Western European countries. These Orders are among the most ancient and illustrious Knighthoods of Europe, besides ranking among the highest in their own countries.

Some of these Orders have retained vestiges of their Catholic past either in their insignia or in their statutes and traditions. Thus "Collar Days", when collars are worn by Knights of the Garter, Thistle and the Knights and Dames Grand Cross or Grand Commanders of the various Orders, comprise religious feastdays, including those dedicated to Our Lady and the Saints. The secularisation of these Orders may have come

about in perfect agreement with the Holy See when, for instance, it was a question of transforming an ancient monastic-military Order into an Order of Merit; or unilaterally, as at the time of the Reformation or when a republican *régime* was installed in place of a monarchy. In the last two cases, Catholic Orders were either completely suppressed or left dormant for a while, but were later revived by the State because it could not ignore the vital place these Orders had occupied in the history and culture of the country.

Though there is at present no structural relationship between these Orders and the Catholic Church, the Holy See fully recognises them as it does all other legally established Orders of Knighthood.

We shall briefly recall the origin and historical development of the more important Orders of Knighthood which were originally Catholic and which are still today bestowed by sovereign States. In doing so we shall once again observe the important part played by the Holy See and the Catholic Church in the history of the different peoples who composed the *Res Publica Christiana*. For merely practical purposes we shall arrange the different Orders of Knighthood alphabetically.

I

THE MILITARY ORDER OF AVIS

or

THE MILITARY ORDER OF ST. BENEDICT OF AVIS

Portugal

The origin of this Order which is the most ancient among the genuine Portuguese Knighthoods, may be traced back to 1162 when some members of the Order of Calatrava established themselves at Coimbra and transferred in 1166 to Evora, which was later to be called Avis. The King of Portugal, D. Sancho I (1185–1211), commanded them to guard the castle of Alcanede and the city of Alpedriz (today called Estremadura), and promised them the Fort of Juromenha if they won the battle against the Moors. Celestine III (1191–1198) approved the Order in 1192 and Innocent III (1198–1216) took it under his protection in 1201 and confirmed its property rights over a large territory stretching from Evora to Panoias. He also granted it many privileges, immunities and indulgences already enjoyed by the Order of Calatrava. The Knights were given the town of Avis in 1211, with the condition that they built a castle there and promoted the population of the area. The Friars of Evora thence came to

Badge worn prior to 1910

Star prior to 1910

be known as the Friars of Avis. The Order rendered many important services while it fought the Moors. After that, the Friars retired to a quiet life in a cloister.

The Order acquired many estates in Portugal as a gift of the Order of Calatrava in 1213 and thus became very wealthy. Without renouncing its identity, it submitted to the Grand Mastership of the Order of Calatrava, until in 1385, John, Grand Master of the Order of Avis and natural son of the King of Portugal, Peter (1357–1367), having become King of Portugal (1385–1433) rebelled against the authority of Calatrava. A serious dispute arose which continued for many years and was finally referred to the Council of Basel for a solution in 1431. The Council approved and confirmed the reunion of the two Orders, but the Order of Avis refused to accept this decision. It thus remained independent of Calatrava, even when Philip II, King of Spain, became King Philip I of Portugal (1581–1598) by marriage. Meanwhile the Holy See attributed the dignity of Grand Master of the Order of Avis to the Crown of Portugal.

Queen Mary of Portugal (1777–1816) reformed the Order in 1789, after obtaining its secularisation from the Holy See, and transformed it into an Order of Military Merit.

King John VI of Portugal (1816–1826), compelled to take refuge in Brazil in 1807 while he was still Regent (1792–1816), when Portugal was occupied by the French revolutionary army, brought the Order to the New World and conferred it upon many residents of Brazil. On his return to Europe in 1816, the Brazilian branch continued as an independent Order, keeping the same decoration with a variant only in the ribbon to which a pink border was added, until it was suppressed in 1891.

Badge and Star after 1917

The Portuguese Order was reformed again and given the title Royal Military Order of St. Benedict of Avis.

The badge of the Order is a gold-rimmed, green enamel cross *fleury*, resembling that of the Order of Calatrava. Until 1910 it was suspended from a white enamel star with gold rays between its seven points and with the image of the Sacred Heart in its centre, placed there by Queen Mary in 1789 to mark her special devotion to the Sacred Heart, under whose protection she had placed Portugal's three main Orders.

The Order was suppressed by the Portuguese Republic in 1910, but revived and revised in 1917, 1918, 1920, 1927, 1929 and 1934 under the name of MILITARY ORDER OF AVIS. The figure of the Sacred Heart was suppressed in all Orders by the Portuguese Republic in the revision of 1917.

The badge of the Order is now suspended from a green ribbon, and the star of the Order consists of an eight-pointed silver plaque with at its centre a green enamel cross *fleury* on a white enamel background.

II

THE MOST HONOURABLE ORDER OF THE BATH

Great Britain

This high Order of British Knighthood is believed to have been founded during the Anglo-Saxon domination of England, or by Richard II, King of England (1377–1399), in 1377 when he conquered Ireland, or more probably by King Henry IV (1367–1413) on the occasion of his coronation in

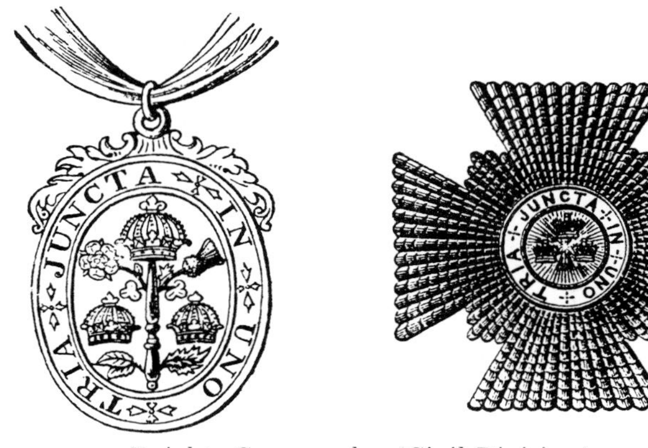

Knights Commander (Civil Division)

399. The Order took its name from the ritual bath which was part of the eremony performed at the inauguration of a knight to symbolise purity. he ritual was followed by a night in prayer, ending with attendance at he mass which was celebrated in the chapel.

This English custom spread to several European countries, notably rance and Italy. The last knights thus created date back to the coronaion of King Charles II, King of England (1660–1685), in 1661. After going nto abeyance the Order was revived by King George I (1714–1727) in 725. In 1815, Frederick, the eldest son of George III, who had become egent in 1811 and later King George IV (1820–1830), used it more as an rder of Merit (civil and military). Finally, Queen Victoria gave a new onstitution to the Order in 1847, decreeing that though once and rimarily a military Order, it would henceforth be conferred for civil and nilitary merit. Revised again in 1925 and 1936, ladies were first admitted nto the Order as Dames by Queen Elizabeth II in 1971.

This is the most important British Order of Chivalry bestowed on ommoners. It has a Bath King of Arms, whose duties are restricted to the rder and who is not an Officer of Arms at H.M. College of Arms. The ean of Westminster Abbey is also the Dean of the Order, and he is ntitled to surround his coat of arms with a gold chain and pendant badge f the Order. There is also a Gentleman Usher of the Scarlet Rod.

Although the Queen is the Sovereign of all British Orders of Knightood, the Grand Master of the Most Honourable Order of the Bath and irst or Principal Knight Grand Cross is H.R.H. The Prince of Wales.

The Order comprises three ranks: Knight Grand Cross (G.C.B.), Knight ommander (K.C.B.), and Companion of the Bath (C.B.).

The collar consists of nine golden crowns separated by a golden rose

Knights Grand Cross (Civil Division)

(for England), a thistle (for Scotland), and a shamrock (for Ireland), connected by white enameled knots.

The badge for military merit is a white enameled, gold ball-pointed Maltese cross with a gold lion between each arm. There are three gold crowns in the centre medallion, separated by a rose, a thistle and a shamrock. There are two mottos. The first one reads: *Tria Iuncta in Uno* (three united in one), which has received three different interpretations: some would say it refers to the three theological virtues faith, hope and love; others to the three Kingdoms of Britain; others, still, to the Holy Trinity under Whose protection the Order was placed. The other motto is *Ich Dien* (I serve) and belongs to the Prince of Wales.

The badge for civil merit is an oval-shaped gold medallion with the centre similar to the military badge.

The star for military merit is a multirayed silver cross, on which the obverse of the military badge is superimposed. The star for civil merit has the centre medallion of the badge imposed on it. The ribbon for both the civil and military divisions is crimson.

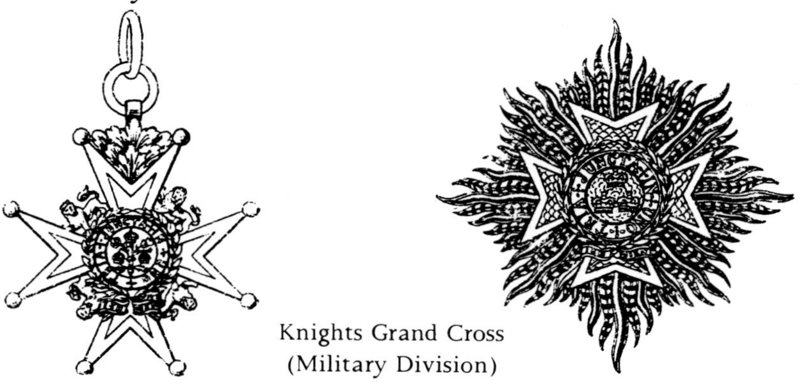
Knights Grand Cross (Military Division)

III

THE MILITARY ORDER OF CHRIST

Portugal

This Order traces its origin back to the Religious Military Order of Jesus Christ which was founded by Denis I, King of Portugal (1279–1325), on 14 August 1318, to replace the Order of the Knights Templars which had been suppressed by Clement V (1305–1314) in 1312. The new Order, originally called the Militia of Jesus Christ, as the Templars had also called themselves, was presented in the bull of recognition by John XXII (1316–1334) in 1319 as a revival of the Order of the Knights Templars, whose estates in Portugal are assigned in the bull to the Order of Christ. In founding the new Order, Denis I was prompted by the need of a military body capable of defending the kingdom against the Moors as efficiently as the Templars had done.

Badge and Star before 1910

The Papacy was the high protecting Power of the Order. It reserved for itself the right to create knights of all ranks. At the same time, the Kings of Portugal could only name knights of noble rank with the obligation of defending the Church and the Dynasty, and expelling the Moors out of the Portuguese confines. Originally the Knights were required to spend three years in the noviciate and to take the vows of poverty, chastity and obedience.

In 1515 the Portuguese branch of the Order was united with the Crown by papal approval under King Manuel I (1495–1521). It thus became an honorary Order, conferred independently by the Portuguese Sovereign as

"Governor and Perpetual Administrator", while the papal branch remained honorary with one class. The Collar of the Supreme Order of Christ was bestowed as an award for civil and military merit on very high personages.

The Portuguese Order was secularised in 1789 by Queen Mary with the agreement of Pius VI (1775–1799).

The Order of Christ was suppressed with other Royal Orders when the Kingdom of Portugal under the reign of King Manuel II (1908–1910) was overthrown in 1910. In consideration of its illustrious past, it was revived and revised in 1918 as Portugal's highest ranking Order, with three classes: Knight Grand Cross, Knight Commander and Knight. It is also given to foreigners, and especially to members of the Diplomatic Corps. This Order was also introduced into Brazil at the time of the Empire, but it was later suppressed by the Republican Constitution in 1891.

The insignia of the Portuguese Order of Christ are somewhat different from the insignia of THE SUPREME ORDER OF CHRIST conferred by the Holy See.

Under the Portuguese crown, the badge was an oval, white enameled, gold-rimmed medallion with a red enameled gold-rimmed cross, containing a smaller white enamel cross in the centre. Queen Mary of Portugal had added a figure of the Sacred Heart above the Cross.

The present badge consists of a red enameled, gold-rimmed cross, similar in form to the corresponding papal decoration, bearing a smaller white enamel cross in its centre.

The present star is similar to the former star: a multirayed silver plaque with the cross of the Order on the white background of the centre medallion.

The ribbon of the Portuguese Order of Christ is scarlet.

Officer's Cross after 1917

Star, Knights Grand Cross after 1917

IV

THE ORDER OF THE DANNEBROG
(or THE ORDER OF THE FLAG OF THE DANES)
Denmark

This is one of the most ancient and illustrious Orders of Knighthood in all Europe. It ranks second among Danish Orders. It is traditionally believed to have been instituted in 1219 by Waldemar II (1202–1241) at a time of close collaboration between the Crown, the Church and the Noblesse. Having remained dormant for a few centuries, it was suppressed during the Reformation and later restored, in 1671, by Christian V (1670–1699) on the occasion of the birth of his first son Frederick. The final revision of the Order took place in 1808 under Frederick VI (1808–1839).

The Order takes its name from a red flag, [*brog* – cloth, flag] with a white cross which according to the legend fell from the heavens, betokening the victory of the Catholic Danes under Waldemar II over the pagan Livonians and Estonians. Some would add that the flag of the victory, according to custom, was sent to the Pope. It is more likely that the Danes adopted the flag used by the inhabitants of the island of Rügen, who came to the help of the Danes, and that the flag was lost in the battle of Meldrop in 1500.

Stars, Knights Grand Cross and Commanders I class

Ceremonial Chain

Following the statutes published in 1693, the Order was reserved for princes of royal blood and the highest dignitaries of the Court. Membership in the Order of the Dannebrog was required for admission to the highest ranking Danish Order of the Elephant. In 1808 Frederick VI made the Order an award for civil and military merit as well. Since 1951 ladies are admitted to the Order. There is also an Association of Men of the Dannebrog, which is open to those whose merits, however outstanding, would not justify the bestowal of the Order itself.

The ranks are: Grand Commander's Cross (reserved for members of the Danish Royal Family and foreign Sovereigns related to the Monarch); Grand Cross with Diamonds; Grand Cross; Commander (first and second degree); Knight (first, and since 1952, second degree).

The badge is a gold-rimmed, red-bordered white enamel cross *patté*, with elongated lower arms and the motto: *Gud Og Kongen* (God and King) on the four arms. A crown and the gold initial W (*Waldemarus*) are in the centre. The reverse bears the figures 1219, 1671, 1808, representing historic dates in the life of the Order. The initial F stands for Frederick VI (1808–1839) who revised the Order. The cross is suspended from a crown, with the gold initials of the reigning Sovereign.

The star is a multirayed silver Maltese cross on which the Order's cross is superimposed. The ribbon is white moiré, bordered with crimson.

Cross, Commander I class, and Badge
"Men of Dannebrog"

H.M. Queen Margrethe II of Denmark
Sovereign of the Order of the Elephant and the Order of the Dannebrog, and H.R.H. Prince Henrik. Her Majesty wears the Grand Commander's Cross of the Order of the Dannebrog and the Star and sash of the Order of the Elephant. His Royal Highness wears the Grand Cross of the Order of the Dannebrog on a chain as neck badge and the sash of the Order of the Elephant with the badge pending from it.
Courtesy: The Royal Danish Embassy in London

V

THE ORDER OF THE ELEPHANT

Denmark

This is Denmark's highest ranking Order of Knighthood. It is believed to have been founded in the twelfth century by Knut IV, King of Denmark (1182–1202). After going into abeyance, it was re-established in 1464 by King Christian I (1448–1481), on the occasion of the marriage of his son John with Christina, the daughter of Ernest, Duke of Saxony The statutes were revised in 1693 by King Christian V (1670 – 1699) limiting membership to princes of royal blood and thirty knights. Previous to 1958 the only ladies admitted to the Order were the Danish Queen and other foreign reigning Queens; now the Order is open to all ladies considered worthy of membership.

The name of the Order is reminiscent of the slaying of a white elephant by a Danish soldier in 1189. The Order was once also called THE ORDER OF ST. MARY. Her image was on the medallion, surrounded by rays and charged with three nails, suspended from a golden chain with alternating figures of the elephant and the patriarchal cross. The first chapter of the Order took place in the metropolitan church of Lunden. The Order had a special chapel in the Cathedral of Roskild, and later in the castle of Frederiksburg.

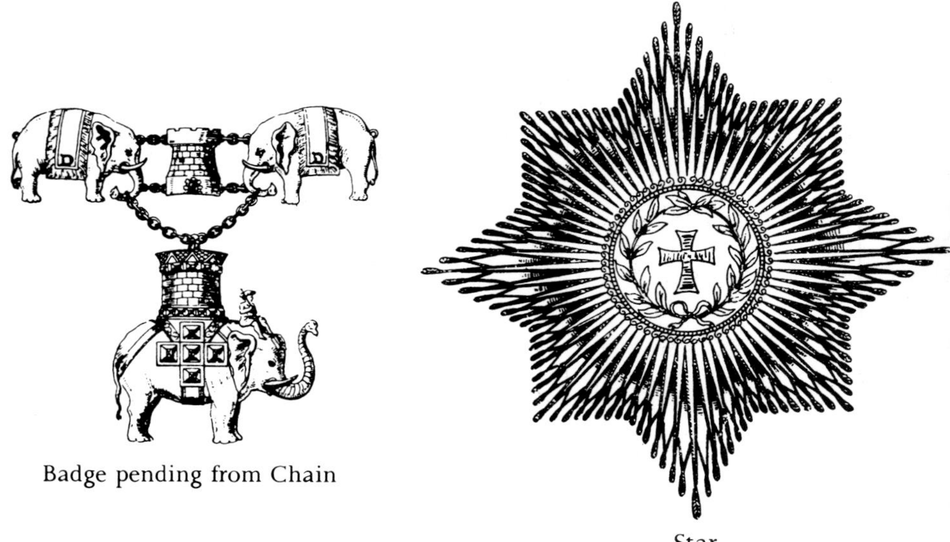

Badge pending from Chain

Star

The Order is now granted only to Sovereigns, princes of royal blood and very meritorious personages, who are already Knights of the Order of the Dannebrog, having attained thirty years of age and professing the Lutheran faith.

The badge of the Order consists of a white enamel elephant covered by a blue enamel blanket bearing a tower with a cross composed of four diamonds on its back and a Hindu driver seated on the elephant's neck. The badge is suspended from a gold chain consisting of alternating elephants and turrets.

The star is silver and multirayed with eight points and with a red enameled centre medallion bearing a silver cross surrounded by a gold laurel wreath.

The ribbon is sky blue moiré, recalling the Order's link with St. Mary.

The insignia of the Order are returned to the Crown on the death of the recipient. There are some exceptions, as in the case of General Eisenhower (1945), whose insignia are kept at the Eisenhower Foundation, Abilene, Kansas. Other distinguished foreign Knights of the Order of the Elephant have included Field Marshal Viscount Montgomery of Alamein, K.G. (1945); Sir Winston Churchill, K.G. (1950); and General Charles de Gaulle (1965).

VI

THE MOST NOBLE ORDER OF THE GARTER

Great Britain

It is the highest Order of English Knighthood and one of the most important of all Knighthoods; the only one, in fact, which has preserved its ancient feudal character. There are different legends about its origin. Some believe it was founded by King Richard I (1189–1199) during the siege of Acre in the Holy Land in 1191, where he distributed garters to the main officers so that they could be recognised. Others maintain it was instituted by King Edward III (1327–1377) either at the battle of Crecy in 1346, where the King raised a garter on a sword to give the signal for the attack and GARTER became the pass-word. Others again believe the Order to have been founded at a court ball in 1344, when the King picked up the blue garter that had fallen off from his lover Joan, Countess of Salisbury, with whom he was dancing. He then diverted the attention of the guests by binding the garter round his own leg and exclaiming *Honi soit qui mal y pense* (Shame on him who thinks evil of it, or: evil is who evil thinks).

The generally accepted date of foundation is 1348 when Edward III obtained from Clement VI (1342–1352) a bull authorising the Bishops of Salisbury and Winchester to erect a collegial chapel in honour of St. George, Windsor, as seat of the Order. The following year, this chapel, by another papal bull, was exempted from the jurisdiction of the local bishop and a Dean was assigned to it, subject to the Bishop of Salisbury. The Order underwent several revisions in 1522, 1551 and 1626 and was reconstituted in 1805 and 1831.

The religious character of the Order was stressed by the good deeds the Knights were required to perform and by the celebration of Masses for the repose of the souls of deceased members, prescribed by Edward III.

Members of the Order became known as "Garters", not to be confused however, with the Knights of the French Order of the Holy Ghost, who were also known as "Garters" because of the blue ribbon or garter (*cordon bleu*) they wore.

From its very beginning the Order's membership was strictly limited to the reigning Monarch as Sovereign of the Order, the consort of the Monarch as Lady of the Garter, a position held by Her Majesty Queen Elizabeth the Queen Mother since her coronation in 1937 as Queen to King George VI, Queen Mary, the King's mother being another Lady of the Garter until her death in 1953, Royal Knights, Extra Knights (who are foreign Sovereigns) and Extra Ladies of the Garter; the actual number of Knights Companions is limited to twenty-four. The Prince of Wales becomes a member of the Order on the occasion of being invested as the Prince of Wales. He is not necessarily immediately invested with the relative insignia by the Sovereign. The Officers of the Order are the Chancellor, who is a Knight Companion, the Prelate, a position always occupied by the Bishop of Winchester, the Registrar who is also the Dean of Windsor, Garter Principal King of Arms, who under the Earl Marshal and Hereditary Marshal of England, the Duke of Norfolk, is *primus inter pares* among the English Kings of Arms, and the Gentleman Usher of the Black Rod, so called from his staff of office, a black wand surmounted by a golden lion.

The King's Queen and the King's eldest daughter as heir presumptive are always admitted as Ladies of the Garter. Foreign sovereign Queens are admitted as Extra Ladies of the Garter. Among those are H.R.H. Princess Juliana of the Netherlands, who was admitted as Queen Juliana in 1958, and H.M. Queen Margrethe of Denmark who was created an

Extra Lady of the Garter in 1979.

In the past foreign ladies have also been received into the Order, among them was Laura Bacio Terracina, a Neapolitan poetess, who was made a Dame of the Garter by King Edward VI (1547–1553).

The first commoner for centuries to be made a member of the Order was Sir Edward Grey, later Viscount Grey, in 1912. The Prime Minister during

Chain and "The George"

"The Lesser George"
pending from sash

Star

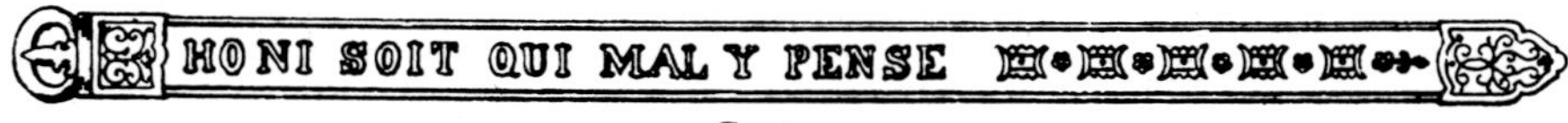

Garter

COLOUR PLATES

PLATE XVII A SECULAR DYNASTIC ORDER OF KNIGHTHOOD
The Royal Victorian Order (Great Britain)
The insignia of a Knight/Dame Grand Cross and Star
The Golden Collar which is worn by Knights and Dames Gran Cross on 'Collar Days' and when ordered to be worn by th Sovereign
The insignia of a Knight Commander with Star (left)
The insignia of a Commander and the Commander's insigni worn by a lady (centre)
The insignia of a Dame Commander with Star (right)

Courtesy: Messrs. Spink & Son, Lond

PLATE XVIII A STATE-FOUNDED CATHOLIC ORDER OF KNIGHTHOOD
The Order of Isabella the Catholic (Spain)
The insignia and Star of a Dame Commander of the Order
(The medallion in the centre of the Star shows only the tw pillars of Hercules; the medallion in the Star of the Grand Cros is identical to the medallion in the cross)

Courtesy: The Countess de Sierragor

PLATE XIX ORIGINALLY CATHOLIC ORDERS OF KNIGHTHOO BESTOWED AS SECULAR ORDERS BY A SOVEREIGN STATE
The Grand Collar of the Three Orders; The insignia worn pendin from the sash and Star (Portugal)
The Grand Collar of the Military Order of the Tower and th Sword, of Valour, Loyalty and Merit (Portugal)

Courtesy: The Portuguese Embassy, Bruss

PLATE XX CEREMONIAL DRESS OF ORDERS OF KNIGHTHOOD
Only Great Britain and the Holy See have retained ceremoni dress for their Orders of Knighthood

A: Knight of the Garter in the Habit and Collar of that Mo Noble Order (Great Britain)

B: Knight Grand Cross of the Most Honourable Order of th Bath in the Habit and Collar of that Order (Great Britain

Reproduced from hand-painted engravings by Sir George Naylor, Garter, 1821, acquired from t Barn Gallery, Pe

C: The ceremonial uniform of a Knight Commander of th Order of Pius IX (Holy See)

D: The ceremonial uniform of a Knight Commander of th Order of St. Gregory the Great (Holy See)

Courtesy: Secretariat of St

PLATE XVII

VICTORIA
BRIT REG
DEF FID
IND IMP
VICTORIA
BRIT REG
DEF FID
IND IMP

PLATE XVIII

A LA LEALTAD ACRISOLADA
A LA LEALTAD ACRISOLADA
POR ISABEL LA CATOLICA

PLATE XIX

PLATE XX

A B

C D

The Garter stall of Charles the Bold (1468), Duke of Burgundy, in St. George's Chapel, Windsor Castle. The star-shaped plate is that of Charles the Bold. Other plates include Victor Emmanuel (1855), first King of Italy, bottom left; and Duke Leopold (1816), later first King of the Belgians, bottom right.

Courtesy: The Dean and Chapter of St. George's Chapel, Windsor Castle the Second World War, Winston Churchill, the most famous commoner, who had steadfastly refused all honours of a peerage, even a Dukedom, offered him by King George VI on behalf of the peoples of Britain and the Commonwealth for his services to the country, accepted the Order of the Garter in 1953 and he wore his Garter robes for the first time at the coronation of Queen Elizabeth II, who had also invested him with the dignity. When the Queen honoured Sir Winston by making an official call on him at his residence on his retirement, the former Prime Minister received her in the court dress of a Knight of the Garter. Another distinguished commoner admitted to the Order was Sir Anthony Eden before he was elevated to the peerage as Earl of Avon.

The higher ranking badge of the Order, *The Great George*, as it is known, consists of a multicoloured enamel figure of St. George slaying the dragon. It is suspended from a collar consisting of gold medallions on which are portrayed red enameled roses surrounded by blue enameled garters bearing the inscription *Honi soit qui mal y pense*. The medallions are linked by gold knots.

The lower ranking badge, also known as *The Lesser George*, is a gold oval medallion, bearing the figure of St. George slaying the dragon, surrounded by a band on which the motto is inscribed. It is suspended from a blue band passing over the left shoulder to the right hip. The Star of the Order is silver and eight-pointed, with the red cross of St. George, surrounded by the blue garter bearing the inscription, portrayed on the centre medallion.

The ribbon, constituting the garter itself, is a band of dark blue velvet, edged and buckled with gold, on which the motto *Honi soit qui mal y pense* is embroidered.

The official and full dress, worn in procession, are the garter, mantle, surcoat, hat and hood. The garter is worn by the Knight under the knee on the left leg and by Dames of the Order on the left arm above the elbow.

The patronal feastday is St. George's Day, 23 April. The admission of new members of the Order takes place on that day. St. George is the official Patron Saint of England and the Knight's Chapel, also often referred to as "the Chapel of the Kings", is named after him though the official Patron of the Chapel is Our Lady.

Knights of the Garter are entitled to the post-nominal letters K.G.

H.M. Queen Elizabeth II and H.R.H. the Duke of Edinburgh wearing the insignia of the Most Noble Order of the Garter during their State Visit to the Vatican in 1961 with John XXIII.

Courtesy: Felici, Pontificia Fotografia, Rome

Twenty years later, in 1981, Her Majesty Queen Elizabeth II, again wearing the insignia of the Sovereign of the Most Noble Order of the Garter, and His Royal Highness Prince Philip made another State Visit to the Vatican where they were most warmly received by John Paul II. His Holiness paid a private visit to Her Majesty during his pastoral visit to Great Britain in 1982.

Courtesy: Felici, Pontificia Fotografia, Rome

VII

THE MILITARY ORDER OF ST. JAMES OF THE SWORD

Portugal

This Order was founded in 1170 by Ferdinand II, King of León and Galicia (1157–1188), and shares its early history with that of the Military Order of Santiago of Spain, with which we dealt in Chapter Eight. The Portuguese branch of this latter Order appeared in Portugal under King Denis I (1279–1325), an admirer of the Order of Santiago. It was recognised by John XXII (1316–1334) in 1320, but became fully independent of the Spanish Order in 1440. In 1556 Julius II (1503–1513) transferred the Grand Mastership of the Order to the Crown of Portugal under King John III (1521–1557). Full nobility remained one of the conditions required for admission. The seat of the Order was established in the Castle of Pamela, near Lisbon. The Order rendered great services to the Kingdom and remained specifically Catholic until 1789 when Queen Mary secularised it, thus opening it to non-Catholic membership as well and making it an Order of Civil Merit. It was then divided into three ranks, with three Knights Grand Cross, apart from the Infants of the Kingdom who were born members of the first rank, fifty Commanders and an unlimited number of Knights. By Royal Decree of 1862 the Order was completely reorganised and reserved for scientific, literary and artistic merit; it was also divided into five classes.

Badge, Knights Grand Cross

Star

Officer's Badge

The original badge

The Order was suppressed in 1910 and revived and revised in 1918 by the Portuguese Republic.

The badge of the Order is suspended from a green and gold laurel wreath and consists of a red enamel cross *fleury*, the lower arm ending in a sharp point resembling a sword, hence the name of the Order. Gold and green palm branches surround the arms of the cross, a gold-rimmed, white band adorns the base with the inscription *Sciencias, Letras e Artes* (Science, Letters and Art), which are the fields in which the recipients have acquired special merit.

The star consists of a multirayed silver plaque bearing the replica of the badge on the white centre medallion, on the rim of which is the same inscription as above.

The figure of the Sacred Heart from which the Grand Cross and the Commander's Cross used to be suspended and which has since been replaced with a green and gold laurel wreath and which also towered above the star of the Order, originally introduced by Queen Mary in 1789, disappeared in 1918 with the revision by the Portuguese Republic. It has been replaced by a green and gold laurel wreath. The ribbon of the Order is dark purple.

Ceremonial Chain

VIII

THE MOST ANCIENT AND MOST NOBLE ORDER OF THE THISTLE

Great Britain

This is a distinctively Scottish Order of Knighthood, ranking second to the Order of the Garter in the list of British Knighthoods. The Order is also known as The Order of St. Andrew, or The Order of the Rue; it was founded, according to an ancient tradition, in 787 by Achaius, King of the Scots who with Hungus, King of the Pitts, is said to have seen a bright cross in the skies the night before undertaking a battle against the English. However, the more likely founder of the Order was James V, King of Scotland (1513–1542), in 1540. After its suppression, following Queen Mary's death in 1587, it was revived by King James VII of Scotland and II of England (1685–1688), in 1687 and placed under the protection of St. Andrew, Patron Saint of Scotland. The Order collapsed in the revolution of 1688 and was again established by Queen Anne (1702–1714) in 1703. Its statutes were repeatedly revised until 1833.

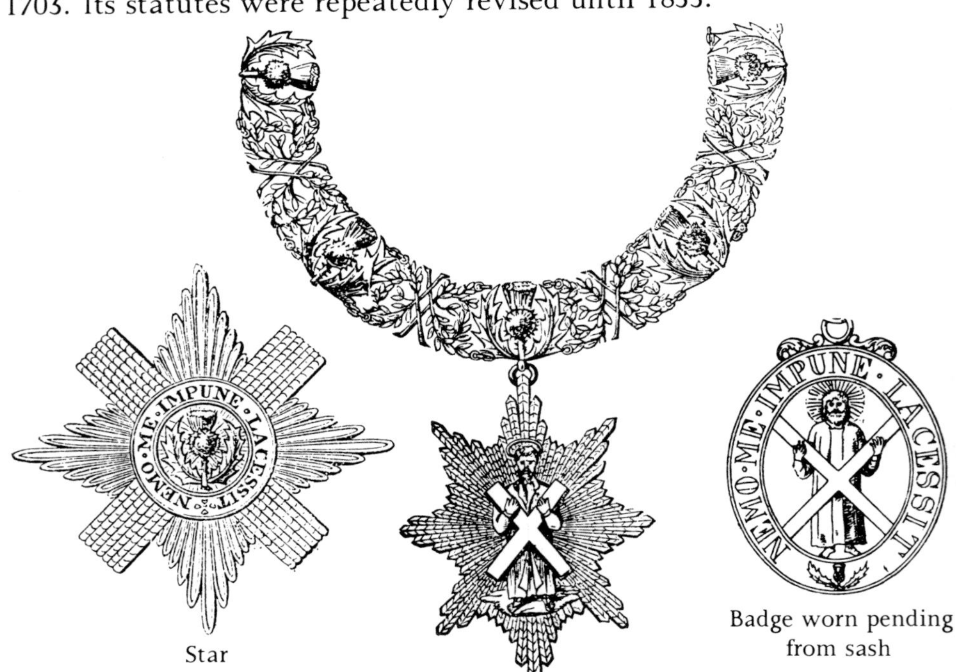

Star

Badge pending from Chain

Badge worn pending from sash

Membership of the Order is confined to sixteen noblemen of Scotland including non-peers, since the nobility of Scotland comprehends technical commoners, who are created Knights of the Thistle for outstanding service to the Monarch. The Monarch is the Sovereign of the Order and the King's Queen is a Lady of the Thistle, an honour held by Queen Elizabeth The Queen Mother since her coronation in 1937. The Order has in addition to the sixteen Knights Royal Knights, such as the Duke of Edinburgh (1952) and the Prince of Wales as Duke of Rothesay (1977), and Extra Knights, who are foreign Sovereigns, who have been admitted on an honorary basis since the eighteenth century. The Officers of the Order are the Chancellor, who is a Knight of the Thistle, a Dean of the Order, who is a member of Her Majesty's Household in Scotland, Lord Lyon King of Arms, who is also Secretary and King of Arms of the Order, and the Gentleman Usher of the Green Rod.

The motto of the Order is: *Nemo me impune lacessit* (Nobody attacks me with impunity), which, incidentally is also engraved on the crown of Lord Lyon King of Arms, who enjoys very wide-ranging powers under the Crown, including the right to issue *Letters Patent of Nobility in the Noblesse of Scotland*. The motto is reminiscent of the victory of the Scots over the Danes at Stirling Castle in the eighth century. The thistle was then adopted as the emblem of Scotland for having caused barefooted scouts to cry out when treading upon it, thus giving the alarm for the Scots to fall upon the Danes.

The badge of the Order consists of an oval medallion, in the centre of which St. Andrew, holding his cross, is portrayed, surrounded by the motto of the Order. The badge is worn suspended from the collar, which is made up of sixteen thistles linked by four sprigs of rue, enameled in natural colours.

The star is silver and four-pointed, with a silver St. Andrew's Cross imposed on it. A green Scottish thistle, surrounded by the motto inscribed in gold letters appears on a green background.

The ribbon, which may be used in lieu of the collar, is green moiré. It is worn passing over the left shoulder with the star on the left hip. Members of the Order are entitled to the initials K.T. behind their names.

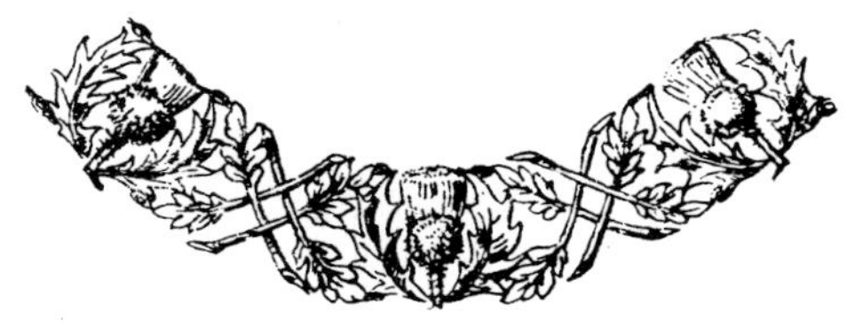

IX

THE GRAND COLLAR OF THE THREE ORDERS

PORTUGAL

This is a peculiar insignia of the First Magistrate of Portugal, the origin of which goes back to King Denis I of Portugal who founded the Grand Collar of the Orders of Christ and of St. Benedict of Aviz as a further reward for additional merits acquired by those who already possessed the highest existing Orders of Christ and Avis. At a later date the Order of St. James of the Sword was added to the other two, thus forming the Grand Collar of the Three Orders.

There was but one rank, the Grand Collar, and its badge, suspended from a gold crown, consisted of a gold *filigree* medallion, bearing in red the emblem of the Order of Christ, in green that of the Order of Avis and in purple the Cross of the Order of St. James of the Sword, all on a white enameled background.

In 1789 Queen Mary of Portugal added the figure of the Sacred Heart to the emblems. The Order was suppressed in 1910, and the figure of the Sacred Heart was omitted when the Order was again revived and revised in 1918 by the Portuguese Republic; a laurel wreath was substituted for the crown.

The Grand Collar is also reserved for foreign Heads of State during their term of office.

Badge worn before 1910

A star to accompany the badge was also instituted, consisting of a multirayed silver plaque on which the obverse of the badge is imposed.

The ribbon of this insignia is made up of equal stripes of red, green and purple colour.

X

THE MILITARY ORDER OF THE SWORD
or
THE ORDER OF THE YELLOW RIBBON

SWEDEN

This Order was founded by Gustav Wasa I (1523–1560), King of Sweden, in 1523 to strengthen the defence of the Catholic religion which was being attacked in his State by the Lutherans. The Order remained dormant after the Reformation until 1748 when Frederick I (1720–1751) gave it entirely new statutes. These were reformed by Gustav III (1771–1792) in 1772, when it became Sweden's main military Order, conferred for outstanding merit. The Order was confirmed again by Gustav IV (1792–1809) in 1798 and by Charles XIII (1809–1818) in 1814. The Princes of the Ruling House are born Commanders of the Order, which has five ranks.

The badge of the Order consists of a white enameled, gold-rimmed Maltese cross, with a gold crown between each arm, crossed swords at the top and bottom, and a sword on each side of the cross, suspended from

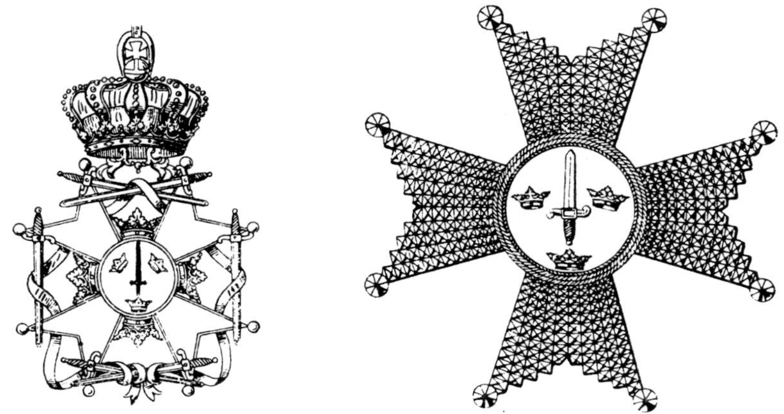

Cross and Star of Knights Commander

Ceremonial Chain, Knights Grand Cross

Star, Knights Grand Cross Commander

a gold crown. On the centre medallion, which is blue, three crowns are portrayed surrounding a sword pointing upwards. The reverse of the badge bears the same sword with a wreath on its tip and the inscription *Pro Patria* (For the Country).

The Star consists of the obverse of the badge superimposed on a silver eight-pointed multirayed cross. The ribbon is yellow moiré with a blue stripe near the border.

XI

THE MILITARY ORDER OF THE TOWER AND THE SWORD, OF VALOUR, LOYALTY AND MERIT

PORTUGAL

This Order was established in 1459 by King Alfonso V of Portugal (1438–1481), called the African, as an award for the Knights who had conquered Fez in Morocco and other African territories. It was placed under the protection of St. James. Having remained dormant for several centuries, the Order was revived by the Prince Regent John (1792–1816), the future King John VI of Portugal (1816–1826), in 1808 as a reward for military services rendered by non-Catholics who, because of their religion, could not be admitted to the other Orders. The Order was subsequently revised under the regency of Dom Pedro, Duke of Bragança (1828–1834), in 1832 and 1833 and was given the name of ANCIENT AND VERY NOBLE ORDER OF THE TOWER AND THE SWORD OF VALOUR LOYALTY AND MERIT with precedence over all other Orders. It was suppressed in 1910 by the Portuguese Republic but revived in 1917.

The Order is now conferred as an award for extraordinary deeds of military or civil significance and for services rendered to mankind, Country and Republic. It comprises five ranks.

The Grand Collar is reserved for Heads of State.

The badge consists of a gold-rimmed, five-pointed, white enameled, ball-tipped star with a green oak wreath and sword in the centre medallion, surrounded by a blue band bearing the inscription *Valor, Lealidad E Merito* (Valour, Loyalty and Merit). A green and gold wreath with a gold tower on the top surrounds the star. The reverse now bears the arms of Portugal with the inscription *Republica Portugesa* (Portuguese Republic). Before the Order's suppression in 1910, the reverse of the badge had an open book on a gold background with the inscription *Pelo Rei e Pela Lei* (For King and for the Law), as illustrated here.

The star is made up of a five-pointed plaque on which the obverse of the badge is imposed. The ribbon of the Order is dark blue.

Badge and Star before 1910

XII

THE IMPERIAL SOCIETY OF KNIGHTS BACHELOR

Great Britain

This is an important dignity conferred upon commoners by the British Sovereign for distinguished service. It is a personal and non-hereditary honour and carries with it the title of "Sir". In the table of precedence in England a Knight Bachelor is placed below Knight Commanders of all Orders of Knighthood and Companions of Honour and above Official Referees of the Supreme Court; in Scotland Knights Bachelor rank below

Sheriffs Principal and above Sheriffs Substitute and Companions of Orders as in England. Wives of Knights Bachelor are given as a matter of courtesy, but not of right, the title of "Lady". [Several distinctions in the usage of the title "Lady" are strictly observed as this title is also used by Peeresses in their own right, wives and daughters of Peers and by Life-Peeresses. The wife of a Knight Bachelor only uses the title Lady before her husband's surname, whereas the Knight Bachelor is addressed by the title Sir, followed by his Christian name. The title "Dame" is strictly reserved for ladies who have received an honour equivalent to that of a Knight Commander in an Order of Knighthood.]

Knights Bachelor do not constitute a Royal Order of Chivalry but they are of interest to our subject because the name used to designate them dates back to Catholic times and customs and recalls the early history of the Knighthood which under the influence of the Church was inspired by Christian principles. The word "knight", as defined in the Oxford Dictionary, is derived from the Old English *cniht, cnecht,* signifying a boy, youth or lad, as the German derivative of the word, *Knecht*, still does. At an early date it added the meaning of a young attendant or servant of follower of the King or other person of high rank, and later, one devoted to the service of a lady as her attendant, or champion in war or the tournament. The title also came to be applied to a feudal tenant holding land from a superior on condition of serving in the field as a mounted and well-armed man. Gradually it took on the meaning of one raised to the honourable military rank by the King or other qualified person. A Knight was usually only a person of noble birth who had served a regular apprenticeship as page or squire to the profession of arms. This was a regular step to be taken even by those of the highest rank.

Badge, Knights Bachelor

A Knight Bachelor was a young knight who was not old enough or who disposed of too few vassals to bring into the field under his own banner. Not being a banneret, he followed the banner of another as novice in arms.

The term is used in this sense in the Prologue to the *Canterbury Tales* (1,80) by Chaucer (c.1340–1400). Hence it is conjecturally suggested that "bachelor" is derived from the French *bas chevalier* in the sense of lower than a Knight of an Order. The late Latin adjective *baccalarius*, however, applied to farm labourers, especially one who worked for the tenant of the land, which was called *baccalaria* or division of land.

Known also as Knights of the Spur, Knights Bachelor were already in existence in the thirteenth century, in the reign of Henry III (1207–1272), who became King of England in 1216, thanks to the influence of Pope Innocent III (1198–1216) and to the military support of a group of barons. He was a pious and learned Sovereign, but quite inept at reigning.

For many centuries Knights Bachelor wore no special insignia. In 1908 a voluntary Association under the title of "The Society of Knights" was set up with the purpose of maintaining and consolidating the dignity of Knights Bachelor. In 1912 King George V (1910–1936) commanded that the Society should thenceforth be known as "The Imperial Society of Knights Bachelor". By Royal Warrant dated 21 April 1926 the King authorised the use of a badge by Knights Bachelor to be worn on the left side of the coat. In 1974, Queen Elizabeth II (1952–) authorised Knights Bachelor to wear a neck badge or a miniature. The badge of a Knight Bachelor is described as: "Upon an oval medallion of vermillion, enclosed by a scroll, a cross-hilted sword belted and sheathed pommel upwards, between two spurs, rowels upwards the whole set about with the sword-belt, all gilt."

Knights Bachelor append the initials Kt. behind their surname.

When The Rt. Hon. Margaret Thatcher was invited by Her Majesty to form the Government following the General Election in 1979, the Prime Minister revived the practice of recommending to the Queen on publication of the Honours List, which takes place on New Year's Day and the Queen's official birthday, to award the honour of Knight Bachelor also for "political services rendered" on a similar basis as many life peerages are proposed to the Queen by the Prime Minister and the Leader of Her Majesty's Opposition.

Chapter Eleven

AUTONOMOUS AND SELF-STYLED ORDERS OF KNIGHTHOOD

The Historical and Juridical Situation

In the aftermath of the Second World War a considerable number of autonomous and self-styled Orders of Knighthood appeared on the public scene, many of which have continued to subsist until the present day. These bodies, which owe their origins to merely private initiative, often claim some kind of connexion with venerable ancient Orders which actually existed and flourished in the course of centuries, frequently under the protection of the Holy See, especially in the heyday of chivalry, but are now completely extinct.

Several of these autonomous and self-styled Orders tend to assume titles and vindicate documents which emanated from the Holy See or State Authorities in centuries past, but which have no juridical value when exploited by these new associations.

Because of such abuses, the Holy See has found it necessary to state its position in this connexion, by making it clear that these Orders do not enjoy any approval or recognition whatsoever on its part. To this effect the Holy See has repeatedly published statements which appeared in *L'Osservatore Romano* and of which the following official statements are merely examples. Such warnings have been made because a good number of self-styled Orders or Federations of Chivalry, claiming some connexion with or approval from the Holy See, appear to be enjoying a luxuriant growth, especially in the United States of America, after having long been active in most European countries.

Official Statement by the Holy See

[Repeatedly published under successive pontificates in *L'Osservatore Romano*. For full text see for example edition of 22 March 1953, under the reign of Pius XII, and 14 December 1970, under the reign of Paul VI].

"Since some time one can observe the deplorable phenomenon of the appearance of alleged Orders of Knighthood originating from private initiatives and aiming at replacing the legitimate forms of chivalric awards.

"As we have previously pointed out, these so-called Orders take thei name from Orders which have in fact already existed but are now extinc since many centuries or from Orders which had been planned but wer never realised or, finally, from Orders which are truly fictitious and hav no historical precedent at all.

"To increase the confusion of those who are not aware of the tru history of Orders of Knighthood and of their juridical condition, thes private initiatives, which style themselves as autonomous, are qualifie by appellations which had reason to exist in the past and which belon exclusively to authentic Orders duly approved by the Holy See.

"Thus, with a terminology which is almost monotonous these allege Orders claim for themselves – in differing degrees – such titles as *Sacred Military, Equestrian, Chivalric, Constantinian, Capitular, Sovereign Nobiliary, Religious, Angelical, Celestial, Lascaris, Imperial, Royal Delcassian etc.*

"Among these private initiatives, which in no way are approved of o recognised by the Holy See, one can find alleged Orders such as th following:

St. Mary or Our Lady of Bethlehem;
St. John of Acre;
St. John the Baptist;
St. Thomas;
St. Lazarus;
St. George of Burgundy or of Belgium or of Miolans;
St. George of Carinthia;
Constantinian Lascaris Angelical Order of the Golden Militia;
The Crown of Thorns;
The Lion of the Black Cross;
St. Hubert of Lorraine or of Bar;
The Concord;
Our Lady of Peace.

"To all these alleged Orders of Knighthood and similar ones, with the adjoining more or less international Gold, Silver and Blue Cross Associa-tions, those Orders must certainly be added which, together with one o the names mentioned above, have taken the titles:

of Mercy;
of St. Bridget of Sweden;
of St. Rita of Cascia;

of The Legion of Honour of the Immaculate;
of St. George of Antioch;
of St. Michael;
of St. Mark;
of St. Sebastian;
of St. William;
of the historical but extinct Order of the Temple;
of The Red Eagle;
of St. Cyril of Jerusalem, etc.

"So as to avoid equivocations which are unhappily possible, also because of the abuse of pontifical and ecclesiastical documents, once granted for religious purposes or for merely monastic Orders, and to put an end to the continuation of such abuses, entailing harmful consequences for people in good faith, we are authorised to declare that the Holy See does not recognise the value of the certificates and insignia conferred to the above-named alleged Orders."

Official Statement by the Holy See
[Concerning the "*Sovereign Order of St. John of Jerusalem*"; the full text of this Official Statement can be found in *L'Osservatore Romano* of 1 December 1976, Paul VI PP.]

"Enquiries have been received from various parties asking for further information regarding the *Sovereign Order of St. John of Jerusalem* and in particular regarding how the Holy See looks on this Order.

"We are authorised to repeat the clarifications previously published in *L'Osservatore Romano* in this connexion. The Holy See, in addition to its own Equestrian Orders, recognises only two Orders of Knighthood: *The Sovereign Military Order of St. John of Jerusalem*, called *The Order of Malta*, and the *Equestrian Order of the Holy Sepulchre in Jerusalem*.

"No other Order, whether it be newly instituted or derived from a mediæval Order having the same name, enjoys such recognition, as the Holy See is not in a position to guarantee its historical and juridical legitimacy. This is also the case with regard to the above-mentioned *Sovereign Order of St. John of Jerusalem* which assumes, in an almost identical form and in such a way as to cause ambiguity, the name of the *Sovereign Military Order of Malta*."

Official Statement by the Holy See

[Concerning the *Sovereign and Military Order of the Temple of Jerusalem*. The full text of this Official Pronouncement can be found in *L'Osservatore Romano* of 24 July 1970, under the reign of Paul VI.]

On 24 July 1970 the Holy See deemed it necessary to publish yet another severe warning in *L'Osservatore Romano* to make its position clear with regard to the pretensions of "Emissaries" of a certain "Knightly Order" which gives itself the title of *Sovereign and Military Order of the Temple of Jerusalem*.

"Their unqualified behaviour" the statement goes on to say, "compels us to put on their guard all the members of the Hierarchy in Italy and in other countries . . .; in the specific case at hand, the historical vicissitudes of the ancient Order of the Temple (The Templars), suppressed by Pope Clement V (1305 – 1314) and never again revived by any of his successors, are well known.

"It is hence obvious that its contemporary revival, aggravated by the pretended appellation of *Sovereign*, appears to be an evident abuse and is therefore illegitimate."

The Holy See is by no means alone in refusing to recognise private or independent Orders of Knighthood. A similar position is generally assumed by the different States with a view to suppressing abuses and protecting the official Orders which have been founded by them or are under their protection. To avoid abuses, there are stringent rules in each State regulating the bestowal, acceptance and wearing in public of the insignia of Orders of Chivalry. In recent years independent Orders mushroomed in Italy to such a point that a special law was published on 3 March 1951 (Law No. 178) stating that "the use of decorations of extinct, suppressed or abolished Orders shall not be tolerated".

René Cornet, an official of the Belgian Ministry of Foreign Relations, commenting on the relevant articles of the Belgian Penal Code, brands the abuse of self-styled orders in the following terms:

"In recent times we have witnessed the flourishing of pretended orders, resulting from private initiatives, whose only aim is to replace legitimate forms of honorific distinctions and whose creators very often are moved by intentions which are not absolutely disinterested.

"Admission to such orders is generally obtained by paying an amount of money which varies according to the rank being granted. Furthermore, in some cases members must pay an annual fee. In most cases the creators of these decorations pretend that their objective is to foster in their followers a spirit of loyalty and generosity. In reality, their main end appears to be to cater to feelings of vanity. Insignia and ranks more or less similar to those of official Belgian or foreign Orders are generally conferred.

"Frequently, people who have been ensnared, are wary to denounce the deceit of which they are victims because that would imply an embarrassing admission of their personal ambition and naïveté, and their silence simply strengthens the position of the founders of false decorations." (René Cornet, *Les Ordres Nationaux Belges*, Heule (Belgium) 1982, p. 39, n. 41.)

M. Cornet furnishes a long list of orders which are not recognised by the Belgian Kingdom and which, in fact, are autonomous or self-styled orders rejected by other States as well. Among them are the following which may appear to have some link with the Church or the Holy See but are in no way acknowledged or recognised by them:

Religious and Military Order of Bethlehem;
Order of Knighthood of Christ The King;
Constantinian Order of St. Stephen;
Real Illustre y muy Noble Confradia del Santisimo Cristo de Perdon;
Supreme Order of the Knights of Peace;
Order of the Redeemer of Jerusalem;
Sacred, Imperial and Angelical Order of the Cross of Constantine The Great;
Order of the Knights of St. Andrew of Serravalle;
Military Order of St. George of Antioch;
Apostolic and Hospitaller Order of Our Lady of Mount Carmel;
International Military Hospitaller Order of St. James of Jerusalem;
Order of Hospitaller Knights of St. John the Baptist of Spain;
Order of St. John of the Lateran;
Order of St. Lion of Vitanval;
Gold Cross of the Holy Apostle and Evangelist Mark;
Order of the Holy House of Loreto;
Military Order of St. Michael and St. James of Holland;
Military Order of the Holy Saviour and St. Bridget of Sweden;
Banneret of the Order of the Knights of St. Sebastian;
Dynastic Order of St. Agatha of Paterno;
Order of the Most Holy Trinity and of Villedieu;

Order of the Corps of Knights of SS. Sebastian and William;
Order of St. George and Victor;
Belgian Association of the Knights of the Sovereign and Military Order of the Temple.
(*Cf. op. cit.* pp. 134–137.)

Several other European States have published penal provisions concerning self-styled and autonomous Orders of Chivalry and decorations conferred by them. The Federal Republic of Germany, for example imposes up to three months imprisonment and/or a heavy fine on those who deceive the public with decorations which could be mistaken for, or give the impression of being, recognised legitimate national or foreign Orders.

The basic reason militating against the official recognition of such bodies is that, to be publicly acknowledged, as we have already said Orders of Knighthood must be founded or sponsored by a Sovereign Power for the purpose of rewarding meritorious service.

Some of the bodies in question bear the names of Orders which in past centuries had been created or recognised by a Sovereign Power, but have long ceased to exist. They cannot be legally resuscitated by a merely private act of re-establishment without sovereign recognition.

Because of the firm stance taken by the Holy See, there is now a new phenomenon of Orders of Chivalry, claiming connexion with various Orthodox Churches. Some of these Churches possess Orders of Chivalry of their own, which are not generally recognised by Western States. Their criterion for founding Orders is different because of the special position held in the past by their chief leaders, who under Islamic law were considered also as civil heads for certain purposes, and Churches themselves were often described as 'Nations'.

Such Orders however are not to be confused with those of more recent and private initiative, claiming an historical connexion with ancient Knighthoods which have become extinct several centuries ago.

Autonomous and self-styled Orders often present themselves as associations which have obtained some form of legal recognition. This, however, is accorded to them not as Orders of Chivalry but as benevolent or social associations, instituted to fulfil some charitable or philanthropic purpose, and are registered as such under the existing corporation laws To justify their existence, these bodies usually support or even found charitable, cultural, social, medical or similar institutions, which may be of undoubted public usefulness. But this does not affect their legal status which, at the most, may be that of a private individual or corporate body, and registered as such, either with the Charity Commissioners or the Registrar of Companies, but always belonging to the sphere of private law.

The lack of appropriate information in this connexion is such that unfortunately even personages of very high ecclesiastical and civil standing accept honours offered by the Orders in question, thus increasing the confusion among common folk.

The argument is often put forward that the acceptance of a decoration or chivalric title from an autonomous or self-styled Order by a high dignitary of the Catholic Church constitutes an *ipso facto* recognition of the Order. The same argument is utilised when, on occasion, misguided prelates allow their names to be mentioned in literature published by such Orders. In certain cases, however, this is done without the knowledge or permission of the prelate.

Such an implication is totally gratuitous and misleading. The Holy See is quite clear and firm in its directives to members of the hierarchy concerning the acceptance of decorations and titles. The acceptance of such honours by a prelate is therefore a matter of merely private initiative. In no way does it weaken or alter the Holy See's attitude concerning its non-recognition of autonomous and self-styled Orders.

It is therefore in the interest of all parties concerned, when they are invited to give their support to, or become members of, an Order of Chivalry, to make a thorough investigation into the historical background and the legal status of the Order so as to be fully satisfied about the legitimacy, value and recognition of the body in question and the real consistence of the honour which is intended to be conferred upon them.

A Corollary on the Association of the Knights of Columbus

None the less there are certain associations which describe their members as Knights but do not pretend to form an Order of Knighthood. Such bodies are not to be confused with the above-described autonomous and self-styled Orders. The term "knight" is used by them as a perfect exemplar of rectitude and ready service, which should inspire their members.

A typical example is the Association of the Knights of Columbus, the leading Catholic laymen's organisation in the world, forming a fraternal society under a Supreme Knight with the general object to unite Catholic laymen for religious and civic usefulness. Their particular object is to be of generous service to the Church and society in the various fields of the social apostolate in complete harmony with the Catholic Hierarchy.

The Society was founded by Father Michael J. McGivney at New Haven, Connecticut, U.S.A., and chartered by the General Assembly of Connecticut on 29 May 1882. It has councils in many countries, besides the United States.

As His Eminence Cardinal Casaroli, the Papal Secretary of State, said in his speech at the meeting of the Association of the Knights of Columbus which took place at Hartford, Connecticut, on 4 August 1982 to celebrate the centenary of its foundation: its very name is meant to express a readiness to take inspiration, in a new form, from the ancient ideals of Knighthood into a modern and practical environment through the practice of "Unity, Charity, Fraternity and Patriotism", which are the values contained in the motto of the Association. (*Cf. L'Osservatore Romano*, 5 August 1982.)

In his speech, Cardinal Casaroli elaborated on the message confided to him in the letter with which Pope John Paul II appointed him as his Personal Envoy to the celebrations. After praising the members of the Association for their spirit of Christian chivalry, His Holiness exhorts them to keep "Christian fraternity for their shield, truth for their sword, and for their banner peace springing from sacrifice". The lofty principles with which the knights are imbued are demonstrated, illustrated and confirmed, the Pope goes on to say, by "the boundless number and wonderful variety of their beneficent initiatives in aid of the Church's every need, the cause of justice as a whole, any human disaster whatever, and everything that is of true benefit to society".

Chapter Twelve

THE SUPERNATURAL IN THE ORDERS OF KNIGHTHOOD

The supernatural, comprising the Deity, the Blessed Virgin Mary, the Angels and the Saints, occupies a very important place in the life of Orders of Knighthood. From the very outset we find Orders dedicated to Christ and to the Holy Ghost, strangely enough, at first sight never to God as such apart from the Trinity, or to God the Father alone. A great number of Orders have the Blessed Virgin Mary as their heavenly Patron, under different titles such as personal attributes: the Immaculate Conception, the Visitation, the Assumption; or even according to places where she is revered in a special way, such as Bethlehem, Nazareth and Mount Carmel. Then there are the Angels and the Saints, the choice of which is often determined by customs of local piety. There are numerous Orders dedicated to St. Michael, St. John the Baptist, St. James, St. Peter, St. Andrew and other Apostles, St. George and other popular Saints of the early Christian era. But there are also more recent Saints, starting with the Middle Ages and running into Modern Times such as St. Dominic, St. Elizabeth, St. Hubert, St. Henry and St. Theresa.

It would be wrong to believe that this custom is relegated to the Orders founded during the mediæval period. Even more recently instituted Orders of the last two centuries are dedicated to Saints of all eras, such as St. Agatha, St. Marinus, St. Charles and St. Rose of Lima.

Three reasons explain such a phenomenon.

There is above all the fact that, originally, Orders of Knighthood were either monastic or religiously motivated. Their aims, way of life and dress were modelled on those of the Religious Orders, the rules of which often inspired their own statutes as is the case of the Rules of St. Basil, St. Augustine, St. Benedict and St. Bernard.

Then there was the spiritual and social cosmology of the mediæval universe, of which God was regarded as the Supreme Ruler and Holder, the source of all authority and power, both spiritual and temporal, so that it was by his grace that human rulers exercised their sovereign attributes. God himself was the Supreme Protector of many Orders, but not in his divine essence, which no living being has even seen, but rather in the forms in which He made himself manifest to man, that is in Christ, his Son, and in the Holy Spirit, appearing as a dove.

Mary, the Angels and the Saints were considered as God's assistants i
ruling the universe. They were the actual lords to whom God had con
fided differents portions of the earth. Human rulers only had a partici
pated form of sovereignty, and not an absolute one, over their estate
which were given to them by God as it were in feudal tenure and to whon
alone they were answerable.

Among the Saints, Mary was the first of all mere creatures. She there
fore enjoyed prime of place in the founding of Orders. As the highes
human ideal of goodness, purity and all beauty, she exercised a powerfu
influence upon the knights, who took her as their Protectress as she ha
been the Protectress of Jesus, her Son, Who on the cross recommended al
humanity to her in the person of St. John the Evangelist. Then came th
Archangel St. Michael, the prince of the Angels, and finally the Saints
under whose protection the different lands were placed.

Finally, the choice of the heavenly Protector was often made accord
ing to the titular Saint of the main shrine of the land where the Order wa
founded. This shrine was either the central chapel of the Order itself o
even the site of important pilgrimages. It was necessary to give materia
and moral assistance to the pilgrims on their way to the shrine because o
the hardships suffered during the voyage, but it was often imperative t
protect them against the assaults of the Moors or other adversaries, suc
as was the case of the shrines of St. James at Compostela and of Our Lad
of Loreto.

In some cases, imagination and familiarity with the Saints thu
revered engendered beliefs which were more of the realm of popula
legend and fancy than of history, as one can see in the case of the lives o
St. George and St. Christopher, and even of more historicall
documented biographies as of St. Dominic, St. Francis and St. Elizabeth
These legends were perpetuated by some Orders because of an under
standable regard for their devotional value and for a desire to protect th
legends themselves against discriminatory researches conducted by hos
tile critics. In its reform of the Liturgical Calendar of the Roman Rite o
9 May 1969, implementing a directive issued by the Second Vatica
Council, the Catholic Church made a decisive effort to purge th
accounts of the lives of the Saints from all the legendary elements whic
at times infringed upon the credibility of their very existence.

It must be stated, in conclusion, that the dedication of Orders o
Knighthood to the Deity and to the Saints is an evident witness of th
Christian belief in the mystery of the Communion of Saints whic
unhappily Churches of the Anglican and of the Protestant tradition hav

either minimised or suppressed in their lives and teachings, erring by defect where they believed Catholics may have sometimes erred by excess.

We shall now give a very brief outline of the biographies of some of the Saints who have been chosen, in the course of the centuries, as titulars and protectors of Orders of Knighthood.

A CHIVALROUS REGISTER OF SAINTS

The following record includes the principal Saints under whose patronage different Orders of Knighthood have been placed and whose names sometimes appear in the title of the Order itself. These Saints all belong to the official Register of the Catholic Church, but a number of them are revered also by the Orthodox Church, are mentioned in the Calendar of Saints of Churches of the Anglican Communion and enjoy the respect of several Protestant Churches as well. Their brief biographical sketches will help understand why these Saints in particular were chosen as patrons and titulars by the founders of Orders of Knighthood.

I

THE BLESSED VIRGIN MARY

MOTHER OF GOD

It is proper to place Mary on top of the list. She is the mother of Jesus and the spouse of Joseph. The various phases of her life are commemorated by different Orders of Knighthood, from the moment she was conceived (the Immaculate Conception) to the appearance of the Angel Gabriel announcing she was to become the Mother of the Son of God (the Annunciation) while preserving her maidenhood intact (the Virginity of

Mary); her visit to her cousin Elizabeth (the Visitation); the boyhood of Jesus, his public life beginning with the marriage at Cana (Mary's Mediation), his passion and death on Calvary (Mary's contribution to the Redemption); and finally to the moment Mary was assumed into heaven (The Assumption). Mary, "full of grace" is revered by the knights as the masterpiece of God's creation, the ideal of womenhood, inspiring them in their respect and defence of all women, especially the widows, and as their example of unfaltering discipline and generous dedication.

The knights of old were invested in the name of God, of Mary, and the Patron Saint of their Order; they consecrated themselves to her in a special way taking their oath before God Almighty and His Immaculate Mother and promising to faithfully observe their religious vows and to live in obedience, poverty and chastity. The cincture they wore was to remind them of Mary's untainted purity. They would recite the little Office of the Blessed Virgin Mary and respect her feastdays. They would regularly visit the Holy Places in any way connected with Mary's life; many Orders took their name from them, such as Nazareth, Bethlehem, Jerusalem, and even Mount Carmel, which looks over the green plain of Galilee and Nazareth as a witness of Mary's life. Mount Carmel was always considered a Holy Place: even the Old Testament speaks of its beauty. Nine centuries before Christ, the Prophet Elijah took refuge there and defended the faith in the living God of the people of Israel. During the Crusading times, its caves were occupied by Christian hermits who in the 13th century formed the Carmelite Order with the aim of leading a contemplative life under the patronage of Mary, Mother of God. Starting with the 14th century, several Orders took the oath of defending the "mystery of the Immaculate Conception".

From the same century an oath to defend the Immaculate Conception was required from all those who took their degrees at the Universities of Paris, Oxford and Cambridge.

Thus the Orders, throughout the centuries, interpreted and stood for all the teachings of the Catholic Church about Mary, the world's first love, who in the *Magnificat* identifies herself with the whole human race and rightly foretells that "All generations will count me blessed, so wonderfully has he dealt with me, the Lord, the Mighty One". Mary has many feastdays in the Liturgical Calendar. The official solemnity of Mary Mother of God, is on 1st January.

"The Immaculate Conception" by Murillo as adapted for the medallion of the Spanish Order of Carlos III. Courtesy: Spanish Embassy in Brussels

2

ST. MICHAEL THE ARCHANGEL

St. Michael the Archangel is venerated as the greatest Prince of all the Angels, whom he led in the war waged upon the dragon. "The dragon and his angels fought, but they had not the strength to win and no foothold was left them in heaven. So the great dragon was thrown out, that serpent of old that led the whole world astray, whose name is Satan or the Devil, thrown down to earth, and his angels with him" (Rev. 12, 7–10). St. Michael is therefore revered as the Protector against all evil spirits. He was very popular among the Crusaders, who considered him the first Knight. He is revered throughout Christendom and especially in England where his festival is one of the quarter-days when rents are paid, magistrates are elected and goose is eaten. There is also a British Order of Knighthood, instituted in 1818 – the Order of St. Michael and St. George – which honours him as co-Patron and has its chapel in St. Paul's Cathedral. He is represented in art as a handsome, severe-looking, winged young man, clad in white or armour, combating a dragon, with lance and shield. He is also depicted as weighing the souls in heaven, with scales, on the day of final judgement.

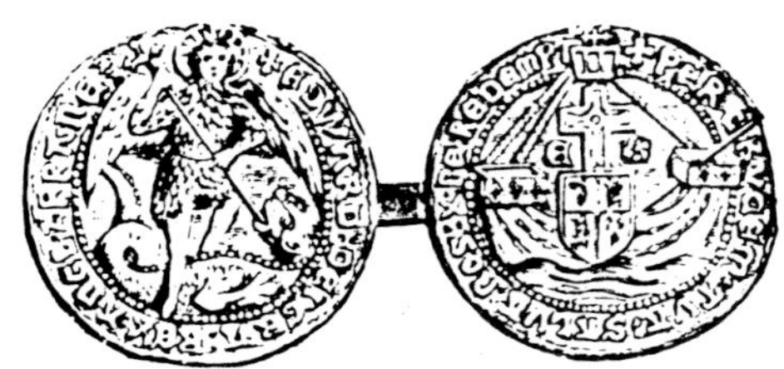

The image of St. Michael the Archangel slaying the dragon appears on the English coin known as Angel-Noble, which was so called because of the device of the Archangel it bore and the excelling quality of the metal. The "Angel" was a re-issue, under King Edward IV in 1465, of the "Noble", which had the current value of 6s 8d when first minted by King Edward III (1327–1377) and remained in use till the time of King Charles I (1600–1649), when it was worth 10s. When this coin ceased to be struck, it was substituted with official medals showing the same device. The "Angel" was presented to persons who, being affected by scrofula, had been touched by the Sovereign. Hence the disease became known as "the King's evil" and the coin itself as a "touch-piece". This practice, still existing in 1712 when Dr. Johnson, then less than three years old, was "touched" by Queen Anne, was based on a belief, prevailing from the reign of Edward the Confessor (1042–1066) to that of Queen Anne (1702–1714), according to which, by divine hereditary right, the Sovereign enjoyed a special healing charism that was exercised by royal touch. The origins of such a belief may be traced back to the time of Clovis, King of the Franks (481–511). King Louis XIV is said to have

The Archangel Michael depicted as Principal Knight of Heaven.

touched 1,600 persons on Easter Sunday 1686, repeating the words: *Le roy te touche, Dieu te guérisse*, meaning "The king touches you, may God heal you."

Archangel Michael's feastday, known as Michaelmas Day, is celebrated on 29 September.

3

ST. AGATHA

VIRGIN AND MARTYR

St. Agatha, a virgin from Catania, in Sicily, suffered martyrdom in the persecution of Decius in 251 for having refused the solicitations of a Roman senator. She was venerated as a saint from the earliest times and her name soon entered the Roman Canon. She is represented in art with a pair of pincers or sheers and a salver, holding her breasts cut off in her martyrdom. Her feastday is 5 February.

4

ST. ANDREW

APOSTLE

St. Andrew was a native of Bethsaida in Galilee and a disciple of John the Baptist. He answered Christ's call, taking his brother Peter with him. He introduced the Gentiles to Christ and preached the Gospel in Greece and other countries. He died on an X-shaped cross at Patrae in Achaia, Greece. According to the legend, his relics were carried to Scotland by a priest of Patrae called Regulus, whose memory is perpetuated by the name Killrule and who founded the town and bishopric of St. Andrews (now archdiocese of St. Andrews and Edinburgh). St. Andrew is the Patron Saint of Scotland and his feastday is celebrated on 30 November.

5

ST. ANNE

MOTHER OF OUR LADY

According to a tradition dating back to the first half of the second century, St. Anne was the mother of the Blessed Virgin Mary and the pouse of St. Joachim. Her veneration spread from East to West from the ixth century. The basilica of St. Mary, erected in Jerusalem in the early enturies on the site of her house, became the church of St. Anne of the Crusaders during the Crusades. Her feastday is 26 July.

6

ST. ANTONY

ABBOT

Renowned father of all monks, St. Antony was born in Egypt, of rich parents, in 250. After his parents' death he distributed his property to the poor and retired to a life of prayer and penitence in the desert, where he gained many followers. He is called Patriarch of Monks, having been the first abbot to form a stable Rule. He gave his full support to those who suffered for their faith during the persecution of Diocletian and to St. Athanasius in his struggle against the Arians. He died in 356 and is revered in the East and the West. Both in art and in literature the story of his temptations by the devil in the form of a pig is often recounted. In heraldry he is emblematically represented by a tau cross with a bell, recalling the legend that one of the proctors of St. Antony's Hospital tied a bell about a pig whose ear had been slit to warn it was unfit for food, so that the pig was not hurt. St. Antony is the Patron Saint of swineherds. His feastday is 17 January.

7

ST. BASIL THE GREAT

BISHOP

St. Basil was born of a Christian family in 330 at Caesarea in Cappadocia. He led a retired life but became well-known for his piety, virtue and learning and was named Bishop of Caesarea. In his ministry he distinguished himself in his love for the poor and in his defence of orthodoxy against the Arian heresy. He wrote many works of theological value. The monastic Rule composed by him is followed by many monasteries of the Eastern Church even today, and exercised a great influence on the establishment of Orders of Knighthood. He died in 379. His feastday is 2 January.

8

ST. BENEDICT

Abbot

St. Benedict was born at Norcia in Umbria, Italy, about the year 480. At 14 he went to study at Rome, where he felt the call to the monastic life. He retired to Subiaco, where he took the religious habit and led a life of solitude, prayer and work. He gathered many disciples whom he distributed in twelve monasteries with twelve monks each. Compelled to leave Subiaco because of the hostility of the local clergy in 529 he went to Mount Cassino where he founded the well-known monastery and wrote his famous Rule, which became the basis for western monasticism and exercised a strong influence on the whole Church, on Orders of Knighthood and on secular society as well. He died in 547. Paul VI proclaimed him Patron Saint of Europe in 1947. His feastday is celebrated on 11 July.

9

ST. BRIDGET

Religious

St. Bridget was born in Sweden in 1303. By birth into the Persson family and marriage with Ulf Gudmarsson (1316) she belonged to the Swedish aristocracy. Mother of eight children, she became a widow in 1344. Though still in the world, she gave herself to an ascetical life and planned the foundation of the Order of the Holy Saviour, went on pilgrimage to Rome in 1350, was outstanding in her practice of Christian virtues, had many mystical experiences, which she describes in her books. She urged the Kings of France and England to conclude the peace, and Clement VI to leave Avignon and return to Rome. She went on a penitential pilgrimage to the Holy Land and died in Rome in 1373. Her feastday is 23 July.

St. Bridget of Sweden giving the rules to members of her Order; sixteenth century painting (altar piece), St. Bridget House in Rome. Courtesy: Mother Theodora, Superior Bridgettine Convent, Iver Heath

HONOREM
VIRGI
MARI

10

ST. CASIMIR

CONFESSOR

St. Casimir, son of King Casimir IV of Poland and Grand Duke of Lithuania, was born at Krakow in 1458. He was well known for his firm faith, pious life, his veneration of the Holy Eucharist and his devotion to the Blessed Virgin Mary. He died in 1484. His feastday is 4 March.

11

ST. CECILIA

VIRGIN AND MARTYR

Of a noble family, St. Cecilia was born in Rome in the third century. She was a perfect example of Christian firmness. She married Valerian who respected her virginity. She suffered martyrdom in Rome, and a basilica was built on the site during the fifth century. She is the Patroness of musicians and is believed to have invented the organ, according to the legend. In reality, her only connexion with music is that she is said to have sung in her soul a song to purity while music was playing at her marriage. The Worshipful Company of Musicians, a Livery Company of London, walks in procession for divine service at St. Paul's Cathedral, on her feastday, 22 November.

12

ST. CHARLES BORROMEO

BISHOP

St. Charles, of the noble Borromeo family, was born at Arona in Lombardy, in 1538. He became a priest, and won a doctorate both in canon and civil law. He was created a cardinal in 1560 by his uncle Pius IV, who named him Secretary of State at the age of 22. He was made a bishop after his uncle's death in 1565 and appointed to Milan. He was a great Reformer of the Church in the 16th century, according to the

Council of Trent. True shepherd of his flock, he distinguished himself for his frequent pastoral visits and wise regulations for the spiritual good of the faithful, erected monasteries, founded charitable institutions, worked tirelessly for the renewal of society, called Synods, and remains an example to all bishops in the apostolate. He died in 1584. His feastday is 4 November.

13

ST. DAVID

Bishop

St. David was probably born in Cardiganshire about the year 520. According to the legend, he was the son of Xantus, Prince of Certicu (Cardiganshire). He was a disciple of St. Illtyd and lived an ascetical life in the Isle of Wight. He preached to the Britons, confuted Pelagius, founded many monasteries, renowned for the austerity of their rule of life. After being preferred to the see of Caerleon, where he had received his early education, he was consecrated a bishop in Jerusalem. Dyvrig having resigned his see in his favour, he moved his archiepiscopal see to Mynnyw (Menevia), later called St. Davids, and was recognised as primate of Wales. He died as abbot of the Mynynw Monastery about 588. He is the Patron Saint of Wales. His feastday is celebrated on 1 March.

14

ST. DOMINIC

Religious

St. Dominic, a member of the noble Guzman family, was born about 1170 at Calaruega in Old Castile, Spain. After studying theology at Palencia he was ordained a priest and made a canon of Osma Cathedral. His apostolate was very fruitful, thanks to his exemplary life, especially in preaching against the Albigensian heresy from which he saved the Western Church. He instituted the Order of Friars Preachers (Dominicans) and died at Bologna in Italy in 1221. His feastday is 8 August.

15

ST. FERDINAND

CONFESSOR AND KING

Ferdinand III, the Saint, King of Castile (1217–1252) and León (1230–1252) was born in 1199, the son of King Alphonse IX of León and Berenguela of Castile. He successfully fought the Moors and drove them out of Granada and Aragon. He was well known for his practice of Christian virtues, the reforms he introduced, his military deeds. He was very pious and devoted to Our Lady, started building the cathedrals of Burgos and Toledo, initiated the *jus patronatus* (the right of presentation to an ecclesiastical benefice). He was a Tertiary of the Friars Minor. He died in 1252, was buried in the Royal Chapel of the cathedral of Seville and was canonised by Clement X in 1671. He is represented in art in an upright position, wearing a red robe and holding a sword and an orb. His feastday is 4 February.

16

ST. FRANCIS

CONFESSOR

Francis, the Seraphic Saint, was born at Assisi in 1182. In the full bloom of his youth he gave up a life of light-heartedness and all his wealth, embraced poverty and lived a life strictly modelled on the Gospel teachings, shining forth in his love of God and neighbour. He preached the Gospel even to the Muslims, founded the Order of Franciscan Friars, laid the foundation of an Order of Nuns. He was favoured with the stigmata and died peacefully in 1226. He is the most extraordinary Saint of all times. His feastday is 4 October.

17

ST. GEORGE

MARTYR

Saint George was a Christian soldier who, according to tradition, suffered martyrdom in the third century during the persecution of Dio-

St. George defeating the dragon. A silver, enameled badge, surrounded by the Garter, struck in the 59th and last year of the reign of King George III of England in 1820. The reverse of the badge bears the image of George III.

Private Collection

cletian at Lydda in the Holy Land, where a church was built in his honour in the fourth century. The extraordinary popularity enjoyed by St. George in the Middle Ages, which spread with his cult in the Christian world, brought numberless pilgrims to the site of his martyrdom. Many legends about St. George took shape over the centuries; some of them were so unlikely that in 1960 the Sacred Congregation of Rites had to suppress much of what was said of him in the Breviary. Contrary to what many believed, this measure placed no doubt on the historical reality of the personage, whose name is found in the liturgical calendars of East and West. The Church's attitude of restraint regarding the legends dates back to the Gelasian decree of the year 496 which placed the "Passion of St. George" among the apocryphal writings.

The earliest legend presented George as an army officer who, having refused to apostatise, underwent long and refined tortures for seven years, was killed and was resurrected by God three times before he was decapitated. Many episodes are recounted, the most famous of which was his struggle with the dragon who kept a young woman in captivity. The legend about St. George slaying the dragon is an allegorical way of expressing the triumph of good over evil, which St. John the Divine represents as a dragon. Bunyan uses the allegory in making Christian prevail against Apollyon. In Percy's ballad *Reliques* St. George is presented as the son of Lord Albert of Coventry.

St. George became popular in England thanks to the early Crusaders who claimed they enjoyed his protection at Antioch in 1099, when the Normans, led by Robert, son of William the Conqueror, chose him as their Patron Saint. "St. George" thus became the battle-cry of English soldiers. He is the favourite Patron Saint of many Orders of Knighthood, archers, armies, cities and countries, among which England and Portugal are prominent.

His feastday is celebrated on 23 April.

18

ST. GREGORY THE GREAT

POPE

See Chapter Three, IV, "The Order of St. Gregory the Great".

19

ST. HENRY

CONFESSOR AND KING

St. Henry was born in Bavaria in 973, son of the Duke of Bavaria. He succeeded his father in 995 and was elected Holy Roman Emperor in 1014. He led a monastic life with his childless wife Cunegond of Luxembourg. He brought about several reforms of the Church, set up dioceses, founded monasteries and encouraged missionary activity. It was thanks to his insistence that Benedict VIII introduced the chanting of the Creed in Sunday and feastday Masses. He died in 1024 and was buried in the cathedral of Bamberg, which he had built. He was canonised by Eugene III in 1146. His feastday is 13 July.

20

ST. HUBERT

Bishop

St. Hubert was born about the year 685, the son of Bertrand, Duke of Aquitania and cousin of Pepin, King of the Franks. Formerly married, he became Bishop of Maastricht in Holland about 705. His successor there was his son Florebert. Having extirpated the remains of idolatry from his diocese, in 717 he transferred the relics of his immediate predecessor, the martyr Lambert, to Liège which he then made his episcopal see and became the apostle of Ardennes and Brabant. He died at Tervuren, with infection from a wound he got while fishing in 727. In 825 some of his relics were given to the newly founded monastery at Andage in the hunting-ground of Ardennes, which received its name from him, St. Hubert-en-Ardenne. According to the legend, he was converted when while chasing he saw a stag with a crucifix between his antlers, threatening him with eternal perdition unless he reformed his life. The legend also says that he received a key from St. Peter and a stole from an Angel; these objects are still preserved as relics at Liège. A race of dogs was bred at the Andage monastery, named after St. Hubert, who is the Patron of huntsmen and is also invoked against rabies. In art St. Hubert is represented with the stag. His feastday is 3 November.

21

ST. ISABELLA OF PORTUGAL

A Holy Woman and Queen

St. Isabella (= Elizabeth) was born in 1271. She was the daughter of King Peter II of Aragon and grandniece of St. Elizabeth, Queen of Hungary. She married Denis I, King of Portugal, by whom she had two sons. She suffered many trials even in her own family life. She enjoyed the gift of settling disputes. She was very pious and accomplished numerous works of mercy. After her husband's death in 1325, she distributed all her personal property to the poor, took the habit of the Franciscan Third Order, lived a most saintly life and died in 1336 while effecting a reconciliation between her son and her son-in-law. She and her saintly Hungarian aunt share many legends. Her feastday is 5 July.

22

ST. JAMES

APOSTLE

St. James the Apostle was born at Bethsaida, the son of Zebedee and brother of the Apostle John. He is not to be confounded with St. James, the son of Alphaeus and a cousin of Jesus, who ruled the Church at Jerusalem. St. James was one of Christ's most beloved disciples. He witnessed the resurrection of the daughter of Jairus and the transfiguration of the Lord. He was the first among the Apostles to offer his life for the Gospel, having been decapitated by King Herod Agrippa about the year 42. Since the ninth century he is venerated especially at Compostela in Spain, where his tomb is visited by millions in the famous shrine dedicated in his honour. His feastday is 25 July.

23

ST. JANUARIUS

BISHOP AND MARTYR

St. Januarius was bishop of Benevento in the third century and was beheaded at Naples during the persecution of Diocletian. He is the Patron Saint of Naples where his blood, kept in a phial, is liquified twice a year through an unknown cause when placed near the head of the martyr, a miracle which had been witnessed by the Duke of Wellington while in Naples on St. Januarius's feastday, which is 19 September.

24

ST. JOHN THE BAPTIST

PRECURSOR OF OUR LORD JESUS CHRIST

St. John the Baptist, John meaning "God is gracious" and Baptist "the Baptiser", was the son of Zechariah and Elizabeth, born to them in old age. He was sanctified in his mother's womb when Mary visited her after the annunciation. As the last and greatest of the Prophets, his mission as Forerunner was to prepare the people for the coming of his cousin Jesus, the Messiah, by proclaiming a baptism of penance. On Jesus's arrival, St. John pointed him out to his own followers and encouraged them to follow him only in the future. Having reproached Herod for his unlawful union with his brother's wife, the adulterous Herodias and her daughter Salome asked Herod to behead John, who was thus martyred at the beginning of Jesus's public life. In some countries fires are burnt on St. John's festival in memory of the Lord's own words: "John was a lamp, burning brightly and for a time you were ready to exult in his light" (Jn.5, 35). He is not to be confounded with John the Apostle, who wrote the Fourth Gospel. St. John the Baptist is represented in art clothed in sheepskin, holding a wooden cross with a pennon on which are inscribed the words: *Ecce Agnus Dei* (Behold the Lamb of God), or with a lamb on his right surrounded by a halo bearing a cross on the right foot. His feastday is 24 June.

25

ST. JOSEPH

Jesus's Foster Father

St. Joseph was the husband of the Blessed Virgin Mary. He belonged to the Royal House of David, but was of humble condition, and gained his living by working as a carpenter. Mary had already conceived Jesus of the Holy Ghost when he married her, reassured by an Angel about her fidelity. He became the foster-father of Jesus. He is mentioned in the Gospels of St. Matthew and St. Luke, where he is described as a just man. Devotion to him developed rather lately in the Church, around the 14th century. He has two feastdays, one celebrating him as foster-father of Jesus on 19 March and the other as a worker on 1 May.

26

ST. LAZARUS OF BETHANY

Confessor

St. Lazarus of Bethany was the brother of Martha and Mary, whom Jesus held as a dear friend and resurrected from the dead. According to the legend, he evangelised Provence together with his two sisters. It also adds he was bishop of Marseilles, after being bishop of Ephesus. The cathedral of Autun, St. Nazarus, changed its name to St. Lazarus in 1147, when it received what was thought to be his relics. The Order of St. Lazarus grew out of the Hospital of St. Lazarus outside the walls of Jerusalem where lepers were cured by Armenian monks who lived according to the rule of St. Basil. There is some confusion at times between him and the Lazarus of the parable, who was a beggar covered with sores and was laid daily at the gate of a rich man (Lk.16, 19–31). This may explain the connexion with leprosy. His feastday in 29 July.

27

ST. LOUIS

CONFESSOR AND KING

St. Louis of France was born in 1114. He became King of France in 1136. As a member of the Third Order of St. Francis he sought to carry the spirit of the Gospel into his daily duties, private and public, giving an outstanding example of Christian virtue in his practice of prayer, penance and brotherly love, especially with regard to the poor. He was married and had eleven children. He was an attentive Sovereign, a promoter of peace and goodwill, an exemplary Knight at arms, always ready to defend good causes. He undertook Crusades to win back the Holy Places to the Christians. Taken prisoner at Mansourah in Egypt, he edified his Muslim captors by his virtuous behaviour. He died as a soldier under a tent at Carthage in 1270, and was canonised in 1297 by Alexander III. In memory of his Crusades, he is often represented in art holding a crown of thorns and the cross, or a standard of the cross, or with the pilgrim's staff. His feastday is 25 August.

28

ST. MARGARET

VIRGIN AND MARTYR

St. Margaret, also known as Marina, was a Roman virgin of the third century. Having refused to marry the pagan Roman prefect Olybrius because she was a Christian, she was tortured, thrown into a tank of boiling oil from which she survived, and finally decapitated. She is no longer in the Liturgical Calendar. She was very popular in the Middle

Ages when many legends were spread about her extraordinary life, during which she was believed to have strangled a dragon with her cincture. Hence she is often represented in art holding a cross and with a dragon at her feet. She was especially invoked by parturient women. Her feastday is 20 July.

St. Margaret; a fifteenth century painting of the Flemish School.

Courtesy: Le Palais de la Nation (Sénat) in Brussels

29

ST. MARK

Apostle

St. Mark was a cousin of Barnabas the Reconciler. He was one of the Apostles and of the Evangelists, a disciple of St. Peter. He enjoyed St. Paul's friendship and went to Rome with him. He is believed to have founded the Church of Alexandria in Egypt. He suffered martyrdom in the latter part of the first century. He is depicted in art as being in the prime of life, sometimes wearing episcopal robes, accompanied by a winged lion, which emblematically recalls that he was the historian of the Resurrection. He holds a pen in his right hand and in his left the Gospel. The lion may also be related to the fact that he starts his Gospel by describing the mission of John the Baptist, crying in the desert. The lion, in fact, is also one of the symbolic living creatures of Ezechiel's vision shaking the desert with its roars. St. Mark's feastday is 25 April.

30

ST. MARY MAGDALENE

Holy Woman

St. Mary of Magdala, hence Magdalene, is one of Christ's most famous converts and disciples, often mentioned in the Gospels. The Oriental Church believes she is not the same Mary as the sister of Lazarus and Martha or who annointed Jesus's feet at the house of Simon the Pharisee and who stood at the foot of the cross. The Western Church believes that these three personages are the same Mary of Magdala. She became a legendary figure, who took refuge in France with Martha and Lazarus and worked with them for the evangelisation of Provence. She is represented in art as a young and beautiful woman, with flowing hair and holding in her hand a box of ointment, or even praying before a scull or a cross. She is the Patron Saint of penitents. Devotion to her spread in the Western Church, especially thanks to the Crusaders, as from the eleventh century. Her feastday is 22 July.

31

ST. MAURICE

MARTYR

St. Maurice is a Roman martyr who is said to have been a member of the Theban Legion whose members all suffered martyrdom at Agaunum in the Gauls for having refused to take part in the persecution of Diocletian. The legion was also called the "Angelical Legion". An abbey and a basilica were erected there in honour of St. Maurice, whose name they still bear, and his companions, by Bishop Theodore in the second half of the fourth century. St. Maurice is depicted as a knight, sometimes with moorish features. His feastday is 22 September.

32

ST. PATRICK

BISHOP

Born in Wales or Scotland around the year 387, the son, as it is thought, of the deacon Calpurnius, a Roman official, St. Patrick spent his youth in Ireland, where he had been sold as a slave, working as a herdsman. Having managed to escape to Gaul, he studied under St. Martin of Tours, became a priest, was commissioned by Pope St. Celestine to evangelise Ireland, landed at Wicklow in 432 and became a bishop. He converted many to the faith in his 31 years of preaching. The Church in Ireland was organised by him. He founded the cathedral and monastery of Armagh, held two synods and died around 464 and was buried, as believed, at Downspatrick or at Glastonbury. He is the Patron Saint of Ireland. There are many legends of his miraculous powers. He is often depicted as banishing serpents and holding a shamrock leaf he used as a symbol to preach the Trinity. His feastday is 17 March.

33

ST. PAUL

APOSTLE

Saul, who took the name of Paul after his conversion, was born at Tharsus in Cilicia in the first decade of the Christian era. He was "a Jew, son of a Jew", but also a Roman citizen, who was trained in Greek and rabbinical schools, persecuted Christians and was finally converted while journeying to Damascus on a punitive mission, when Jesus appeared to him and said: "Saul, Saul, why do you persecute me?" (Acts,9, 1–19). Baptised by Ananias, he became an indefatigable and brave missionary, journeyed extensively in the East and the West, organising the Church in many countries, suffering hard trials including shipwreck at Malta before arriving in Rome in the year 60. A prodigious writer of fourteen Epistles filled with fundamental Christian teachings, he suffered martyrdom under Nero at *Aquae Salviae* near Rome, where he was decapitated. He is the Patron Saint of missionaries and also of tentmakers, having himself earned his living for a time as one of the latter. He is represented in art often with St. Peter, and as of short stature, with a bald head and a grey beard, holding a sword (emblematic of the word of God) and an open book. His feastday is 29 June, with St. Peter's.

34

ST. PETER

APOSTLE

St. Peter, son of Jonah, was born at Bethsaida. He was the brother of the Apostle Andrew, who introduced him to the Master, whose company he joined after being a follower of John the Baptist. He was very close to Jesus, who admired his ardour, and changing his original name of Simon to Cephas, that is Peter, the Rock, made him the foundation stone of his future Church. He witnessed many of Jesus's miracles, spread the Gospel in Syria and then journeyed to Rome where he set up the Church, becoming Bishop of the Eternal City, whence the Popes derive their primatial authority over the universal Church. His faithful companion was Mark, who received from him much of the contents of the second Gospel he wrote, while Peter wrote two letters with fundamental teachings to the Christians. With St. Paul he is revered as the Prince of the Apostles. He suffered many trials and having confuted Simon Magnus, a magician at Nero's court, he was crucified, head downwards at his own request, feeling unworthy to take the upright position in which Christ was crucified, on the very spot over which St. Peter's Basilica was built. The location of his tomb under the high altar was verified in 1950. In art he is usually represented as an old man of 70 (he was martyred in the year

66), with a flowing beard, holding a book or a scroll in his hand and with the Keys of the Kingdom of Heaven. He is the first Patron of the universal Church, and also of fishermen. His feastday is 29 June, together with St. Paul's.

35

ST. RAYMOND OF PEÑAFORT

Priest

St. Raymond was born at Barcelona, Spain, in 1175. He became a priest and a canon of the cathedral, and professor of philosophy and law. He joined the Dominican Order in 1222, shortly after St. Dominic's death. By order of Gregory IX he wrote five "Books of Decretals" which became a valuable part of the canon law of the Catholic Church. Elected Master General of his Order, he governed it with wise laws. His rules for the fruitful administration of the Sacrament of Penance, given in his "Summary of Cases", are of outstanding and everlasting importance. He was also a brave and zealous missionary. Together with St. Peter Nolascus he founded the Sacred and Military Order of Our Lady of Mercy for the redemption of Christians made captives by the Moors. He also endeavoured to establish a dialogue with the Muslims and encouraged his religious to study Arabic and the Koran. He died in 1275. His feastday is 7 January.

36

ST. ROSE OF LIMA

Religious

St. Rose was born at Lima, Peru in 1586. After spending her young years at home in the practice of all Christian virtues, at fifteen years of age she took the habit of the Third Order of St. Dominic and modelled her life on that of St. Catherine of Siena, progressing in piety, goodness and penance. She enjoyed many mystical experiences. She died in 1617 and became the first American to be canonised. She is revered by South American Orders of Knighthood. Her feastday is 23 August.

37

ST. STEPHEN OF HUNGARY

Confessor and King

St. Stephen was born in Hungary about the year 975. He was the founder of the Hungarian State and was crowned King of Hungary in the year 1000. To avoid Hungary's integration into the German Empire, he proclaimed himself vassal of the Holy See. Profoundly respectful of the laws of the Church, he strengthened its position by establishing sixteen dioceses, over which he kept the *jus patronatus*, invited many Italian missionaries and favoured the spread of Latin culture in his kingdom, which became one of the most consolidated monarchies in Europe. Stephen was a just, pious, charitable and peace-loving king, who always sought the good of his subjects, especially the poor and suffering. He declared Our Lady Patroness of Hungary. He died at Szekesfehérvar in 1038, and was immediately revered as the Apostle of Hungary. His feast day is 16 August.

38

ST. SYLVESTER

Pope

See Chapter Three, V, "The Order of Pope St. Sylvester".

39

ST. THERESA OF AVILA

Religious and Doctor of the Church

St. Theresa was born at Avila in 1515. Highly privileged by extraordinary spiritual charisms, she joined the Carmelite Order at 20 years of age and had many mystical experiences. She bravely and successfully endured many trials in the reform of her Order and wrote works of great theological and literary value, considered to be equal to those of a doctor of the Church by Gregory XV and Urban VII. Paul VI proclaimed her Doctor of the Church in 1970. She died at Avila in 1582. Her feastday is 15 October.

40

ST. THOMAS

Apostle

St. Thomas was one of the Twelve Apostles. Little is known of his origin. He is introduced into St. John's Gospel by the appellative "the Twin". He was a man of courage, but also a doubter, rebuked by Christ for seeking evidence of his Master's resurrection. According to tradition, he preached the Gospel in Syria, Persia and India, and suffered martyrdom at Calamina, India, where the Christians of St. Thomas claim him as their first evangeliser, as Vasco da Gama witnessed when he arrived there in 1498. Many legends are told of him in the apocryphal "Acts of St. Thomas". On his feastday a custom exists in certain parts of Britain of collecting small sums of money or obtaining drink from employers while in London members of the Common Council are either elected or re-elected. He is represented in art either holding a square to indicate his tendency of desiring to ascertain facts he is told about or putting his finger in Christ's wounds to scatter his doubts about Christ's resurrection. His relics rest at Edessa in Turkey certainly since the year 232. His feastday is 3 July.

41

ST. WENCESLAUS

Martyr and Duke

St. Wenceslaus was born in Bohemia about the year 907 and raised in the Catholic faith by his grandmother. He lived a penitent life, filled with love of God and neighbour, especially the poor, in the midst of a very corrupted court. He became Duke of Bohemia in 925, and promoted the Christian faith in his dukedom. Deeply attached to "our holy mother the Church", his preference went to German missionaries rather than to Slavic ones, which caused much opposition, especially on the part of his brother Boleslav. This opposition reached its climax when King Henry I of Germany appeared before the walls of Prague with a powerful army, seeking to impose his authority on the Bohemians. Wenceslaus was taken prisoner in a plot organised by his brother Boleslav and put to death between 929–935. He was immediately revered as a Saint and recognised as principal Patron of Bohemia. His feastday is 28 September.

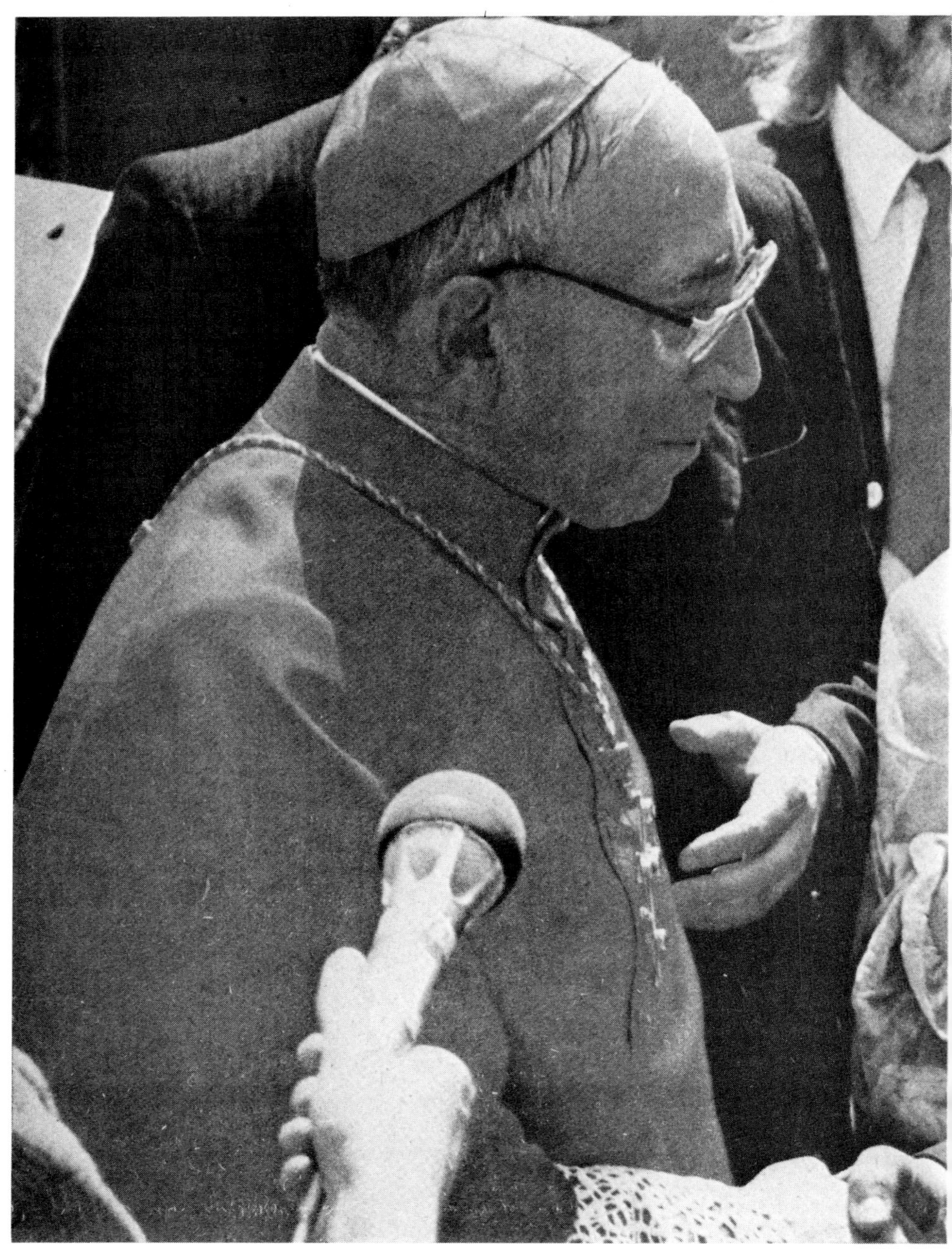

His Eminence Agostino Cardinal Casaroli, Papal Secretary of State and Prefect of the Council for Public Affairs of the Church. Courtesy: Felici, Pontificia Fotografia, Rome

CHAPTER THIRTEEN

THE SPIRIT OF CHRISTIAN CHIVALRY TODAY

The spirit of Christian Chivalry was summed up by the Papal Secretary of State, His Eminence Agostino Cardinal Casaroli, in the following terms:

"A Knight was a man who intended to place himself completely at the service of a noble and difficult cause, a pure and arduous ideal. Fighting evil, promoting good, defending the weak and the oppressed against injustice. Bringing low the arrogance of the more powerful. Courage and unselfishness, generosity and readiness to make sacrifices: to the point of heroism, even to the point of death, if necessary. This is the picture – the *ideal* picture, let us say – of the Knight in the original accepted meaning of the term. Not for nothing was St. George the martyr, who fought the dragon to protect the defenceless maiden, the prototype of the Knight; and he still is.

"In early times, becoming a Knight did not merely mean receiving a title of honour, even though it was well deserved. It also demanded a vocation and a call, a preparation and a period of trial; it was an achievement and it presupposed a solemn commitment; and in its totality it was crowned by an austere and almost religious ceremonial.

"Becoming a Knight meant taking on a mission, before God and man."

(*Cf. L'Osservatore Romano*, 5 August 1982)

The reader who has had the patience to bear with us until now will need no further words to convince him of the Church's favourable attitude towards the bestowal of titles and decorations of legitimately instituted Orders of Knighthood as well as other honours and awards.

Though chivalry was not originally founded by the Church, but by the laity, it was the Church who set about immediately to refine it according to the spirit of the Gospel. In fact it was the Church who, more than any other body, understood and appreciated the spirit which moved the first Crusading Orders of Knighthood, spiritualised their military zeal and valour, granted them her approval and support, inspired their so-called "chivalric system of virtues" based on ethico-aesthetic categories of a secular nature with the high Christian ideals which transformed the rude and violent soldiers into disciplined, self-controlled, refined, gentle and strong defenders of the rights of God, of Christendom, of the Church and of society, consciously endeavouring to bring religion into daily life with service to the less fortunate, honour and courtesy to all.

In return, the constitutional codes of the ancient Orders of Chivalry would ask all their members to submit obediently and lovingly to the authority of the Church, to obey her commandments, and to protect her against her enemies, seeing in her the sweet Spouse of Christ. This explains why these ancient Orders, many in fact were also Monastic Orders, as well as more recent ones, claim some link with the Church or with religion in general. And this also explains why the Church has found it normal, especially in the sixteenth century and then again in the nineteenth and twentieth centuries to found, revise, suppress, re-establish her own Orders of Knighthood and other means of giving official and public awards to well-deserving persons, even of other obediences, who have rendered conspicuous service to good causes.

Indeed it can be said that through the history of the ancient Orders of Knighthood from the beginning up to modern times, one can trace the history of European Christendom. The Catholic Church was deeply involved in the life of the European nations forming the *Res Publica Christiana*. The great Catholic values and beliefs were present and operative in the minds and lives of its peoples. Many Orders were founded for the glory of God, the defence of the Church and Christendom and in honour of the Blessed Virgin Mary, for whom they professed a tender devotion and deep commitment. As we have seen, several of them honoured Our Lady under the title of the Immaculate Conception many centuries before this traditional belief was defined as a dogma by Pius IX in 1854.

After the breaking-up of the *Res Publica Christiana* in the sixteenth century, the Catholic inspiration was drained out of the lifestream of most of the ancient Orders of Knighthood which had contributed so significantly to forging the sense of a common bond between northern and southern countries. Another pillar was thus overthrown of that solidarity in one Catholic faith which had kept Western Europe together as a Christian commonwealth of nations and which, until then, had found adequate expression even in and through the ancient Orders of Knighthood.

Nevertheless chivalry, with all its pageantry of armoured knights and hierarchy of classes and titles and corresponding chains, badges and medallions, has survived almost unscathed the simplifying trends of our progressive technological era. The study of chivalry continues to be a matter of deep interest and an indispensable aid to comprehend the development and folklore of European history from the Middle Ages to our present day. But it also remains a fascinating reality to which, responding to a sort of inborn appetite, some appear to be drawn more than others in an irresistible way.

Some people feel that it is vain and futile to accept decorations. Others would go so far as to believe that it is against the virtue of humility. Others instead crave for any kind of distinction they can add to their personal collection, which they wear proudly upon their breast. We have no intention of valuing beyond measure the bestowal of titles, decorations and medals. But we should like to stress that even though our praise and admiration may be very high for those who shun such honours *sub specie aeternitatis* [when seen in the light of eternity] we find no wrong in those who in good conscience delight in receiving them, if and when they are well deserved; and indeed in those lawful authorities who, for justifiable reasons, confer these marks of esteem and distinction on people who merit them.

The saintly Pius X puts all this in a nutshell when he writes (*Multum ad excitandos*) on 7 February 1905:

> "Rewards which are given to honour valour are very useful to encourage men to accomplish praiseworthy deeds because, as they do credit to persons worthy of the grateful recognition of Church and society, they also stimulate others to follow their path leading to praise and honour. So it was that Our Predecessors, the Roman Pontiffs, turned their special attention to Orders of Knighthood, as a spur towards glory. Some of them founded new Orders, others either restored ancient ones to their pristine lustre or increased this lustre with extraordinary privileges."

Chivalry, as an institution, may well be something belonging to the past, and the ages in which it flourished may have differed widely from our own. The spirit, however, which permeates the very notion of chivalry is timeless because it is based on the strength of Christian spiritual and social values, which are expressed so clearly in the codes of honour of the ancient Orders aiming at rendering the upper classes worthy of their exceptional advantages.

Those who in our time have the privilege of being associated in some way with a lawful Order of Knighthood, should indeed endeavour to translate the ideals of the knights of old into the modern texture of social life where their need is so sorely felt. They too are called to engage all their efforts for the triumph of Christ's cause in the world. They should "put on all the armour which God provides, so that they may be able to stand firm against the devices of the devil" [Eph.6, 11]. Thus "wielding the weapons of righteousness in right hand and left", they should recommend themselves by the innocence of their behaviour, their grasp of truth, their patience and kindliness in order that their service may not be brought into discredit [2 Cor.3 – 6], and God's glory may shine forth and be extolled in their efforts to liberate the world from the evils impending over it.

In so doing they can be sure that "His faithfulness will be their true buckler and shield" [Ps.91, 7].

AUTHOR'S ACKNOWLEDGEMENTS

The author is deeply grateful to all those who by their assistance and advice have encouraged him in writing this book.

In particular he desires to thank the Papal Secretariat of State and the Sovereigns, the Head of the Imperial and Royal House of Austria and the Heads of other Royal Houses who either directly or through the officers of their Courts have placed original photographs and documents at his disposal.

Moreover he would like to witness his warm appreciation of the valuable co-operation offered by the Count de Sierragorda of the Spanish Foreign Service, Mr. Pierre Blanchard, member of the National Foundation of the *Pieux Etablissements de la France à Rome et à Lorette*, Dr. Mario Belardo, Procurator of the Apostolic Palaces, and indeed Mr. Peter Bander van Duren and his colleague Mr. Leslie Hayward, his publishers in Great Britain, whose interest in the subject matter involved them far beyond their professional obligation to the advantage of the book itself.

Material and photographs to the Orders of Knighthood were kindly supplied also by the Embassies of Denmark (London and Brussels), Great Britain (Brussels), Portugal (Brussels), Monaco (Brussels), Spain (Brussels), Sweden (London), and the Consulate General of San Marino (Brussels).

He likewise owes a special gratitude for their help to the Central Chancery of British Orders of Knighthood; Mr. S.J. Connelly of Messrs. Spink and Son, London; Mme. Ruth M.M. de Wohl, Swiss Lieutenancy of the Equestrian Order of the Holy Sepulchre; the Marquess di Lorenzo, Grand Chancellor of the Sacred and Military Constantinian Order of St. George; Mr. Drummond-Murray, Chancellor of the British Association of the Sovereign Military Order of Malta; Archbishop Bruno B. Heim, Apostolic Pro-Nuncio to Great Britain, London; Mr. Douglas Jenkins, London, Member of the Grand Magistry of the Equestrian Order of the Holy Sepulchre; Malteser Hilfsdienst, Köln, Bundesrepublik Deutschland; the Rev. Canon J. Robinson, Master of the Temple, London; Mr. Kenneth Rose, London; Mr. Colin P. Smythe, Gerrards Cross; Miss S. Stockwell, the Peter Grugeon Studio, Reading; Mr. W.T. Taylor, MVO, OBE, Curfew Tower, Windsor Castle, and Mr. Brian Hockey of Messrs. Inforum, Portsmouth.

Finally, he wishes to express his indebtedness to the following: Biblioteca Apostolica Vaticana, Vatican City, (several photographs of Popes); L'Osservatore Romano, Vatican City, (photographs of Pope John

Paul II and the Cardinal Secretary of State); Editalia, Edizioni d'Italia, Rome, (illustrations appearing in *La Cavalleria e gli Ordini Cavallereschi* by Arrigo Pecchioli); Stablimento Giovanni Johnson, Milan and Rome, (reproductions of coloured photographs of several Orders of Knighthood, taken by Oscar Savio, Rome); the Dean and Chapter of St. George's Chapel, Windsor Castle, for the photograph of the Garter Stall.

He owes a large dept of gratitude to the pontifical photographer Felici (*Pontificia Fotografia Felici, Roma*) who supplied many photographs taken on solemn occasions at the Vatican.

The painting of Pope John Paul II on page 2 is by the eminent Flemish painter Felix de Boeck (1898–). The portrait was painted shortly before the assassination attempt on the Holy Father in 1980. The artist announced at the time that this was to be his last portrait because of failing eye sight. He presented the painting to the author and it is reproduced here for the first time. The portrait of Pope Paul VI was painted by Felix de Boeck in 1970 and was presented to the Apostolic Nunciature in Brussels. Felix de Boeck was appointed a Knight Commander of the Order of Pope St. Sylvester by Paul VI.

H.E.C.

APPENDICES

STATUTES OF PONTIFICAL ORDERS OF KNIGHTHOOD

DE SUPREMO EQUESTRI
ORDINE
MILITIAE D.N. IESU CHRISTI

DE EQUESTRI ORDINE
MILITIAE AURATAE

DE EQUESTRI ORDINE
PIANO

DE EQUESTRI ORDINE
S. GREGORII MAGNI

DE EQUESTRI ORDINE
S. SILVESTRI PAPAE

APOSTOLIC LETTER

DE ORDINUM EQUESTRIUM
DIGNITATE IIS DEFERENDA
QUI CIVITATIBUS PRAESUNT

APOSTOLIC LETTER

DE CRUCE "PRO ECCLESIA ET PONTIFICE"

Excerpta Brevi SS. D. N. Pii PP. X " De Ordinibus Equestribus " pro Supremo Ordine Militiae D. N. Iesu Christi.

PIUS PP. X

AD perpetuam rei memoriam. – Multum ad excitandos ad egregia facinora hominum animos praemia virtuti reddita valent, quae, dum ornant egregios bene de re sacra vel publica meritos viros, ceteros exemplo rapiunt ad idem laudis honorisque spatium decurrendum. Hoc quidem sapienti consilio Romani Pontifices Decessores Nostri Equestres Ordines, quasi gloriae stimulos, singulari studio prosequuti sunt, horumque alios instituere, alios iam institutos, vel pristino decori restituerunt, vel novis ac potioribus privilegiis ditarunt.

Nunc autem, cum peropportunum visum sit gravibus de causis quaedam immutare de nonnullis Equestribus Pontificiis Ordinibus, Nos collatis consiliis cum dilecto filio Nostro Aloisio S. R. Ecclesiae Diacono Cardinali Macchi, a Brevibus apostolicis Literis Secretario, et Pontificiae Sedis Equestrium Ordinum Magno Cancellario, omnibus rei momentis attente ac sedulo perpensis, ex certa scientia ac matura deliberatione Nostris haec quae infrascripta sunt decernenda existimavimus.

Oculos mentis Nostrae convertentes ad Militiae Iesu Christi nobilissimum Ordinem, quem anno MCCCXVIII post Ordinis Templi ruinam Dionysius I Portugalliae et Algarbiorum Rex auctore et auspice Ioanne PP. XXII rec. mem. Praedecessore Nostro instituit, hunc Equestrium Pontificiae Sedis Ordinum Supremum esse auctoritate Nostra per praesentes edicimus ac mandamus, quo non alter sit dignitate potior, sed ceteris amplitudine ac splendore superemineat. Una sit Equitum classis. Sed quo magis per Nos consultum sit huius Supremi Ordinis decori volumus ut posthac Crux, Ordinis propria, collo dependeat ex aureo torqui, qui constet alternis clypeolis Crucem Ordinis ac Pontificium Emblema enchausto referentibus, nodis aureis inter se iunctis. Traditum enim memoriae est, et ipsos veteres dictae Militiae Equites simili torqui iamdiu usos fuisse alternis ensibus ac tiaris caelato. Similiter volumus ut in magno Numismate corona laurea ex auro, parva taenia ex enchausto rubro inferius vincta, Crucem concludat; tandem ut femoralia alba e serico rasili genua vix praetergrediantur; caligae sint sericae, et item albae; aureae denique fibulae calceolos ornent. Quoad vestem, ensem et alia ornamenta nihil immutetur.

Verum tamen expresse mandamus, ne inter Equites eiusdem Militiae discrimen contingat, sed unusquisque Ordo stemmata, insignia, arma, atque ornamenta, a Sancta Sede praescripta servet integerrime, ut praefata insignia Cruces, Numismata, vestes, enses, opera phrygia, atque ornamenta, tum propria Supremi Ordinis Militiae Iesu Christi, cum ceterorum quos Apostolica Sedes conferre solet, sint adamussim confecta ad normam exemplarium et declarationum quas a Cancelleria Equestrium Ordinum edi et penes Nostram a Brevibus Apostolicis Literis Secretariam iussimus asservari; utque prae oculis habeantur apposita schemata, quae singulis vicibus cuilibet equestri dignitate aucto de more traduntur.

Haec statuimus, mandamus, praecipimus, decernentes praesentes Literas firmas, validas, atque efficaces semper fore et existere, suosque plenarios atque integros effectus sortiri atque obtinere, illisque, ad quos spectat et pro tempore spectabit, in omnibus et per omnia plenissime suffragari: sicque in praemissis per quoscumque iudices ordinarios et delegatos et alios quoslibet quacumque praeeminentia et potestate fungentes, sublata eis et eorum cuilibet quavis aliter iudicandi et interpretandi facultate et auctoritate, iudicari et definiri debere: irritumque et inane si secus quidquam super his a quocumque quavis auctoritate scienter vel ignoranter contigerit attentari. Non obstantibus Nostra et Cancellariae Apostolicae regula de iure quaesito non tollendo, aliisque Constitutionibus et Ordinationibus Apostolicis, nec non supradictorum et aliorum quorumcumque Equestrium Ordinum etiam iuramento, confirmatione Apostolica, vel quavis firmitate alia roboratis Statutis et consuetudinibus, ceterisque contrariis, licet speciali mentione dignis, quibuscumque, privilegiis quoque, indultis, et Literis Apostolicis, in contrarium praemissorum quomodolibet concessis, confirmatis et innovatis; quibus omnibus et singulis, illorum tenores praesentibus pro plene et sufficienter expressis ac de verbo ad verbum insertis habentes, illis alias in suo robore permansuris, ad praemissorum effectum hac vice dumtaxat specialiter et expresse derogamus. Datum Romae apud Sanctum Petrum sub Annulo Piscatoris die 7 Februarii anno MDCCCCV, Pontificatus Nostri anno secundo.

ALOISIUS Card. MACCHI.

Ex Cancellaria Ordinum Equestrium

Die 7 Februarii 1905.

SSm̃us Dominus Noster Pius Papa X, animo repetens omnia, quae ab Apostolica Sede sive ad homines virtute formandos sive ad praemia iisdem pro recte factis rependenda iugiter emanant, iis legibus servanda esse quibus et decori eiusdem Sedis et congrue rationi consultum sit, opportune mentem suam ad Equestres Ordines admovit.

Hinc est quod, re prius acta cum infrascripto Cardinali a Brevibus, magno Equestrium Ordinum Cancellario, sacrum et perillustrem illum Ordinem, ab eo appellatum Nomine in quo omnes genuflectantur oportet, Militiae nempe Domini Nostri Iesu Christi, iis praerogativis et insignibus commendatum voluit quibus, ut decet, ceteros Equestres Ordines antecellat.

Honorarias hasce praerogativas sartas tectasque praestitit per Breve hoc ipso die datum et specialia insignia adamussim statuta per leges quae hic sequuntur.

Pro Equitibus a Magno Torqui
Supremi Ordinis Militiae D. N. Iesu Christi.

Vestis e panno rubri coloris siet in longos post tergum producta limbos.

Circa collum atque ad extremas manicas sit e panno albo.

E panno item albo gestet pectorale.

Opera phrygia, omnia acu picta ex auro, circa collum, pectorale et extremas manicas taeniola dentata sint et laciniae laureas referentes; iuxta et supra peras pariter sint laureae acu pictae, quae inter utramque in sertum copulentur.

Posteriores vestis limbi ad quatuor extremas oras acu picto trophaeo Ordinis decorentur.

Duplex pectorali globulorum series, pro unoquoque latere novem; tres minoris moduli sive manicis sive circa peras, duo vero moduli maioris sub laurearum serto sint globuli.

Humeralia, aureo panno squamante prout in schemate contecta, superne globulo firmentur Crucemque Ordinis propriam acu pictam referant: aureis sint distincta circumdependentibus ut in schemate fimbriis exercituum Ducum propriis.

Femoralia, e serico rasili albo, brevia sunto: fibula et duobus parvis globulis sub genu nectantur.

Sint caligae e serico albo.

Calceoli nigri, lucidi, ornentur fibula aurea.

Galero nigro ex sericis coactilibus, aurea fascia praedivite circumornato, alba superemineat pluma; eique Insigne Pontificium quatuor ex auro funiculis globulo coniunctis innexum sit.

Globuli, omnes ex auro, Crucem Ordinis caelato opere referant.

Item et ensis aurato cingulo suffultus, Crucem Ordinis prout a schemate apparet, in capulo caelatam referat; capulus ipse sit e concha albida ornatus auro, cum aureo dependente fimbriato funiculo; vagina ex corio nigro aureis fulcro et cuspide terminetur.

Torquis, Crux, Numisma, globuli quoad modulos et formam a schemate non differant.

ALOISIUS Card. MACCHI
MAGNUS CANCELLARIUS ORDINUM EQUESTRIUM.

NOTANDUM. - *Cum aliquem huius Supremi Ordinis Equitem ex hac vita migrare contingat, haeredibus curae sit huic Cancellariae decessum significare.*

Excerpta Brevi SS. D. N. Pii PP. X "De Ordinibus Equestribus" pro Ordine Militiae Auratae.

PIUS PP. X

Ad perpetuam rei memoriam. – Multum ad excitandos ad egregia facinora hominum animos praemia virtuti reddita valent, quae dum ornant egregios bene de re sacra vel publica meritos viros, ceteros exemplo rapiunt ad idem laudis honorisque spatium decurrendum. Hoc quidem sapienti consilio Romani Pontifices Decessores Nostri Equestres Ordines, quasi gloriae stimulos, singulari studio prosequuti sunt, horumque alios instituere, alios iam institutos vel pristino decori restituerunt, vel novis ac potioribus privilegiis ditarunt.

Nunc autem, cum peropportunum visum sit gravibus de causis quaedam immutare de nonnullis Equestribus Pontificiis Ordinibus, Nos collatis consiliis cum dilecto filio Nostro Aloisio S. R. Ecclesiae Diacono Cardinali Macchi, a Brevibus Apostolicis Literis Secretario, et Pontificiae Sedis Equestrium Ordinum Magno Cancellario, omnibus rei momentis attente ac sedulo perpensis, ex certa scientia ac matura deliberatione Nostris haec, quae infrascripta sunt, decernenda existimavimus.

Quod attinet ad Ordinem Militiae Auratae, sive ab Aureo Calcari, auctoritate Nostra ab Ordine Sancti Silvestri Papae seiunctum, animo repetentes vetustissimas et gloriosas Ordinis illius memorias, Nos eum non solum ad pristinum gradum restituere sed novo etiam splendore cohonestare, ac funditus sub coelesti Immaculatae Virginis patrocinio per praesentes instaurare statuimus. Et sane cum Pontificia Sedes Ordine Equestri careat, quod sit sub Virginis praesidio constitutus, hoc potissimum anno a solemni definitione Dogmatis Immaculatae Conceptionis quinquagesimo, atque hac tempestate qua tot tantaque mala videt lugetque christianus orbis, placet Nobis huic Equestri Ordini, in quem dumtaxat fortissimi Ecclesiae Dei vindices atque adsertores erunt cooptandi, coelestem Patronam Immaculatam illam Deiparam Virginem adsignare, quae « terribilis sicut castrorum acies ordinata » draconis inferni caput victrix usque conteret. Quocirca praecipimus ut in Ordinem Militiae Auratae, sive ab Aureo Calcari, ii tantum inserantur praestantissimi viri, qui vel armis, vel scriptis, vel praeclaris operibus rem Catholicam auxerint, et Ecclesiam Dei virtute tutarint, aut doctrina illustraverint, ideoque tribui poterit tum iis qui qualibet alia equestri dignitate sint expertes, cum illis qui iam splendidioribus titulis et ipso Supremo Militiae Iesu Christi Ordine potiantur. Ordo Militiae Auratae constet unica Equitum classi; Nostro et Romani Pontificis pro tempore existentis motu proprio conferatur: liber esto a iuribus Cancellariae;

Equites pro universo Catholico orbe centum numerum non excedant, ne dignitas ex frequentia minuatur. Quoad huius Ordinis propriam Crucem, iuxta tenorem similium Benedicti PP. XIV rec. mem. Nostri Decessoris in forma Brevis Literarum sub die VII Septembris mensis anni MDCCXXXXVII quibus cautum est ne Equites Militiae Auratae Crucem Hierosolymitani Ordinis usurparent, volumus ut Crux Ordinis eiusdem Auratae Militiae, sit octogona, aurea, enchausto flavo obducta, cum aureo inferius dependente calcari; referatque in medio parvum numisma album, aureo adversa parte inclusum circulo, et Augustissimo Virginis Mariae Nomine inscriptum, aversa vero numerum referat praesentis anni MDCCCCV et in circulo « PIUS X RESTITUIT »; Cruci armorum trophaeum ex auro superemineat. Eadem Crux, argenteae stellae radiis super imposita, Ordinis Numisma sit. Careant Equites torqui, sitque eorum vestis rubri coloris tunica, duplici ordine globulorum ex auro, circa collum atque ad extremas manicas serico villoso nigro distincta cum fimbriis aureis. Humeralia sint, tum aureis laciniis, tum Ordinis Emblemate superne ornata. Femoralia praelonga, sint e panno nigro, cum aurea fascia. Calcaria aurea. Oblongus, duplici cuspide, fimbriatus auro galerus, Pontificios referat aureo nodo inclusos colores. Crucem gladii capulus imitetur: vagina sit nigra, balteus aureus cum fimbriis rubris. Sicuti priscis temporibus Ordinis taenia sit rubri coloris, sed circumdata albo. Gestent Equites Crucem taenia serica rubra extremis oris alba, collo circumducta dependentem; inserant ad pectus sinistro lateri Numisma. Quibus animi ingeniique dotibus lectissimos viros, hoc ordine decorandos, praeditos esse oporteat clare superius significavimus, ideoque ut hi semper meritis dumtaxat propriis commendentur, omnes concessiones etiam a Decessoribus Nostris Militiae auratae Equitibus factas, circa privilegium nobilitatis, et Palatini Comitis titulum, quae fortasse nondum sublatae fuerint vi similium Apostolicarum Literarum Gregorii PP. XVI sub die XXXI Octobris anni MDCCCXXXXI, quas ante recensuimus, per praesentes auctoritate Nostra interposita omnino abrogamus, easque in posterum nullius roboris esse decernimus ac statuimus.

Verum tamen expresse mandamus, ne inter Equites eiusdem Militiae discrimen contingat, sed unusquisque Ordo stemmata, insignia, arma atque ornamenta, a Sancta Sede praescripta, servet integerrime, ut praefata insignia Cruces, Numismata, vestes, enses, opera phrygia, atque ornamenta, tum propria Ordinis Militiae Auratae, cum ceterorum quos Apostolica Sedes conferre solet, sint adamussim confecta ad normam exemplarium et declarationum quas a Cancelleria Equestrium Ordinum edi et penes Nostram a Brevibus Apostolicis Literis Secretariam iussimus asservari; utque prae oculis habeantur apposita schemata, quae singulis vicibus cuilibet equestri dignitate aucto de more traduntur.

Haec statuimus, mandamus, praecipimus, decernentes praesentes Literas firmas, validas, atque efficaces semper fore et existere, suosque plenarios atque integros effectus sortiri atque obtinere, illisque ad quos spectat et pro tempore spectabit, in omnibus et per omnia plenissime suffragari: sicque in praemissis per quoscumque iudices ordinarios et delegatos et alios quoslibet quacumque praeeminentia et potestate fungentes, sublata eis et eorum cuilibet quavis aliter iudicandi et interpretandi facultate et auctoritate, iudicari et definiri debere: irritumque et inane si secus quidquam super his a quocumque quavis auctoritate scienter vel ignoranter contigerit attentari. Non obstantibus Nostra et Cancellariae Apostolicae regula de iure quaesito non tollendo, aliisque Constitutionibus et Ordinationibus Apostolicis, nec non supradictorum et aliorum quorumcumque Equestrium Ordinum etiam iuramento, confirmatione Apostolica, vel quavis firmitate alia roboratis Statutis et consuetudinibus, ceterisque contrariis, licet speciali mentione dignis, quibuscumque: privilegiis quoque, indultis, et Literis Apostolicis, in contrarium praemissorum quomodolibet concessis, confirmatis et innovatis; quibus omnibus et singulis, illorum tenores praesentibus pro plene et sufficienter expressis ac de verbo ad verbum insertis habentes, illis alias in suo robore permansuris, ad praemissorum effectum hac vice dumtaxat specialiter et expresse derogamus. Datum Romae apud Sanctum Petrum sub Annulo Piscatoris die 7 Februarii anno MDCCCCV, Pontificatus Nostri anno secundo.

ALOISIUS Card. MACCHI.

Ex Cancellaria Ordinum Equestrium

Die 7 Februarii 1905.

SSmus Dominus Noster Pius Papa X, animo repetens omnia, quae ab Apostolica Sede sive ad homines virtute formandos sive ad praemia iisdem pro rectefactis rependenda iugiter emanant, iis legibus servanda esse quibus et decori eiusdem Sedis et congrue rationi consultum sit, opportune mentem suam ad Equestres Ordines admovit.

Hinc est quod, re prius acta cum infrascripto Cardinali a Brevibus, Magno Equestrium Ordinum Cancellario, vetustissimum et praeclarum illum, unicum apud Pontifices Maximos per saecula, Ordinem Auratae nempe Militiae sub auspiciis praepotentis illius Virginis, quae primum Dei profligavit inimicum, ad pristinum duxit revocandum esse decus: in quo lectissimi ex omni gradu cives pro suis tantum in religionem meritis adscribi valeant.

Honorarias eiusdem Ordinis praerogativas sartas tectasque voluit per Breve, hoc ipso die datum, et specialia insignia adamussim statuta per leges quae hic sequuntur:

Pro Equitibus Militiae Auratae.

Tunica e panno rubri coloris siet ante pectus duplex.

Circa collum atque ad extremas manicas nigrum gestet sericum villosum, taeniola dentata ex auro fimbriatum.

Duplex pectori globulorum ordo, pro unoquoque latere novem: tres minoris moduli sint manicis, quatuor ad extremas post tergum tunicae oras, duo maioris tamen moduli ad renes globuli sunto.

Humeralia, aureo panno contecta, superne globulo firmentur, Crucemque Ordinis acu pictam referant: aureis sint distincta circumdependentibus ut in schemate fimbriis exercituum Ducum propriis.

Femoralia praelonga e panno nigro sunto: fascia ornentur auro et rubri coloris lineolis contexta.

Galero nigro ex sericis coactilibus aurea fascia fimbriato Pontificium Insigne quatuor ex auro funiculis globulo coniunctis innexum siet.

Globuli, omnes ex auro, Crucem Ordinis propriam caelato opere referant.

Balteus aureus tribus coloris rubri lineis distinctus super tunicam fibula aurea Ordinis Crucem referente nectatur.

Gladii capulus aureus esto et, prouti a schemate apparet, crucis formam imitetur; vagina e corio nigro aureis pariter fulcro, Cruce Ordinis distincto, et cuspide terminetur.

Calcaria aurea sunto.

Crux, Numisma, globuli quoad modulos et formas, taenia quoad colores et altitudinem a schemate non differant.

ALOISIUS Card. MACCHI
MAGNUS CANCELLARIUS ORDINUM EQUESTRIUM.

NOTANDUM. - *Cum aliquem huius Ordinis Equitem ex hac vita migrare contingat, haeredibus curae sit huic Cancellariae decessum significare ut de superstitum Equitum numero ratio semper habeatur.*

Breve Pii Pp. IX pro Equestris Piani Ordinis institutione

PIUS PP. IX

Ad perpetuam rei memoriam. – Romanis Pontificibus Praedecessoribus Nostris, quorum sapientiam non latuit quot uberes lectosque fructus incitamenta honoris producere soleant, non dedecere Apostolicum ministerium visum est certa laudis insignia rebus praeclare géstis tribuere, quo magis hominum animi ad optimas quasque disciplinas et omnigenas virtutes excolendas inflammarentur. Itaque quoniam Nobis, ad summi Apostolatus apicem divina favente clementia evectis, non solum aeternam animarum salutem verum etiam temporalem populi regimini Nostro commissi felicitatem exquirere incumbit; ita ad tantum tamque sublimem finem consequendum eorumdem Praedecessorum Nostrorum vestigia sectantes, praesertim vero fel. rec. Pii IV, qui Equitum Ordinem instituens eos a suo nomine Pianos voluit appellare ac pluribus nobilitatis titulis augere, nova et Nos honoris insignia decernenda statuimus per quae adeo in civili Societate praefulgeant ii, quibus fuerint conlata, ut aliis non modo exemplo, sed stimulo quoque ad egregia facinora obeunda et ad bene de Apostolica Sede merendum esse possint. Maximae porro amoris significationes ab ipso Nostri Pontificatus exordio Nobis oblatae, et eximii indicia obsequii supremae B. Petri Cathedrae in persona Nostrae humilitatis exhibita Nos certam in spem adducunt fore ut benedicente Domino consilium Nostrum ea, quae nunc edere decrevimus, iis ad quos praecipue spectant grato animo respondentibus, felicem sortiantur effectum. Quapropter hisce Nostris Apostolicis Litteris Equestrem Ordinem creamus et constituimus, qui, renovando praedictam illam denominationem a memorato Praedecessore Nostro Pio IV olim inductam, Ordo Pianus a nostro item Nomine nuncupabitur; qua quidem denominatione cum plurium ea de re votis annuere voluimus, tum id potissime propositum habuimus, ut Nostram peculiarius quoque benevolentiam viris praestantibus in Ordinem ipsum adlegendis testaremur. Ordo in duos dividetur gradus, quorum alter Equitibus primae classis, alter Equitibus secundae classis constabit. Qui in primam classem fuerint cooptati privilegio nobilitatis in filios quoque transmittendae potientur: Secundae classis Insigne nobilitatis titulo personam tantummodo afficiet. Proprium Ordinis Insigne ex auro stellae instar superficiem habebit, in octo radios caeruleos divisam, referentem in medio parvum numisma album in quo scriptum sit aureis litteris « PIVS IX »: circulus aureus numisma claudet, in eoque caeruleis literis inscripta sit epigraphe « VIRTVTI ET MERITO »: in parte numismatis aversa scriptum erit « ANNO MDCCCXLVII ». Primae classis Equites Insigne ipsum gestabunt ita ut e taenia collo inserta dependeat; taenia autem erit serica caerulea, duplici linea rubra extremis oris distincta. Equites secundae classis idem Insigne, minoris tamen moduli, eadem ex taenia pendens sinistro pectoris latere iuxta communem equitum morem deferent. Praeterea Equites propriam habebunt vestem caeruleo colore, rubris oris, aureis ornamentis decoratam : quae quidem ornamenta pro vario Equitum ipsorum gradu different; maiora scilicet pro prima classe, minora vero pro secunda erunt iuxta schema cuiusque classis proprium. Poterunt etiam primae classis Equites privilegium adipisci gestandi latere pectoris sinistro magnum Numisma argenteum Insigni simile; declaramus tamen nulli ex Equitibus licere eodem privilegio uti nisi peculiaris et expressa facultas facta sit. Reservamus autem Nobis Romanisque Pontificibus Successoribus Nostris ius eligendi Equites, itemque concedendi Equitibus primae classis memorati argentei Numismatis usum. Ceterum cum huiusmodi Ordo non ad vanitatem ambitionemque fovendam sed ad praemia virtutibus meritisque praestantibus retribuenda unice spectet, plene confidimus illos, qui hisce insignibus fuerint decorati, Pontificiae erga eos voluntati communique bonorum suffragio cumulatius in dies responsuros, splendoremque Ordinis, in quem relati fuerint, amplificaturos. Haec statuimus ac declaramus non obstantibus in contrarium facientibus, etiam speciali mentione dignis quibuscumque.

Datum Romae apud S. Mariam Majorem, sub Annulo Piscatoris, die XVII Junii MDCCCXLVII, Pontificatus Nostri anno primo.

A. Card. LAMBRUSCHINI

Breve Pii Pp. IX de ratione gestandi Insignia Piani Ordinis propria

PIUS PP. IX

Ad perpetuam rei memoriam. – Cum hominum mentes animique ita sint comparati, ut ad virtutis et justitiae semitam terendam atque ad optimas excolendas artes et pulcherrima quaeque peragenda facinora honorum et laudum gloria vehementer excitentur, tum Romani Pontifices Decessores Nostri provido sane consilio Equestres Ordines instituerunt, quo viris de christiana et civili republica ob egregia facta optime meritis debitos tribuerent honores, et alios ejusmodi stimulo ad illustria virtutum exempla imitanda inflammarent. Hac quidem mente per similes Nostras Apostolicas Litteras, die XVII Iunii Anno MDCCCXLVII editas, Equestrem Ordinem a Nostro Nomine Ordinem Pianum appellatum constituimus, illumque in duos gradus divisimus, quorum alterum Equitibus primae classis, alterum vero Equitibus secundae classis attribuimus: atque concessimus, ut primae tantum classis Equites pollerent privilegio transmittendi in filios nobilitatis titulum. Iisdem in Litteris proprium ejusdem Ordinis Insigne statuimus, quod ex auro confectum stellae instar superficiem habet in octo caeruleos radios divisam, parvum album numisma in medio referentem, in quo aureis litteris scriptum « PIVS IX », quod numisma aureo circulo clauditur, et in eo inscriptio caeruleis litteris posita « VIRTVTI ET MERITO », atque in parte aversa numismatis scriptum « ANNO MDCCCXLVII ». Statuimus quoque ut primae classis Equites illud Insigne e taenia serica caerulea, duplici linea rubra extremis oris distincta, collo inserta dependens gestarent, utque secundae classis Equites Insigne ipsum minoris moduli, atque eadem ex taenia pendens in sinistra vestis parte juxta communem equitum morem deferrent. Propriam quoque Equitum vestem sancivimus, quae caeruleo colore, rubris oris, ac variis aureis ornamentis est ornata pro vario ipsorum Equitum gradu. Insuper manifestavimus, primae classis Equites consequi posse privilegium gerendi magnum argenteum Numisma Insigni simile in sinistro pectoris latere innexum, declarantes nulli ex Equitibus licere ejusmodi uti privilegio nisi peculiaris et expressa facultas facta fuisset, ac Nobis et Romanis Pontificibus Successoribus Nostris jus reservavimus tum eligendi Equites, tum concedendi primae classis Equitibus commemorati argentei Numismatis usum. Iam vero hisce Nostris Apostolicis Litteris statuimus, atque decernimus, ut ii omnes qui in posterum Equites Piani Ordinis primae classis fuerint renunciati pollere debeant privilegio gestandi commemoratum magnum argenteum Numisma in sinistro pectoris latere, utque alterum proprium Ordinis Insigne, jam primae classis Equitibus attributum, non amplius e fascia collo inserta dependens veluti antea, sed ita deferant, ut idem Insigne fascia serica praelonga caerulei pariter coloris duplici linea rubri coloris extremis oris distincta dextero humero sustineatur. Et quoniam plures clarissimi Viri a Nobis in primam Piani Ordinis classem fuerunt cooptati cum privilegio gerendi memoratum magnum argenteum Numisma, iccirco per praesentes Litteras declaramus, ut ii tantum primae ipsius Ordinis classis Equites, quibus eiusdem Numismatis usus a Nobis fuit concessus, alterum Ordinis Insigne deferre possint et debeant quemadmodum Nostris hisce Litteris nunc praescribitur. Insuper primae Piani Ordinis classis Equites memoratum magnum argenteum Numisma coruscantibus quoque gemmis exornatum in posterum deferre poterunt, quando tamen id a Nobis et Romanis Pontificibus Successoribus Nostris peculiari et expressa facultate fuerit concessum, sine qua nemini umquam licebit magnum Numisma gemmis ornare. Haec statuimus, concedimus, et declaramus non obstantibus quibuscumque in contrarium facientibus, praesertim vero commemoratis Nostris Apostolicis Litteris die XVII Junii Anno MDCCCXLVII editis, quas in iis omnibus, quae praesentibus hisce Litteris minime adversantur, firmas atque in suo robore permansuras volumus atque mandamus.

Datum Cajetae, sub Annulo Piscatoris, die XVII Junii MDCCCXLIX, Pontificatus Nostri anno tertio.

IACOBUS Card. ANTONELLI
De speciali mandato SSmi

Decretum Pii Pp. IX pro triplici Equitum classe in Piano Ordine constituenda

In ipso Nostri Pontificatus exordio animum mentemque intendentes ad inflammandos hominum animos, ut egregia facinora obire et de Apostolica Sede benemereri contendant, Apostolicis Litteris sub Annulo Piscatoris expeditis die XVII Junii MDCCCXLVII Equestrem Ordinem creavimus et instituimus Pianum appellatum, eumque in duos gradus divisimus, quorum alterum Equitibus primae classis, alterum vero Equitibus secundae classis attribuimus; quorum primis Insigne Ordinis proprium collo appensum, reliquis in sinistra vestis parte gerere fas esset: itemque declaravimus ut Equites primae classis consequi etiam possent privilegium ferendi magnum argenteum Numisma in sinistro pectoris latere innexum.

Aliis praeterea Apostolicis Litteris Cajetae die XVII Junii anni MDCCCXLIX datis statuimus atque decrevimus ut omnes Equites Piani Ordinis primae Classis renunciati pollere deberent privilegio gestandi commemoratum Numisma, itemque praescripsimus ut alterum proprium Ordinis Insigne non quidem taenia e collo inserta penderet sed taenia praelonga e dextero ad sinistrum humerum sustineretur.

Nunc vero, quum opportunum existimavimus eundem Ordinem novo augere decore ejusque gradus amplificare, ut major inde Nobis Nostrisque Successoribus pateat aditus ad virtutem rectaque facta pro merito rependenda, iccirco Motu Proprio plenaque auctoritate Nostra per praesentes decernimus et statuimus ut deinceps Ordo Pianus tribus constet gradibus: nempe Equitum primae classis, Equitum secundae classis, seu Commendatorum, et Equitum tertiae classis; primi Insigne et Numisma prout in commemoratis Litteris XVII Junii MDCCCXLIX praescriptum est: alteri seu Commendatores Insigne tantum e collo appensum: Equites demum tertiae classis Insigne ipsum minoris moduli sinistra vestis parte innexum gerent; firmis tamen remanentibus circa reliqua iis omnibus, queis per hoc Nostrum Decreto minime derogatur. Et quoniam Equites Piani propria utuntur veste caeruleo colore, rubris oris, aureis ornamentis decorata, ita et vestem conformem quae media sit inter primum et tertium Equitum gradum Commendatoribus attributam volumus iuxta schema cum diplomate tradendum. Id statuimus atque decernimus in contrarium facientibus non obstantibus quibuscumque.

Datum Romae ex Nostris aedibus in Quirinali die XI Novembris MDCCCLVI, Pontificatus Nostri anno undecimo.

PIUS PP. IX

Breve Pii Pp. XII de nobilitatis privilegio iam Ordinis Piani proprio abolendo

PIUS PP. XII

Ad perpetuam rei memoriam. – Litteris suis Apostolicis sub anulo Piscatoris obsignatis die decima septima m. Iunii, an. MDCCCXLVII ac die pariter decima septima mensis Iunii, an. MDCCCXLIX, necnon decreto ex Aedibus in Quirinali dato die XI m. Novembris an. MDCCCLVI, Praedecessor Noster Pius Pp. IX Equestrem Ordinem creavit atque instituit, Pianum nuncupatum, qui tribus Equitum classibus constaret. Apostolicis autem Litteris praelaudatis statutum etiam fuit Equites in primam eiusdem Ordinis Classem cooptatos privilegio nobilitatis in filios quoque transmittendae, illos vero, qui secundae Classis insigni essent honestati, nobilitatis titulo ad personam tantummodo gavisuros esse. Quod, habita praesertim temporum nostrorum ratione, minus opportunum videtur, cum ceteri, etiam potiores, Equestres Ordines, quorum insignia a Romanis Pontificibus conferuntur, nullo modo nobilitatis privilegio aliquo fruantur. Itaque, omnibus rei momentis attente perpensis, Nos, ut huiusmodi iure Ordo quoque Pianus ceteris Equestribus Ordinibus adaequetur Pontificiis, motu proprio statuendum censemus ut, iis abolitis quae iam Litteris Apostolicis supradictis decreta fuerant, ex nunc et in posterum omnes et singuli, in quamlibet ex tribus classibus praefati Ordinis Piani classem adsciti, insignibus tantum ac titulo proprio Classis, absque ullo nobilitatis iure privilegioque licite uti, frui possint et queant. Contrariis non obstantibus quibuslibet; decernentes praesentes Litteras firmas, validas atque efficaces iugiter extare ac permanere, suosque plenos atque integros effectus sortiri et obtinere; sicque iudicandum esse ac definiendum, irritumque ex nunc et inane fieri si quidquam secus super his a quoquam, auctoritate qualibet, scienter sive ignoranter attentari contigerit.

Datum Romae, apud Sanctum Petrum, sub anulo Piscatoris, die XI m. Novembris, an. MCMXXXIX, Pontificatus Nostri primo.

A. Card. MAGLIONE
a Secretis Status

Ex Cancellaria Ordinum Equestrium

Die 7 Februarii 1905.

SSmus Dominus Noster Pius Papa X, animo repetens omnia, quae sive ad homines virtute formandos sive ad praemia iisdem pro rectefactis rependenda ab Apostolica Sede proveniunt, iis legibus jugiter moderanda esse quibus et decori eiusdem S. Sedis et congrue rationi consultum sit, opportune mentem suam ad Equestres Ordines admovit.

Hinc est quod re acta cum infrascripto Cardinali a Brevibus, Magno Equestrium Ordinum Cancellario, praeter ordinationes de caeteris Equestribus Ordinibus hoc ipso die latas, voluit ut, quae etiam de Piani Ordinis vestibus et Insignibus propriis illorumque usu adhuc non satis certa et definita viderentur, eadem forent adamussim statuta per leges, quae hic sequuntur:

Equites Primae Classis, seu a Magna Cruce, Ordinis Piani potientur privilegio nobilitatis in filios transmittendae.

Eorum vestis e panno coeruleo nigrante siet in longos post tergum producta limbos.

Circa collum et extremas manicas, itemque super peras, gestet pannum rubri coloris.

Opera phrygia, omnia acu picta ex auro, circa collum, extremas manicas, et supra peras laciniae sint laureas referentes: duplex ante pectus lacinia quae laureas pariter imitetur: dentata insuper taeniola quae extremas totius vestis oras circumeat.

Novem pectori globuli: tres vero sint, minoris moduli, manicis.

Posteriores vestis limbi, inter utramque peram, duobus maioribus globulis nec non laureo serto decorentur; ipsisque peris tres subsint globuli minores.

Sit humeris impositus tortus ex auro funiculus, globulo iuxta collum innexus.

Femoralia praelonga sunto e panno coeruleo nigrante; fascia ornentur ex aureo laureis intexta, cuius altitudo quatuor centesimarum metricae mensurae partium siet.

Galero nigro ex sericis coactilibus, aurea fascia praedivite circumornato, et aureo parvo flocco in utraque cuspide distincto, alba superemineat pluma: eique Insigne Pontificium quatuor ex auro funiculis, globulo coniunctis, innexum sit.

Globuli, omnes ex auro, Insigne Ordinis caelato opere referant.

Item et ensis aurato cingulo suffultus, Insigne Ordinis, prout a schemate apparet, in capulo caelatum referat; capulus ipse sit e concha albida ornatus auro, cum aureo dependente fimbriato funiculo; vagina e corio nigro aureis fulcro et cuspide terminetur.

Numisma Ordinis sit Insigne ipsum argenteae stellae radiis impositum.

Insigne, Numisma, globuli quoad formas et modulos, sic et fascia quoad colores et altitudinem a schemate non differant.

Equites Secundae Classis, seu Commendatores, cum Numismate Ordinis Piani potientur privilegio nobilitatis absque iure transmissionis.

Eorum vestis e panno coeruleo nigrante siet in longos post tergum producta limbos.

Circa collum et extremas manicas, itemque super peras, gestet pannum rubri coloris.

Opera phrygia; omnia acu picta ex auro, circa collum, extremas manicas et supra peras laciniae sint laureas referentes, et dentata taeniola quae extremas totius vestis oras circumeat.

Novem pectori globuli: tres vero sint, minoris moduli, manicis.

Posteriores vestis limbi inter utramque peram duobus maioribus globulis, nec non laureo serto decorentur; ipsisque peris tres subsint globuli minores.

Femoralia praelonga sunto e panno coeruleo nigrante; fascia ornentur ex auro laureis intexta, cuius altitudo quatuor centesimarum metricae mensurae partium siet.

Galero nigo ex sericis coactilibus, duplici transversa utrinque et circum ducta limbos, ut in schemate, nigra undati operis fascia ac parvo aureo flocco in utraque cuspide distincto, nigra superemineat pluma; eique Insigne Pontificium quatuor ex auro funiculis globulo coniunctis innexum sit.

Globuli, omnes ex auro, Insigne Ordinis caelato opere referant.

Item et ensis aurato cingulo suffultus Insigne Ordinis, prout a schemate apparet, in capulo caelatum referat; capulus ipse sit e concha albida ornatus auro, cum aureo dependente fimbriato funiculo; vagina e corio nigro aureis fulcro et cuspide terminetur.

Numisma Ordinis sit Insigne ipsum argenteae stellae radiis impositum.

Insigne, Numisma, globuli quoad formas et modulos, sic et taenia quoad colores et altitudinem a schemate non differant.

Equites Secundae Classis, seu Commendatores, Ordinis Piani potientur privilegio nobilitatis absque iure transmissionis.

Eorum vestis e panno coeruleo nigrante siet in longos post tergum producta limbos.

Circa collum et extremas manicas, itemque super peras, gestet pannum rubri coloris.

Opera phrygia, omnia acu picta ex auro, circa collum, extremas manicas et supra peras laciniae sint laureas referentes, et dentata taeniola quae extremas totius vestis oras circumeat.

Novem pectori globuli: tres vero sint, minoris moduli, manicis.

Posteriores vestis limbi inter utramque peram duobus maioribus globulis, nec non laureo serto decorentur; ipsisque peris tres subsint globuli minores.

Femoralia praelonga sunto e panno coeruleo nigrante; fascia ornentur ex auro laureis intexta cuius altitudo quatuor centesimarum metricae mensurae partium siet.

Galero nigro ex sericis coactilibus, duplici transversa utrinque et circum ducta limbos ut in schemate nigra undati operis fascia ac parvo aureo flocco in utraque cuspide distincto, nigra superemineat pluma; eique Insigne Pontificium quatuor ex auro funiculis globulo coniunctis innexum sit.

Globuli, omnes ex auro, Insigne Ordinis caelato opere referant.

Item et ensis aurato cingulo suffultus Insigne Ordinis, prout a schemate apparet, in capulo caelatum referat; capulus ipse sit e concha albida ornatus auro, cum aureo dependente fimbriato funiculo; vagina e corio nigro aureis fulcro et cuspide terminetur.

Insigne Ordinis et globuli quoad formas et modulos, sic et taenia quoad colores et altitudinem a schemate non differant.

Equitibus Tertiae Classis Ordinis Piani vestis e panno coeruleo nigrante siet in longos post tergum producta limbos.

Circa collum et extremas manicas, itemque super peras, gestet pannum rubri coloris.

Opus phrygium sit circa totius vestis oras, extremas manicas et peras dentata taeniola ex auro.

Novem pectori globuli: tres vero sint, minoris moduli, manicis.

Posteriores vestis limbi, inter utramque peram, duobus maioris moduli globulis necnon parvo laureo serto decorentur: ipsisque peris tres subsint globuli minores.

Femoralia praelonga sunto e panno coeruleo nigrante: fascia ornentur ex auro laureis intexta, cuius altitudo trium centesimarum metricae mensurae partium siet.

Galero nigro ex sericis coactilibus, duplici transversa utrinque et circum ducta limbos, ut in schemate, nigra undati operi fascia ac parvo aureo flocco in utraque cuspide distincto, nigra superemineat pluma; eique Insigne Pontificium quatuor ex auro funiculis globulo coniunctis innexum sit.

Globuli, omnes ex auro, Insigne Ordinis caelato opere referant.

Item et ensis aurato cingulo suffultus Insigne Ordinis, prout a schemate apparet, in capulo caelatum referat; capulus ipse sit e concha albida ornatus auro, cum aureo dependente fimbriato funiculo; vagina e corio nigro aureis fulcro et cuspide terminetur.

Insigne Ordinis et globuli quoad formas et modulos sic et taenia quoad colores et altitudinem a schemate non differant.

ALOISIUS Card. MACCHI
MAGNUS CANCELLARIUS ORDINUM EQUESTRIUM.

BREVE GREGORII PP. XVI PRO INSTITUTIONE EQUESTRIS ORDINIS S. GREGORII MAGNI

GREGORIVS PP. XVI

AD perpetuam rei memoriam. – Quod summis quibusque Imperatoribus maximae curae est praemia virtutis et insignia honoris et monumenta laudis iis decernere, quos optime de re publica meritos noverint, id et Romani Pontifices Praedecessores Nostri praestare pro personarum, temporum, actuumque ratione consueverunt erga eos, qui Sanctae Romanae Ecclesiae imperium ope, armis, consiliis, aliisque recte factis iuvarent. Haec reputantibus Nobis, ac de honore iis habendo deliberantibus, qui fidelem assiduamque asperioribus etiam temporibus operam Principatui navarunt, placuit ex more institutoque maiorum Ordinem Equestrem constituere, in quem homines spectatae in Sedem Apostolicam fidei ex Summorum Pontificum auctoritate cooptentur, quos vel praestantia generis, vel gloria rerum gestarum, vel insignium munerum procuratione, vel demum gravibus aliis ex causis dignos ipsi censuerint qui publico Pontificiae dilectionis testimonio honestentur. Inde enim nedum praemium virtuti conferri, sed et stimulos addi ceteris palam est quibus ad bonum rectumque impensius in dies excitentur. Quare hisce Nostris Apostolicis Litteris Equestrem Ordinem constituimus, quem, et ex praecipuo Nostrae in Sanctissimum Praedecessorem Gregorium Magnum venerationis affectu, et ob assumptum ipsius Nomen quando Humilitati Nostrae impositum Pontificatum suscepimus, a Sancto Gregorio Magno volumus nuncupari; reservantes Nobis ac Romano Pontifici pro tempore existenti ius eligendi Equites, quos constet virtutum laude, condicionis honestate, splendore munerum, atque eximia in rebus gerendis sedulitate, communi demum bonorum suffragio commendari. Erit porro peculiare Ordinis Insigne Crux octangula ex auro artificiose elaborata, rubram superficiem habens, in cuius medio, veluti parvo in numismate, exstet affabre caelata imago S. Gregorii Magni. Taenia ad eam sustinendam erit serica rubra, cuius extrema ora flavo colore distinguatur. Cum vero stati quidam in Equestribus Ordinibus gradus dignitatem illorum, qui iisdem accensentur, designent, quattuor in Gregoriano Ordine gradus Equitum praefinimus; quorum primi Equites Magnae Crucis primae classis, secundi Equites Magnae Crucis secundae classis, tertii Equites Commendatores, quarti Equites simpliciter nuncupabuntur. Serica fascia praelonga binis Ordinis coloribus picta, dextero humero imposita, transversaque ad latus sinistrum propendens, et magnam Crucem sustinens, Insigne erit Equitum primi generis; qui insuper medio sinistro latere pectoris innexam vestitui gestabunt alteram maiorem Crucem radiis undique ac gemmis circumornatam, opereque magnifico caelatam. Equites secundae classis Crucem magnam, instar Numismatis, latere pectoris sinistro habebunt, praeter Crucem alteram grandem collo ex fascia serica appensam. Equites Commendatores Crucem magnam gerent, quae e fascia collo inserta dependeat; privilegio tamen carebunt ferendi praedictum numisma seu Crucem alteram in latere pectoris sinistro. Equites quarti ordinis Crucem parvam, iuxta communem Equitum morem, ad pectus apponent in parte vestis sinistra. Ceterum eos omnes, qui publico hoc Pontificiae voluntatis testimonio sint honestati, monitos volumus ut animadvertant sedulo praemia virtutibus addici, nihilquè diligentius curandum ipsis esse quam ut rebus praeclare gestis expectationem ac fiduciam quam excitarunt cumulate sustineant, delatoque sibi honore dignos sese in dies magis exhibeant. Haec quidem suscepti huiusce consilii ratio est, haec praecipua muneris ipsius condicio, cui apprime satisfiet constanti erga Deum et Principem fide, prout in aversa Crucis parte scriptum est; atque ita boni omnes et ii praesertim, quorum maxime interest ob Ordinis coniunctionem, de fausto felicique Nostri Instituti progressu gratulabuntur. Haec statuimus ac declaramus non obstantibus in contrarium facientibus, etiam speciali mentione dignis, quibuscumque. Datum Romae apud Sanctam Mariam Maiorem sub Annulo Piscatoris die 1 Septembris MDCCCXXXI, Pontificatus Nostri anno primo.

TH. Card. BERNETTI

BREVE GREGORII PP. XVI PRO TRIBUS TANTUM GRADIBUS IN EQUESTRI GREGORIANO ORDINE SERVANDIS ET PRO INSIGNIBUS SINGULORUM GRADUUM PROPRIIS STATUENDIS

GREGORIVS PP. XVI

Ad perpetuam rei memoriam. – Cum amplissima honorum munera iure meritoque parta hominum mentes atque animos ad virtutem amplectendam, gloriamque assequendam vel maxime excitent atque inflamment, tum Romani Pontifices provide sapienterque praecipuos honorum titulos iis tribuere ac decernere semper existimarunt, qui egregiis animi ingeniique dotibus praestantes nihil non aggrediuntur, nihilque intentatum relinquunt, ut de Christiana et Civili Republica quam optime mereri conentur. Hac sane mente in ipso Pontificatus Nostri exordio, ob tantam temporum asperitatem iniucundo ac permolesto, singulare praemium rectefactis impertiri, itemque ad suas cuique partes demandatas impensius obeundas quoddam veluti incitamentum addere in animo habentes illis praesertim viris, qui singulari studio, consilio, fide, integritate Nobis et Romanae Petri Cathedrae omni ope atque opera adhaererent, novum Equestrem Ordinem instituere decrevimus, quem ob praecipuum Nostrae in Sanctissimum Praedecessorem Gregorium Magnum venerationis affectum, et ob assumptum ipsius Nomen quando ad Universae Ecclesiae regimen evecti fuimus, a Sancto Gregorio Magno voluimus nuncupari. Quapropter Apostolicas dedimus Litteras die primo Septembris Anno MDCCCXXXI Annulo Piscatoris obsignatas, quarum vi omnibus notam perspectamque fecimus novi Gregoriani Ordinis institutionem, simulque praescripsimus eius Insigne Crucem esse octogonam ex auro affabre elaboratam, rubra superficie imaginem S. Gregorii Magni in medio referentem, taenia serica rubra, extremis oris flava, sustinendam. Clare insuper significavimus quibus dotibus viros hoc honore decorandos praeditos esse oporteat, Nobisque et Romanis Pontificibus Successoribus Nostris ius reservavimus eiusmodi Equites renuntiandi, quos virtutis et religionis laude, condicionis honestate, muneris splendore, eximia in rebus gerendis sedulitate, communi denique bonorum suffragio pateat esse commendatos. Ad designandam autem eorum dignitatem, qui huic Ordini sunt adscribendi, Nobis opportunum visum est eumdem ipsum in quattuor classes dividere; quarum altera Equitibus Magnae Crucis primi ordinis, altera Equitibus Magnae Crucis secundi ordinis, tertia Equitibus Commendatoribus, quarta Equitibus tantummodo constat. Praescripsimus idcirco, ut Equites a Magna Cruce primi ordinis magnam Crucem e serica fascia praelonga binis Ordinis coloribus picta, dextero humero imposita, transversaque ad latus sinistrum descendente sustineant, ac praeterea medio sinistro pectoris latere innexam vesti gestent alteram maiorem Crucem radiis undique ac gemmis circumornatam: ut Equites a Magna Cruce secundae classis praeter magnam Crucem, ut supra appensam, medio sinistro pectoris latere alteram Crucem nullis coruscantibus gemmis refulgentem deferant: ut Equitibus Commendatoribus liceat Crucem magnam gerere, quae e fascia collo inserta dependeat, haud tamen Crucem alteram in latere pectoris sinistro: ut Equites demum quarti ordinis Crucem parvam ex communi Equitum more in parte vestis sinistra ad pectus apponant. Quin etiam ad removendum quodcumque discrimen, quod in hoc gestando Insigni posset contingere, cuiusque Crucis schema typis excudi mandavimus, novis quibusque Equitibus una cum Diplomate tradendum. Iam vero, cum honoris ac dignitatis splendor eo magis refulgeat quo minor est eorum numerus quibus confertur, Nostris profecto fuisset in votis in Gregoriano Ordine constituendo eorum numerum praefinire, qui in singulas illius classes essent cooptandi. Sed quoniam eo tunc praecipue spectavimus, ut praemium iis potissimum rependeremus, qui incorrupta fide et egregio in Nos atque hanc Sanctam Sedem studio et obsequio effervescentes id temporis seditionis impetus propulsarent, et Religionis causam et Civilem Apostolicae Sedis Principatum pro viribus tuerentur, haud potuimus extemplo consilia Nostra certis quibusdam limitibus circumscribere. Nunc vero rebus divini Numinis ope conversis, atque exoptato in Pontificiis Nostris Provinciis ordine restituto, cum fidis fortibusque viris mercedem proposuerimus, in eam venimus sententiam, aliquid in commemoratis Nostris Litteris immutare, pluraque etiam ab integro decernere, quae ad eiusdem Ordinis splendorem augendum maiestatemque amplificandam pertinere posse videntur. Hisce igitur Litteris statuimus atque mandamus, ut posthac ex utraque classe Magnae Crucis una tantum constet, cui nomen erit primae classis. Nobis vero et Romanis Pontificibus Successoribus Nostris reservamus Magna Cruce gemmis ornata in peculiaribus quibusdam casibus eos decorare, qui Nostro eorumdemque Successorum Nostrorum iudicio singulari ratione honestandi videantur. Quapropter eos omnes qui Magnam Crucem secundae classis iam fuerint adepti, ad primam classem pertinere omnino volumus et declaramus. Itaque deinceps Gregorianus Ordo tribus tantummodo constabit classibus, nempe Equitibus a Magna Cruce, Commendatoribus et Equitibus. Numerum autem cuiuslibet ex tribus iis classibus praefinire volentes, quemadmodum in pluribus Militiis vel Equestribus Ordinibus provide sapienterque factum est et Nos ipsi vehementer optabamus, plena Auctoritate Nostra edicimus atque praecipimus ut Equites a Magna Cruce numerum triginta non praetergrediantur: Commendatores septuaginta, Equites demum tercenti esse possint. Quem quidem singularum classium Equitum numerum pro iis tantum viris, qui Civili Apostolicae Sedis Principatui subsunt praescriptum volumus; propterea quod ad Nostrum et Successorum Nostrorum arbitrium semper pertinebit homines etiam exterarum gentium in cuiusque classis coetum praeter hunc numerum adlegere. Praeterea, ut huius Ordinis ratio perpetuo servetur neque temporis lapsu diuturna vetustate ullatenus immutetur, mandamus ut Summus ab Actis Gregoriani Ordinis seu, ut dicitur, Magnus Cancellarius sit S. R. E. Cardinalis a Brevibus Apostolicis Litteris; penes quem Equitum nomina, gradus, admissionis dies, ac numerus diligenter servetur. Haec decernimus atque statuimus, non obstantibus editis Nostris Litteris, de quibus habitus est sermo, nec non etiam speciali mentione dignis in contrarium facientibus quibuscumque. Nobis quidem sperare fas est novam hanc consilii Nostri instaurationem optatum exitum assequuturam, eosque simili honore auctos vel in posterum augendos votis Nostris ac fini, ad quem referuntur, quam cumulatissime responsuros, ac Pontificia benevolentia magis magisque dignos futuros, praesertim quod ipso in Insigni inscriptum legant hoc munus eorum potissimum esse, qui Pro Deo et Principe vel maxime praestant. Datum Romae apud S. Petrum sub Anulo Piscatoris die xxx Maii mdcccxxxiv, Pontificatus Nostri anno quarto.

Pro Domino Card. ALBANO
A. PICCHIONI, substitutus

Ex Cancellaria Ordinum Equestrium

Die 7 Februarii 1905.

SSm̃us Dominus Noster Pius PP. X, animo repetens omnia, quae sive ad homines virtute formandos sive ad praemia eisdem pro rectefactis rependenda ab Apostolica Sede proveniunt, iis legibus iugiter moderanda esse, quibus et decori eiusdem S. Sedis et congrue rationi consultum sit, opportune mentem suam ad Equestres Ordines admovit.

Hinc est quod re acta cum infrascripto Cardinali a Brevibus, magno Equestrium Ordinum Cancellario, praeter ordinationes de ceteris Equestribus Ordinibus hoc ipso die latas, voluit ut quae etiam de Gregoriani Ordinis vestibus et Insignibus propriis illorumque usu adhuc non satis certa et definita viderentur, servata eiusdem Ordinis, quae hactenus usu venit, in Civilem unam et Militarem alteram Classem partitione, omnia forent adamussim statuta per leges quae hic sequuntur:

Pro Equitibus a Magna Cruce Classis Civilis.

Vestis e panno viridi nigrante siet in longos post tergum producta limbos.

Opera phrygia omnia acu picta ex argento, circa collum, extremas manicas, et supra peras laciniae sint quernea folia referentes: duplex ante pectus lacinia quae folia quernea pariter imitetur: dentata insuper taeniola quae extremas totius vestis oras circumeat.

Novem pectori globuli: tres vero sint, minoris moduli, manicis.

Posteriores vestis limbi, inter utramque peram, duobus maioribus globulis nec non corona querna decorentur; ipsisque peris tres subsint globuli minores.

Sit humeris impositus tortus ex argento funiculus, globulo iuxta collum innexus.

Femoralia praelonga sunto e panno viridi nigrante; fascia ornentur ex argento querneis foliis intexta, cuius altitudo quatuor centesimarum metricae mensurae partium siet.

Galero nigro ex sericis coactilibus, argentea fascia praedivite circumornato, et argenteo parvo flocco in utraque cuspide distincto, alba superemineat pluma: eique Insigne Pontificium quatuor ex argento funiculis, globulo coniunctis, innexum sit.

Globuli, omnes ex argento, Crucem Ordinis caelato opere referant.

Item et ensis argenteo cingulo suffultus, Crucem Ordinis, prout a schemate apparet, in capulo caelatam referat; capulus ipse sit e concha albida ornatus auro, cum aureo dependente fimbriato funiculo; vagina e corio nigro aureis fulcro et cuspide terminetur.

Crux Ordinis Magna e transversa, ut in schemate, fascia binis Ordinis coloribus distincta dependens, nec non argenteum magnum Numisma, nullis tamen gemmis ornatum, sinistro pectoris lateri ingestum Insignia sunto.

Crucem corona laurea ex enchausto viridi ut in schemate, parva taenia ex auro inferius vincta, superemineat.

Crux, Numisma, globuli quoad formas et modulos, sic et fascia quoad colores et altitudinem a schemate non differant.

Pro Equitibus Commendatoribus cum Numismate Classis Civilis.

Vestis e panno viridi nigrante siet in longos post tergum producta limbos.

Opera phrygia, omnia acu picta ex argento, circa collum, extremas manicas et supra peras laciniae sint quernea folia referentes, et dentata taeniola quae extremas totius vestis oras circumeat.

Novem pectori globuli: tres vero sint, minoris moduli, manicis.

Posteriores vestis limbi inter utramque peram duobus maioribus globulis, nec non corona querna decorentur; ipsisque peris tres subsint globuli minores.

Femoralia praelonga sunto e panno viridi nigrante; fascia ornentur ex argento querneis foliis intexta, cuius altitudo quatuor centesimarum metricae mensurae partium siet.

Galero nigro ex sericis coactilibus, duplici transversa utrinque et circum ducta limbos, ut in schemate, nigra undati operis fascia ac parvo argenteo flocco in utraque cuspide distincto, nigra superemineat pluma; eique Insigne Pontificium quatuor ex argento funiculis globulo coniunctis innexum sit.

Globuli, omnes ex argento, Crucem Ordinis caelato opere referant.

Item et ensis argenteo cingulo suffultus Crucem Ordinis, prout a schemate apparet, in capulo caelatam referat; capulus ipse sit e concha albida ornatus auro, cum aureo dependente fimbriato funiculo; vagina e corio nigro aureis fulcro et cuspide terminetur.

Praeter Crucem, non aliter ac serica taenia e collo dependentem, Numisma Ordinis argenteum sinistro pectoris lateri ingestum deferre fas esto.

Crucem corona laurea ex enchausto viridi ut in schemate, parva taenia ex auro inferius vincta, superemineat.

Crux, Numisma, globuli quoad formas et modulos, sic et taenia quoad colores et altitudinem a schemate non differant.

PRO EQUITIBUS COMMENDATORIBUS CLASSIS CIVILIS

Vestis e panno viridi nigrante siet in longum post tergum producta limbos.

Opera phrygia, omnia acu picta ex argento, circa collum, extremas manicas et supra peras laciniae sint quernea folia referentes, et dentata taeniola quae extremas totius vestis oras circumeat.

Novem pectori globuli: tres vero sint, minoris, moduli, manicis.

Posteriores vestis limbi inter utramque peram duobus maioribus globulis, nec non corona querna decorentur; ipsisque peris tres subsint globuli minores.

Femoralia praelonga sunto e panno viridi nigrante; fascia ornentur ex argento querneis foliis intexta cuius altitudo quatuor centesimarum metricae mensurae partium siet.

Galero nigro ex sericis coactilibus, duplici transversa utrimque et circumducta limbos, ut in schemate, nigra undati operis fascia ac parvo argento flocco in utraque cuspide distincto, nigra superemineat pluma; eique Insigne Pontificium quattuor ex argento funiculis globulo coniunctis innexum sit.

Globuli, omnes ex argento, Crucem Ordinis caelato opere referant.

Item et ensis argenteo cingulo suffultus Crucem Ordinis, prout a schemate apparet, in capulo caelatam referat; capulus ipse sit e concha albida ornatus auro, cum aureo dependente fimbriato funicolo; vagina e corio nigro aureis fulcro et cuspide terminetur.

Crux tantum non aliter ac per sericam taeniam e collo dependens, Insigne Commendatoribus siet.

Cruci corona laurea ex enchausto viridi ut in schemate, parva taenia ex auro inferius vincta, superemineat.

Crux et globuli quoad formas et modulos sic et taenia quoad colores et altitudinem a schemate non differant.

PRO EQUITIBUS CLASSIS CIVILIS

Vestis e panno viridi nigrante sit in longum post tergum producta limbos.

Opus phrygium sit circa totius vestis oras, extremas manicas et peras taeniola dentata ex argento.

Novem pectori globuli: tres vero sint, minoris, moduli, manicis.

Posteriores vestis limbi, inter utramque peram, duobus maioris moduli globulis necnon parva corona querna ex argento decorentur: ipsique peris tres subsint globuli minores.

Femoralia praelonga sunto e panno viridi nigrante: fascia ornentur ex argento querneis foliis intexta, cuius altitudo trium centesimarum metricae mensurae partium sit.

Galero nigro ex sericis coactilibus, duplici transversa utrimque et circumducta limbos, ut in schemate, nigra undati operis fascia ac parvo argento flocco in utraque cuspide distincto, nigra superemineat pluma; eique Insigne Pontificium quattuor ex argento funiculis globulo coniunctis innexum sit.

Globuli, omnes ex argento, Crucem Ordinis caelato opere referant.

Item et ensis argenteo cingulo suffultus Crucem Ordinis, prout a schemate apparet, in capulo caelatam referat; capulus ipse sit e concha albida ornatus auro, cum aureo dependente fimbriato funicolo; vagina e corio nigro aureis fulcro et cuspide terminetur.

Crucem minoris moduli in sinistro pectoris latere, ut in ceteris Equestribus Ordinibus serica taenia Ordinis coloribus picta pendentem Equitibus gestare ius sit.

Cruci corona laurea ex enchausto viridi ut in schemate, parva taenia ex auro inferius vincta, superemineat.

Crux et globuli quoad formas et modulos sic et taenia quoad colores et altitudinem a schemate non differant.

ALOISIUS Card. MACCHI
MAGNUS CANCELLARIUS ORDINUM EQUESTRIUM

Ex Cancellaria Ordinum Equestrium

Die 7 Februarii 1905.

SSmus Dominus Noster Pius PP. X, animo repetens omnia, quae sive ad homines virtute formandos sive ad praemia eisdem pro rectefactis rependenda ab Apostolica Sede proveniunt, iis legibus iugiter moderanda esse quibus et decori eiusdem S. Sedis et congrue rationi consultum sit, opportune mentem suam ad Equestres Ordines admovit.

Hinc est quod, re acta cum infrascripto Cardinali a Brevibus, magno Equestrium Ordinum Cancellario, praeter ordinationes de ceteris Equestribus Ordinibus hoc ipso die latas, voluit ut quae etiam de Gregoriano Ordine adhuc non satis certa et definita viderentur, servata eiusdem Ordinis, quae hactenus usu venit, in Civilem unam et Militarem alteram Classem partitione, omnia forent adamussim statuta per leges quae hic sequuntur:

Equitum Classis, quae Militaris appellatur, ex iis constituitur viris, qui sive in Pontificiis sive in quarumcumque gentium copiis stipendia facientes, suis PRO DEO ET PRINCIPE meritis hoc Ordine cohonestantur.

In hanc Classem adlectis nulla specialis statuitur vestis, cum propriam sui exercitus eorum quisque induatur.

Cruces quidem et Numismata ab unoquoque iuxta suum in Ordine gradum gestentur.

Equitibus a Magna Cruce praeter grande Numisma lateri pectoris sinistro innexum, Magnam Crucem transversa praedivite serica fascia Ordinis coloribus distincta deferre ius esto.

Cruci non laurea corona sed aureum armorum trophaeum, ut in schemate, superemineat.

Numisma argentea stella siet, cuius radiis Crux Ordinis sit superposita.

Crux, Numisma quoad formas et modulos, fascia quoad colores et altitudinem a schemate non differant.

Equitibus Commendatoribus cum Numismate, praeter Crucem serica taenia coloribus Ordinis picta e collo pendentem, etiam Numisma lateri pectoris sinistro innectere fas esto.

Cruci non laurea corona sed aureum armorum trophaeum, ut in schemate, supereмineat.

Numisma argentea stella siet, cuius radiis Crux Ordinis sit superposita.

Crux, Numisma quoad formas et modulos, taenia quoad colores et altitudinem a schemate non differant.

Equitibus Commendatoribus Crucem serica taenia Ordinis coloribus picta e collo pendentem gestare ius esto.

Cruci non laurea corona sed aureum armorum trophaeum, ut in schemate, superemineat.

Crux quoad formam et modulos, taenia quoad colores et altitudinem a schemate non differant.

Equitibus Crucem minoris moduli e serica taenia Ordinis coloribus picta pendentem in sinistro pectoris latere deferre ius esto.

Cruci non laurea corona sed aureum armorum trophaeum, ut in schemate, superemineat.

Crux quoad formam et modulos, taenia quoad oolores et altitudinem a schemate non differant.

ALOISIUS Card. MACCHI
MAGNUS CANCELLARIUS ORDINUM EQUESTRIUM.

EXCERPTA BREVI SS. D. N. PII PP. X «DE ORDINIBUS EQUESTRIBUS» PRO ORDINE SANCTI SILVESTRI PAPAE

PIUS PP. X

Ad perpetuam rei memoriam. – Multum ad excitandos ad egregia facinora hominum animos praemia virtuti reddita valent, quae, dum ornant egregios bene de re sacra vel publica meritos viros, ceteros exemplo rapiunt ad idem laudis honorisque spatium decurrendum. Hoc quidem sapienti consilio Romani Pontifices Decessores Nostri Equestres Ordines, quasi gloriae stimulos, singulari studio prosequuti sunt, horumque alios instituere, alios iam institutos, vel pristino decori restituerunt, vel novis ac potioribus privilegiis ditarunt.

Nunc autem, cum peropportunum visum sit gravibus de causis quaedam immutare de nonnullis Equestribus Pontificiis Ordinibus, Nos collatis consiliis cum dilecto filio Nostro Aloisio S. R. Ecclesiae Diacono Cardinali Macchi, a Brevibus Apostolicis Literis Secretario, et Pontificiae Sedis Equestrium Ordinum Magno Cancellario, omnibus rei momentis attente ac sedulo perpensis, ex certa scientia ac matura deliberatione Nostris haec, quae infrascripta sunt, decernenda existimavimus.

Neminem latet Ordinem Militiae Auratae, sive ab Aureo Calcari, inter vetustissimos iure esse enumerandum. Sed rerum humanarum ac temporum vicissitudine de veteri splendore ac dignitate excidit. Illum per Apostolicas Literas, die XXXI mensis Octobris anno MDCCCXXXXI eadem hac forma datas, Gregorius PP. XVI rec. mem. Decessor Noster ad pristinum decus curavit revocandum: ipsi vero titulum a Sancto Silvestro Papa tribui iussit, atque exinde novum quasi constituit Equestrem Ordinem Sancti Silvestri Papae, sive Auratae Militiae appellatum. Eundem Ordinem duabus tantum constare classibus praescripsit, Commendatorum et Equitum; sed in praesens iuxtae et rationabiles causae suadent ut etiam Equester Ordo Sancti Silvestri, non minus atque ordines Pianus et Gregorianus, tribus in posterum classibus constet, Equitum scilicet, Commendatorum, et Equitum a Magna Cruce. Nos itaque superiorem classem Ordini Sancti Silvestri tribuentes, eundem a prisco Militiae Auratae Ordine penitus seiungendum esse arbitramur.

Quae cum ita sint, hisce Literis, auctoritate Nostra perpetuum in modum decernimus ac mandamus ut Equester Ordo Sancti Silvestri Papae ab illo Militiae Auratae omnino separetur, atque alterum ab altero per praesentes ita seiungimus, ut duo diversi ac distincti in posterum Ordines exinde efformentur: alter a Sancto Silvestro Papa appellandus, et alter a Militia Aurata sive Aureo ex Calcari. Ordo Sancti Silvestri, non aliter ac Pontificii Ordines supradicti Pianus et Gregorianus, tribus constet classibus: nempe Equitum sive tertia, Commendatorum sive secunda, et Equitum a Magna Cruce sive prima classi. Crux Ordinis propria eadem esto atque hodierna, dempto aureo dependente calcari: sit videlicet aurea, octangula, alba superficie, imaginem cum circum scripto nomine Sancti Silvestri Papae in medio adversa parte referens, aversa vero emblema Pontificium caeruleo inclusum circulo, quo tum Gregorianae instaurationis cum hodiernae renovationis anni aureis literis imprimantur, MDCCCXLI-MDCCCCV. Ipsa Crux argenteae stellae radiis imposita Ordinis numisma sit. Similiter ruber ac niger sint fasciae Ordinis propriae colores. Sit vestis nigri coloris, unico globulorum ordine, et ad extremas manicas et circa collum villoso serico nigro ornata, ac phrygiis ex auro operibus distincta. Femoralia nigra sunto praelonga, cum fascia ex auro. Niger ex sericis coactilibus galerus oblongus, duplici cuspide, emblemate Pontificio ac parvo aurato flocco insignis. Ensi, aurato cingulo innexo, capulus sit e concha albida ornata auro. Tum Crucis moduli ac numismatis, tum vestis opera phrygia, tum galeri ornamenta pro vario Equitum gradu different, minora scilicet pro Equitibus simplicibus, pro superioribus classibus maiora. Gerant Equites Crucem sinistro pectoris latere dependentem e taenia serica, rubro et nigro distincta colore extremis oris rubris. Gerant Commendatores Crucem eandem maioris moduli, simili taenia collo circumducta pendentem, galerum nigra ornent pluma. Equites denique a Magna Cruce gerant Crucem maximi moduli, quae fascia serica praelonga, binis Ordinis coloribus picta, a dextero humero ad extremum sinistrum transversa latus, sustineatur; sinistro item vestis pectori innexum proprium primae classis numisma maius deferant; albam galero plumam imponant. Cum vero contingat ut viri ad gradum Commendatorum evehendi seu iam evecti egregiis iis meritis eniteant, quae quasi potiora Pontificiae voluntatis testimonia exposcant, volumus ut, sicuti fieri interdum solet in ordinibus Piano et Gregoriano, nonnulli etiam Commendatores Ordinis Sancti Silvestri Papae ex singulari prorsus gratia numismate uti queant minori, secundae classis proprio sive Commendatorum, illudque ad pectus sinistro lateri innexum gestent.

Verum tamen expresse mandamus, ne inter Equites eiusdem Militiae discrimen contingat, sed unusquisque Ordo stemmata, insignia, arma, atque ornamenta, a Sancta Sede praescripta, servet integerrime, ut praefata insignia Cruces, Numismata, vestes, enses, opera phrygia, atque ornamenta, tum propria Ordinis Sancti Silvestri Papae, cum ceterorum quos Apostolica Sedes conferre solet, sint adamussim confecta ad normam exemplarium et declarationum quas a Cancelleria Equestrium Ordinum edi et penes Nostram a Brevibus Apostolicis Literis Secretariam iussimus asservari; utque prae oculis habeantur apposita schemata, quae singulis vicibus cuilibet equestri dignitate aucto de more traduntur.

Haec statuimus, mandamus, praecipimus, decernentes praesentes Literas firmas, validas, atque efficaces semper fore et existere, suosque plenarios atque integros effectus sortiri atque obtinere, illisque, ad quos spectat et pro tempore spectabit, in omnibus et per omnia plenissime suffragari: sicque in praemissis per quoscumque iudices ordinarios et delegatos et alios quoslibet quacumque praeeminentia et potestate fungentes, sublata eis et eorum cuilibet quavis aliter iudicandi et interpretandi facultate et auctoritate, iudicari et definiri debere: irritumque et inane si secus quidquam super his a quocumque quavis auctoritate scienter vel ignoranter contigerit attentari. Non obstantibus Nostra et Cancellariae Apostolicae regula de iure quaesito non tollendo, aliisque Constitutionibus et Ordinationibus Apostolicis, nec non supradictorum et aliorum quorumcumque Equestrium Ordinum etiam iuramento, confirmatione Apostolica, vel quavis firmitate alia roboratis Statutis et consuetudinibus, ceterisque contrariis, licet speciali mentione dignis, quibuscumque: privilegiis quoque, indultis, et Literis Apostolicis, in contrarium praemissorum quomodolibet concessis, confirmatis et innovatis; quibus omnibus et singulis, illorum tenores praesentibus pro plene et sufficienter expressis ac de verbo ad verbum insertis habentes, illis alias in suo robore permansuris, ad praemissorum effectum hac vice dumtaxat specialiter et expresse derogamus. Datum Romae apud Sanctum Petrum sub annulo Piscatoris die 7 Februarii anno MDCCCCV, Pontificatus Nostri anno secundo.

ALOISIUS CARD. MACCHI

EX CANCELLARIA ORDINUM EQUESTRIUM

DIE 7 FEBRUARII 1905

SS.mus Dominus Noster Pius Papa X, animo repetens omnia, quae ab Apostolica Sede sive ad homines virtute formandos sive ad praemia iisdem pro rectefactis rependenda iugiter emanant, iis legibus servanda esse quibus et decori eiusdem Sedis et congrue rationi consultum sit, opportune mentem suam ad Equestres Ordines admovit.

Hinc est quod, re prius acta cum infrascripto Cardinali a Brevibus, Magno Equestrium Ordinum Cancellario, ad memoriam S. Silvestri I Papae honorificentius excolendam edixit, ut Pontificius Ordo, qui hactenus iuxta literas in forma Brevis a f. r. Gregorio XVI die XXXI Octobris MDCCCXLI datas ab Aurata Militia et a S. Silvestro appellabatur, posthac non quasi adscititium sed proprium unice ab eodem Divo Decessore suo, primo Christianorum Equitum Patrono, nomen mutuetur; utque, item ac alii Equestres Ordines, non Equitibus et Commendatoribus tantum sed et iis et Equitibus a Magna Cruce constet.

Honorarias eiusdem Ordinis praerogativas sartas tectasque voluit per Breve, hoc ipso die datum, et specialia insignia adamussim statuta per leges quae hic sequuntur:

PRO EQUITIBUS A MAGNA CRUCE ORDINIS S. SILVESTRI PAPAE

Vestis e panno nigro siet in longos post tergum producta limbos.

Circa collum et extremas manicas gestet sericum villosum nigri coloris.

Opera phrygia, omnia acu picta ex auro, circa collum, extremas manicas et supra peras taeniola dentata sint et laciniae laureas referentes: duplex ante pectus lacinia, quae laureas pariter imitetur.

Novem pectori globuli; tres vero sint, minoris moduli, manicis.

Posteriores vestis limbi, inter utramque peram, duobus maioribus globulis nec non laureo serto decorentur.

Sit humeris impositus tortus ex auro funiculus, globulo iuxta collum innexus.

Femoralia praelonga e panno nigro sunto: fascia ornentur ex auro laureis intexta et altitudinis quatuor centesimarum metricae mensurae partium.

Galero nigro ex sericis coactilibus, duplici transversa utrinque, ut in schemate, undati operis nigra fascia ac parvo aureo flocco in utraque cuspide distincto, alba superemineat pluma: eique Insigne Pontificium quatuor ex auro funiculis, globulo coniunctis, innexum sit.

Globuli, omnes ex auro, Crucem Ordinis caelato opere referant.

Item et ensis aurato cingulo suffultus Crucem Ordinis, prout a schemate apparet, in capulo caelatam referat: capulus ipse sit e concha albida ornatus auro, cum aureo dependente fimbriato funiculo: vagina e corio nigro aureis fulcro et cuspide terminetur.

Crux, Numisma, globuli quoad modulos et formas, sic et fascia quoad colorem et altitudinem a schemate non differant.

PRO EQUITIBUS COMMENDATORIBUS CUM NUMISMATE ORDINIS S. SILVESTRI PAPAE.

Vestis e panno nigro siet in longos post tergum producta limbos.

Circa collum et extremas manicas gestet sericum villosum nigri coloris.

Opera phrygia, omnia acu picta ex auro, circa collum, extremas manicas, et supra peras taeniola dentata sint et laciniae laureas referentes.

Novem pectori globuli; tres vero sint, minoris moduli, manicis.

Posteriores vestis limbi, inter utramque peram duobus maioribus globulis nec non laureo serto decorentur.

Femoralia praelonga e panno nigro sunto: fiscia ornentur ex auro laureis intexta et altitudinis quatuor centesimarum metricae mensurae partium.

Galero nigro ex sericis coactilibus, duplici transversa utrinque, ut in schemate, undati operis nigra fascia ac parvo aureo flocco in utraque cuspide distincto, nigra superemineat pluma: eique Insigne Pontificium quatuor ex auro funiculis, globulo coniunctis, innexum sit.

Globuli, omnes ex auro, Crucem Ordinis caelato opere referant.

Item et ensis aurato cingulo suffultus Crucem Ordinis, prout a schemate apparet, in capulo caelatam referat: capulus ipse sit e concha albida ornatus auro, cum aureo dependente fimbriato funiculo: vagina e corio nigro aureis fulcro et cuspide terminetur.

Crux, Numisma, globuli quoad modulos et formas, sic et taenia quoad colores et altitudinem a schemate non differant.

PRO EQUITIBUS COMMENDATORIBUS ORDINIS S. SILVESTRI PAPAE

Vestis e panno nigro sit in longos post tergum producta limbos.

Circa collum et extremas manicas gestet sericum villosum nigri coloris.

Opera phrygia, omnia acu picta ex auro, circa collum, extremas manicas, et supra peras taeniola dentata sint et laciniae laureas referentes.

Novem pectori globuli; tres vero sint, minoris moduli, manicis.

Posteriores vestis limbi, inter utramque peram duobus maioribus globulis nec non laureo serto decorentur.

Femoralia praelonga e panno nigro sunto: fascia ornentur ex auro laureis intexta et altitudinis quatuor centesimarum metricae mensurae partium.

Galero nigro ex sericis coactilibus, duplici transversa utrinque, ut in schemate, undati operis nigra fascia ac parvo aureo flocco in utraque cuspide distincto, nigra supəremineat pluma: eique Insigne Pontificium quatuor ex auro funiculis, globulo coniunctis, innexum sit.

Globuli, omnes ex auro, Crucem Ordinis caelato opere referant.

Item et ensis aurato cingulo suffultus Crucem Ordinis, prout a schemate apparet, in capulo caelatam referat: capulus ipse sit e concha albida ornatus auro, cum aureo dependente fimbriato funiculo: vagina e corio nigro aureis fulcro et cuspide terminetur.

Crux et globuli quoad modulos et formam, sic et taenia quoad colores et altitudinem a schemate non differant.

PRO EQUITIBUS ORDINIS S. SILVESTRI PAPAE

Vestis e panno nigro sit in longos post tergum producta limbos.

Circa collum et extremas manicas gestet sericum villosum nigri coloris.

Opus phrygium sit circa collum, extremas manicas et peras taeniola dentata ex auro.

Novem pectori globuli; tres vero sint, minoris moduli, manicis.

Posteriores vestis limbi, inter utramque peram, duobus maioribus globulis nec non laureo serto acu picto ex auro decorentur.

Femoralia praelonga e panno nigro sunto: fascia ornentur ex auro laureis intexa et altitudinis trium centesimarum metricae mensurae partium.

Sit galerus niger ex sericis coactilibus, fimbriatus serico undati operis nigro, parvo aureo flocco in utraque cuspide distinctus; eique Pontificium Insigne quatuor ex auro funiculis, globulo coniunctis, innexum sit.

Globuli, omnes ex auro, Crucem Ordinis caelato opere referant.

Item et ensis aurato cingulo suffultus Crucem Ordinis, prout a schemate apparet, in capulo caelatam referat: capulus ipse sit e concha albida ornatus auro, cum aureo dependente fimbriato funiculo: vagina e corio nigro aureis fulcro et cuspide terminetur.

Crux et globuli quoad modulos et formam, sic et taenia quoad colores et altitudinem a schemate non differant.

ALOISIUS CARD. MACCHI

MAGNUS CANCELLARIUS ORDINUM EQUESTRIUM

LITTERAE APOSTOLICAE

MOTU PROPRIO

DATAE

DE ORDINUM EQUESTRIUM DIGNITATE IIS DEFERENDA QUI CIVITATIBUS PRAESUNT

PAULUS PP. VI

EQUESTRES ORDINES a Romanis Pontificibus, varia quidem ratione, instituti sunt vel immutati, amplificati, quibus bonam existimationem, propensam voluntatem, gratum animum ii significarent egregiis Viris, in publica re versantibus aut alio modo spectabilibus et honoris provectione dignis. Hoc inductus consilio, Pius Pp. XII, Decessor Noster rec. mem., Litteris Apostolicis sub anulo Piscatoris die XXV mensis Decembris anno MCMLVII datis, Ordinem Pianum magnopere auxit, aureum torquem inducendo; quem gradum ad populorum Moderatores voluit pertinere vel ad alios, qui amplissima pollerent auctoritate. Iisdem vero Litteris statuit, ut in Supremum Ordinem Militiae D̃. N. Iesu Christi et in Ordinem Militiae Auratae seu ab aureo calcari, ob peculiarem prorsus et singularem causam, referrentur merentes. Cum vero hac nostra accidat aetate, ut Apostolica Sedes saepius in dies, ac quidem ea ipsa, non aliorum opera, nationum Moderatores attingat atque adeo crebrius humanitatis officia cum his exerceat et ab iisdem accipiat, expedire visum est rem ad praedictos Ordines Equestres spectantem, congruenti ratione componi et accuratius definiri. Itaque, omnibus attente perpensis, haec, quae sequuntur, constituimus atque decernimus:

I. - Torques aureus Ordinis Piani iis tantum, qui Civitatibus praesunt, tribuatur, idemque solus deferatur ob sollemnes eventus, veluti cum ii pro muneris sui officio Summum Pontificem invisunt.

II. – Supremus Ordo Militiae D. N. Iesu Christi et Ordo Militiae Auratae, cum honores sint ob extraordinariam causam conferendi, iis, qui Civitatibus praesunt, solummodo ob maximas celebritates, quibus ipse Summus Pontifex intersit, impertiantur aut propter singulares eventus, qui tanti momenti sint, ut per totum orbem terrarum pervagentur et hominum ubivis incolentium animos moveant. Cum praeterea ambo hi Ordines Equestres indolem potius religiosam praeferant, alter enim nomine D. N. Iesu Christi, alter nomine Beatae Mariae Virginis decoratur, convenire videtur, ut ii tantum Civitatum Moderatores in illos asciscantur, qui fidem profitentur christianam.

Quaecumque autem a Nobis hisce Litteris motu proprio datis sunt decreta, ea omnia firma ac rata esse iubemus, contrariis quibusvis nihil obstantibus.

Datum Romae, apud Sanctum Petrum, die XV mensis Aprilis, anno MCMLXVI, Pontificatus Nostri tertio.

PAULUS PP. VI

LITTERAE APOSTOLICAE

DE HONORIS SIGNO IIS TRIBUENDO
QUI FAUSTUM EVENTUM
SACERDOTALIS IUBILAEI SUMMI PONTIFICIS
SINGULARI STUDIO SUNT PROSEQUUTI.

—

LEO PP. XIII.

AD FUTURAM REI MEMORIAM.

Quod singulari Dei concessu et munere adeo provecti sunt Nostrae aetatis anni, ut potuerit a Nobis quinquagesimus sacerdotii natalis feliciter agi, id profecto Nos non tam Nostra, quam Ecclesiae atque huius Apostolicae Sedis caussa delectat. Faustitas enim eius eventus plene, cumulateque confirmat, quam miro pietatis ardore quantaque voluntatum consensione soleant catholici homines Iesu Christi Vicarium colere et observare, utque difficultates rerum et temporum dirumpere, aut perturbare nequeant officiorum et studiorum vicissitudinem, quae populis christianis cum Romano Pontifice intercedit. Siquidem ex omnibus orbis terrarum partibus, quacumque invectum est catholicum nomen, tot ac tam praeclarae amoris et obsequii significationes sunt nobis exhibitae, ut institui quodammodo visa sit inter populos voluntatis erga Nos et liberalitatis honesta certatio. De rebus sermo est, quas quidem norunt omnes et quas auctori bonorum omnium Deo Nos referimus acceptas. Ceterum nullum est pietatis testimonium, nullum officii genus, quod christiani homines, ea sibi oblata occasione, Nobis non detulerunt. Revera neminem latet, ut multis in locis festus ille habitus atque auctus sit dies, quo quinquagenariam Sacerdotii Nostri memoriam celebravimus, ut de vita et incolumitate Nostra, tamquam de publico bono, decretae sint gratiarum actiones et gratulationes; ut ad commemorationem auspicati diei non pauca sint christianae plena caritatis opera instituta: videlicet comparata calamitosis adiumenta, aperta perfugia puellis, pueri recepti in scholas, redempta a servitute mancipia. Testis vero est alma Urbs Nostra, quam ingens vis peregrinorum continenter menses huc confluxerit, qui haberent ad Nos aditum et eximia erga Nos animi sensa coram profiteretur. Vidimus sane plurimos genere, sermone, moribus inter se dissimiles non solum ab Europae regionibus, sed vel a dissitis Africae, Asiae, Americae et Oceaniae oris Romam conferre eiusdem omnes fidei et paris observantiae testimonium Pontifici Maximo daturos. Res quidem cum valde per se mirabilis, tum Nobis, qui gentes universas una eademque caritate complectimur, summopere iucunda. Verum sunt alia etiam officia, quorum non excidet Nobis memoria et gratia: ea enim animo tam lubenti, gratoque accepimus, quam obsequenti ac prono sunt delata. De donis nimirum loquimur, muneribusque omnis generis, quae ex orbe terrarum fere universo catholici homines quasi pietatis tributum, Nobis conferenda curaverunt. Sunt ea quidem et plurima numero et genere varia, propter dissimilitudinem locorum, dissimilem rationem habentia: quorum alia divitias et artificia referunt naturae, alia opificum industriam prudentiamque artis testantur: multa vel materia, vel opere valde sunt conspicua, multa contuentium animos vel ipsa peregrinitate delectant. Huiusmodi vero dona cum collecta sint et comportata ab omnibus orbis partibus, omnemque civium ordinem ita attingant, ut pretiosis Regum procerumque donariis proxima videantur munuscula pauperum, Nos non parvi referre ducimus ad Apostolicae Sedis laudem, ea omnia simul congerere et in Nostris Vaticanis aedibus ad spectandum proponere. Quod quidem bene ac prospere cessisse, institutisque rebus exitum contigisse quem optabamus, et laetamur maxime et gratias Deo, uti par est, plurimas agimus et habemus. Sed libet Nobis animum Nostrum et memorem et gratum profiteri etiam viris iis, qui honorum Nobis habendorum fautores extitere. Etsi enim probe novimus ob faustitatem proximi eventus studium populorum alacrius fuisse, quam ut incitari oporteret, non sumus tamen nescii in instituendis sodalitatibus pia peregrinatione ad Nos adeuntibus, in muneribus perferendis, ordinandis, custodiendis, in omnibus denique amoris pietatisque officiis praestandis eorum virorum solertiam industriamque mirifice excelluisse. Iis vero se socias et administras addidisse scimus pias feminas, quae in eiusmodi voluntatis erga Nos significationibus impertiendis suas sibi partes deposcere voluerunt. Quibus e rebus placet Nobis, ut apud eos omnes cum eventus memoria, tum benevolentiae Nostrae maneat testimonium. Idcirco volumus iubemus ex argyrometallo nec non ex auro argentoque conflari insigne formam Crucis habens, quod tamen quatuor interiectis liliis efficiatur octogonon. Media in coniunctione numisma parvum extet, cuius in adversa parte nomen et imago Nostra effingatur; in aversa autem exprimatur Pontificale insigne, inscribaturque « Pro Ecclesia et Pontifice ». Extremae vero partes Crucis, quae obversae sunt, ornentur cometa, qui una cum liliis insigne efficit gentis Nostrae: quae autem aversae, signentur « Pridie Kal. Ianuar. 1888 ». Huiusmodi honoris signo, quod e toenia serica purpurei coloris linea alba flavaque ad utramque oram virgata dependeat, merentium pectus sinistro latere decorari concedimus. Omnibus vero et singulis qui tali honore digni habiti fuerint, auspicem caelestium munerum, Apostolicam benedictionem peramanter in Domino impertimus.

Datum Romae apud S. Petrum sub anulo Piscatoris die XVII Iulii MDCCCLXXXVIII, Pontificatus Nostri anno undecimo.

M. CARD. LEDOCHOWSKI

SELECT BIBLIOGRAPHY

ASHMOLE, Elias, *The Institution, Laws and Ceremonies of the Most Noble Order of the Garter*, London, 1672.

BASCAPE', Giacomo C., *Gli Ordini Cavallereschi in Italia*, Milano, 1972.

BURKE, Sir Bernard, *The Book of Orders of Knighthood and Decorations of Honour*, London, 1858.

CORNET, René, *Les Ordres Nationaux Belges*, Bruxelles, 1982.

CUOMO, R., *Ordini Cavallereschi Antichi e Moderni*, Napoli, 1894.

DE FESTI, Cesare, *Sull 'Origine, Istituzione e Prerogative dei Conti Palatini e dei Cavalieri Aurati*, Pisa, 1888.

de la BERE, IVAN, *The Queen's Orders of Chivalry*, London, 1961.

de VILLARREAL de ALAVA, Marques, *La Maison Royale des Deux Siciles, l'Ordre Constantinien de Saint-Georges et l'Ordre de Saint-Janvier*, Madrid, 1964.

DUPUY de CHINCHAMPS, Ph., *La Cavallerie*, Paris, 1961.

FERNANDEZ de la PUENTE y GOMEZ, Federico, Condecoraciones Españolas, Madrid, 1953.

GILLINGHAM, A.E., *Italian Orders of Chivalry and Medals of Honour*, Rochester, N.Y., 1967

GRAN MAGISTERO dell'ORDINE, *Il Sacro Militare Ordine Constantiniano di San Giorgio*, Napoli, 1978.

GRAN MAGISTERO dell'ORDINE, *Statuto dell'Ordine Equestre del Santo Sepolcro di Gerusalemme*, Città del Vaticano, 1977

GRITZNER, Maximilian, *Handbuch der Ritter und Verdienstorden aller Kulturstaaten der Welt innerhalb des XIX Jahrhunderts*, Leipzig 1893, (Reprinted Graz 1968).

HEIM, Bruno B., *Heraldry in the Catholic Church, its origin, customs and laws*, Gerrards Cross, 1981.

HISTORIA, *Les Chevaliers Teutoniques, les Chevaliers de Malta, les Ordres Militaires et Hospitaliers*, n.403 bis (special issue), Paris, 1980.

JOSLIN, E.C., *The Standard Catalogue of British Orders, Decorations and Medals*, London, 1979, (with regular supplements also published by Spink & Son).

KIRCHNER, H. & TRUSZCZYNSKI, G.v., *Ordensinsignien und Auszeichnungen des Souveränen Malteser-Ritterordens*, Köln 1974.

KLIETMANN et alii, *Ordenskunde, Beiträge zur Geschichte der Auszeichnungen*, Berlin (No. 1–29), 1957–1967.

KRANTZ, H.V., *Handbuch Europäischer Orden in Farben*, Berlin, 1966.

MALECOT, *Décorations Françaises, Paris 1956.*

MENENIUS, F., Deliciae Equestrium seu Militarium Ordinum, Coloniae 1608.

MENESTRIER, C.F., *De la Chevalerie Ancienne et Moderne*, Paris, 1683.

MERICKA, V., *Orden und Auszeichnungen*, Praha, 1966.

MIGNE, W., *Dictionnaire Encyclopédique des Ordres de Chevalerie Civile et Militaire Créés chez les Différents Peuples depuis les Temps les plus Reculés*, Paris 1861.

NEUBECKER, O., *Ordens-Lexikon*, Berlin, 1955.

PECCHIOLI, Arrigo, *La Cavalleria e gli Ordini Cavallereschi*, Editalia, Roma, 1980.

RISK, James C., *British Orders and Decorations*, New York, 1945; *History of the Order of the Bath*, London, 1972.

RUBBI, Ugo, *Ordini Cavallereschi Esistiti ed Esistenti nel Mondo*, Roma, 1948.

SECRETARIA STATUS SEU PAPALIS, *De Supremo Equestri Ordine Militiae D.N. Iesu Christi*, Città del Vaticano, 1905; *De Equestri Ordine Militiae Auratae*, Città del Vaticano, 1905; *De Equestri Ordine Piano*, Città del Vaticano 1905, 1958; *De Equestri Ordine S. Gregorii Magni*, Città del Vaticano, 1905, 1947, 1979; *De Equestri Ordine S. Silvestri Papae*, Città del Vaticano, 1905, 1968, 1969, 1976.

SOLANO, Emma, *La Orden de Calatrava en el Siglo XV*, Sevilla, 1978.

VAN HEYDEN, H., *Segni d'Onore del Regno d'Italia e degli Stati Italiani*, Bologna 1966.

WAHLEN, Adolphe, *Ordres de Chevalerie et Marques d'Honneur*, Bruxelles, 1864.

WERLICH, R., *Orders and Decorations of all Nations*, Washington, 1974.

WYLLIE, Robert E., *Orders, Decorations and Insignia*, New York, 1927.

Index

Abbreviatores, College of 37
absolute monarchy 159
Absolutism 174, 175
Academia dei Nobili Ecclesiastici 61
Accademia di San Luca 21
Achaius, King of Scots, 222
Acre 107, 213
Acre, St. John of 93
Acta Apostolica Sedis 85
Acts of St. Thomas 265
Ad ea quibus 27
Adelbert, (Bibi), M.M.M., Sr., 74
Adenauer, Dr. Konrad, 42
Admission to Orders of Knighthood 113–118
Adrian VI 161, 163
Adrienne Mary, O.S.U., Sr., 74
Agatha, St., 165, 166, 239, 246
Agatha, Equestrian Order of St. 165, 166
Agustin de Iturbide, Emperor of Mexico, 190
Ahmad Pasha, Bey of Tunis, 42
Albano, Cardinal, 294
Albert, Duke of Bavaria (Wittelsbach), 143
Albert, King of the Belgians, 33, 140
Albert of Apeldera 188
Albert of Coventry, Lord, 254
Albert, Prince of Liège and of Belgium, 143
Albigenses 183
Alcantara, Military Order of (Spain) 24, 160–162, 184
Alden Biesen, Castle, (Teutonic Order), 106
Alexander III 161, 163, 184, 258
Alexander IV 173, 186
Alexander VI 27, 94, 163
Alexander, Czar of Russia, 84
Alfonso, Count of Caserta, 147
Alfonso, son of Carlos, Bourbon of Spain, 147, 148
Alfonso, King of Naples, 63
Alfonso XIII, King of Spain, 132, 168, 170, 171
Alfonso V, King of Portugal, 226
Alfonso Enriquez I, King of Portugal, 188
Alphaeus, father of St. James, 257
Alphonse IX, King of Leòn, 252
Altopascio 187
Amadeo of Savoy, King of Italy, G.M. of the Order of the Golden Fleece, 134
Amadeus V, Count of Savoy, 136
Amadeus VI, Count of Savoy, 136
Amadeus VIII, first Duke of Savoy, 137
Amalfi pilgrims 82
Amalia Walburga of Saxony 151
Amanullah, King of Afghanistan, 42
Amelia, Queen of Portugal, 66
Americas 85, 263
Amiens, Treaty of 84
Ananias 262
Ancient Nobility of the Four Emperors, Order of (Empire) 182
Andrew, St., Apostle, 53, 54, 126, 222, 223, 239, 246, 262
Andrew, Order of St. see: Thistle, Order of
Andrew, Prince of Thessaly, 145
Angel-Noble, English Coin, 244
Angelical Knights 145
Angelical Legion 261
Angels 239, 240, 244, 255, 257
Anglican tradition (Register of Saints) 241
Anna, Princess of Lithuania, 190
Anna Maria von Dernbach 192
Anna Maria Sophia, Empress, 192
Anne, Queen of Great Britain, 222, 245
Anne, St., 192, 246, 247
Anne,-München-, Order of St. (Bavaria) 192
Anne,-Würzburg-, Order of St. (Bavaria) 192
Annuario Pontificio 40
Annuciation, Our Lady of the 136, 137
Annunciation, Supreme Order of the Most Holy 135–137
Annunziata, Ordine Supremo della SS. 135–137
Anthony of Hainault, Order of St. 177
Anthony of Vienna, Order of St. 177
Antonelli, Card. Iacobus, 284
Antony, St., 247
Aparecida, Shrine of Our Lady of 66
Apocrisarius 53
Apostolic and Hospitaller Order of Our Lady of Mount Carmel 235
Aquae Salviae 262
Archbishop Assistant at Papal Throne 37
Armagh, See of (Ireland) 261
armorials 176
Arnold of Egmont 153
Athanasius, St. 247
Auger de Balbens 83
Augustine, Abp, of Canterbury, 54
Augustine, Rule of St. 83, 137, 163, 185, 239
Augustus II, King of Poland, 190
Augustus III, King of Poland, 151, 196
Aureate Knights 184
Australia 87
Austria 87, 108, 140–143
  Act of Suppression 108
  Republic 140
  H.I. and R.H. Godfrey Archduke of, Grand Duke of Tuscany, 157, 158
  H.I. and R.H. Otto von Habsburg – Lorraine, Archduke of 140–142, 157

Autonomous Orders 20, 86, 87, 173, 177, 181, 191, 231–237
Avignon 63
Avis, Friars of 203
Avis, Military Order of St. Benedict of (Portugal) 192, 202–204, 224
Avis, Military Order of (Brazil) 203

Baccalarius 229
Baldwin II, King of Jerusalem, 179
Banneret of the Order of the Knights of St. Sebastian 235
Bar, Order of the (France) 187
Barnabas the Reconciler 260
Baronets (British) 117
Bas Chevalier 229
Basel, Council of 137, 203
Basil the Great, St., 247
Basilus, Rule of St. 35, 184, 239, 247, 258
Bath King of Arms, England, 205
Bath, Most Honourable Order of the (Great Britain) 117, 204–206, 216
Baudouin I, King of the Belgians, 30–33, 134, 135
Bavaria (Wittelsbach), Royal House of 143, 153
Baw, Catherine 174
Belgian Association of the Knights of the Soveriegn and Military Order of the Temple 236
Belgium, Kingdom of 142, 186, 235
and self-styled Orders 234–236
Belgium, Order of 186, 232
Beltritti, Patriarch G.G., 103
Benedict VIII 254
Benedict XIII (antipope) 162, 186
Benedict XIV 35, 151
Benedict XV 67
Benedict, St., 202, 248
Benedict, Rule of St. 161, 178, 188, 239, 248
Benemerenti Medal 61, 70–75, 113, 115
Benemerenti Medal for Palatine Guard 71
Bernadine of Siena 125
Bernard, St., 178
Bernard, Rule of St. 161, 239
Bernetti, Card. Th., 291
Bertie, Frà Andrew (SMOM), 89
Bertrand, Duke of Aquitania, 255
Biglietto (appointment of Papal Knights) 115
Bishop Assistant at Papal Throne 37
Bismarck, Otto von, Chancellor, 33, 62
Blessed Virgin Mary of Mercy, Religious Order of the 185
Boleslav, brother of St. Wenceslaus, 265
Bourbon, Duchy of Parma, 146, 147
Bourbon of France, Royal House of 130, 186
Bourbon of Spain, Royal House of 120, 132, 134, 146, 147, 150, 151
Bourbon of the Two Sicilies, Royal House of 120, 139, 140, 145–148, 150, 151
Bourbon-Orléans, Royal House of 154
Brandenburg 188
Brazil 203, 208
Bretheren of the Militia of Christ, Order of the 189
Bretheren of the Sword, Order of 189
Bridget of Sweden, St., 248, 249
Bridget of Sweden, Order of St. 178, 232
Brief, Apostolic 66, 115
British Royal Orders of Knighthood 117, 121, 123–125, 204–206, 213–219, 222, 223, 228, 244
Brotherly Love, Order of 178
Brothers of Christ, Order of the 189
Buckingham Palace 62, 90
Bulgaria, Socialist Rep. and Orders of Knighthood 176
Bull, Papal 77, 106, 119, 207, 214
Bunyan, John, 254
Burgundy, Royal House of 126, 132, 143

Calatrava, Military Order of (Spain) 24, 160–162, 184, 202–204
Calatrava, Order for Ladies, 161
Callistus II 93
Calpurnius, Roman deacon, 261
Cambrai, Congress of 132
Camerlengo 22, 62, 75, 79
Campoformio, Treaty of 132
Canali, Card. Nicola, 173
Canova, Antonio, 40
Canterbury Tales (Chaucer) 229
Caracciolo, Marino, Prince of Avellino, 145
Cardinal Patron 148
Cardinal Protector 94, 95
Cardinal Secretary of State 115, 238, 250, 267
Cardinale, Archbishop H.E., (author), 3, 19, 20, 114, 118, 271, 272
Cardinals, Sacred College of 75, 186
Cardinals, Tribunal of 84, 85
Carl Gustav XVI, King of Sweden, 122
Carlos, Infant of Spain, 147, 151
Carlos, King of Naples (of the Two Sicilies) 145, 146
Carlos II, King of Spain, 130
Carlos III, King of Spain, 145–147, 151, 164, 165
Carlos IV, King of Spain 134
Carlos III, Most Distinguished Order of (Spain) 132, 151, 164, 165, 242
Carmelite Order 242, 264
Casaroli, Card. Agostino, 115, 238, 267

Casimir IV, King of Poland, Duke of Lithuania, 250
Casimir, Prince of Poland, 190
Casimir, St., 250
Casimira, Queen of Poland, 63, 66
Castille, Crown of 163
Catherine of Siena, St., 263
Catholic Orders of Knighthood
Pontifical 19, 21–61, 72, 113–118, 216, 273–307
Religious 80–110, 117, 118
Dynastic 126–143, 145–158
State-founded 159–172
formerly Catholic 122, 201–229
extinct 177–200
Catholic Reformation (Counter-Reformation) 45
Cecilia, St., 250
Cecilia, Musical Academy of St. 22
Cecilia, Order of St. 21
Celestial Collar of the Holy Rosary, Order of 178
Celestine, St. Pope, 261
Celestine III 202
Ceremonial Dress of Knights (Great Britain and Holy See) 30, 40, 51, 56–58, 113, 216, 218, 276, 280, 287–289, 295–299, 303–305
Cevdet, Sunay, Pres. of Turkey, 50
Chancery fee for Pontifical Orders of Knighthood 114
Chapel of the Kings
see: Windsor, St. George's Chapel
Chaplain General 148, 150
Charity Commissioners, Orders of Knighthood or Associations registered with the 237
Charlemagne 105
Charles I, Emperor, 140
Charles V, Emperor, 37, 83, 128, 130, 161, 163
Charles VI, Emperor, 63, 130, 140
Charles VII, Emperor, 63
Charles I, King of England, 244
Charles II, King of England, 205
Charles IX, King of France, 130
Charles XIII, King of Sweden, 125, 225
Charles III, Duke of Parma, 197
Charles III, Duke of Savoy, 137
Charles III, Prince of Monaco, 166
Charles Borromeo, St., 193, 239, 250, 251
Charles Louis of Bourbon, Duke of Parma, 197
Charles, Order of St. (Mexico) 193
Charles, Order of St. (Monaco) 166–168
Charles the Bold 128, 129, 217
Charles Theodor, Elector of Bavaria, 193
Charlotte, Grand Duchess of Luxembourg, 66, 67, 73
Charlotte, Princess of Spain, Queen of Portugal, 196
Chaucer (Canterbury Tales) 229
Chevalière 174
Chibesakunda, Miss L.P., Ambassador, 61
Chief of Protocol
Holy See 114
Belgian Court 118
Christ, Military Order of (Portugal) 27, 28, 207, 208, 224
Christ, Supreme Order of (Holy See) 21, 22, 24, 26–33, 38, 42, 50, 63, 72, 113, 115, 159 207, 208, 274–276, 306, 307
Christian I, King of Denmark, 212
Christian V, King of Denmark, 209, 212
Christopher, St., 240
Churchill, K.G., Sir Winston, 213, 218
Cisneros, Card. Francisco Jiménez, 165
Cisneros, Order of (Spain) 165
Clement IV 137
Clement V 27, 162, 180, 207, 234
Clement VI 214, 246
Clement VII 83, 131
Clement VIII 63
Clement IX 156
Clement X 252
Clement XI 145
Clement XIII 146, 183, 193
Clement XIV 164
Clovis I, King of the Franks, 183, 245
Collegia Militum 21
Collegium S. Petri 21
Collegium Militum S. Pauli 21
Collar Days 201
Collar, Order of the
see: Annunciation, Order of the
College of Arms, H.M., London, 205
Columbus 169
Columbus, Knights of 237, 238
Comes Palatii
see: Counts Palatine
Communist States and Orders of Knighthood 176
Comnenus, Imperial Family, 145
Comnenus, Isaac II Angel, Byz. Emperor, 145
Companions of Honour, Order of the (Great Britain) 117
Concord, Order of the 232
Constance, Council of 182
Constantine, ex-King of the Hellenes, 132, 135
Constantine the Great, Emperor, 57, 58, 145, 150
Constantinian Order of St. Stephen 235
Cornet, René, 234, 235
Corporation Law, Orders of Knighthood or Associations registered under 236
Corporations (Orders of Knighthood) 22, 24, 26

Cortèges, papal, 24
Cortes, General, 168
Coty, René, Pres. of France, 33
Counts Palatine 22, 35, 37, 38, 45
Counts of the Holy Roman Empire 37
Crecy, Battle of 213
Cross, Gold, Silver, Blue Associations 232
Cross, Lateran, 111
Cross, Lauretan, 111, 112
Cross of Lorraine 105
Cross *Pro Ecclesia et Pontifice* 61, 67, 68, 73, 74, 113, 115, 308–311
Cross, The Holy Land Pilgrim's – 106, 111, 112
Crown of Thorns, Order of 232
Crusader Knights/Crusaders 35, 93, 108, 176, 244, 247, 254, 260, 267
Crusades (general) 83, 93, 105, 107, 126, 142, 153, 174, 242, 247, 258
  First Crusade 82, 93, 106, 137, 178
  Third Crusade 107
Cum hominum mentes 38, 57
Cunegond of Luxembourg 254
Curia, Roman, 21, 45
Cyprus 83
Cyril of Jerusalem, Order of 233

Da Costa e Silva, Artur, Pres. of Brazil, 50
Dame, use of title, 61, 88, 104, 105, 109, 205, 228
Dames of the Starry Cross, Order of the 156, 157, 200
d'Andalò, Rodrigo, 173
d'Angiò, Count Fulco, 63
Dannebrog, Association of the Men of 210
Dannebrog, Order of the 209–211, 213
da Silva Passoa, Epitacio, Pres. of Brazil, 33
David, King, 143
David, Royal House of 257
David, St., 251
de Chizelle, le général, 102
Decius, Roman Emperor, 246
Decorations, right to accept and wear:
  in Belgium 234–236
  in Germany (Federal Rep.) 236
  in Great Britain 26, 116–118
  in Italy 116, 139, 148, 234
  in the U.S.A. 116
  general rules 24, 26, 116–119, 234
Decretals, Books of 263
Defeated Dragon, Order of (Empire) 182
de Fürstenberg, Card. Maximilien, Gr. Master of the Order of the Holy Sepulchre, 93, 100
de Gaulle, Charles, Pres. of France, 32, 33, 213
Deity, the 239, 240
de'Medici, Cosimo, Duke of Florence, 158
de Mojana, Angelo, Gr. Master of the Sovereign Military Order of Malta, 80, 143
de Molay, Jacques, 181
de Moor, Rittweger, Ambassador, 118
de Mowbray, Roger, first Baron Mowbray, 138
Denis I, King of Portugal, 27, 207, 220, 224, 255
Denmark, 209, 213
de Payens, Hugues, 178
de Valera, Eamon, Pres. of Ireland, 33
de Wohl, Capt. Louis, 104
de Wohl, Mme, Ruth M.M., 105
Diocletian, Roman Emperor, 171, 247, 253, 256, 261
Diploma (awarding the Cross *Pro Ecclesia et Pontifice* and the *Benemerenti* Medal) 115
Diplomats and decorations 61, 114, 116, 208
  see also: Special Missions
Dominic, St., 239, 240, 251, 263
Dominic, Militia of St. 177, 207
Dominicans (O.P.) 251, 263
Donizetti, Gaetano, 40
Dove, Order of the 177
Downspatrick 261
Dragon as a symbol 182
Dubbing ceremonial 94, 115
Dutch Reformed Church 108
Dynastic Order of St. Agatha of Paterno 235
Dynastic Orders of Knighthood
  see: Orders of Knighthood, Dynastic
Dyvrig, Archbishop, 251

Eagle, Order of the Red 233
Eagle, Order of the White (Poland) 189, 190
Eagle, Russian, 189
Earl Marshal of England 214
Ecclesiastical Knights 150
Eden, Sir Anthony (later Earl of Avon) 218
Edict of Milan 57, 58
Edinburgh, Prince Philip Duke of 219, 223
Edward the Confessor, King, 245
Edward II, King of England, 180
Edward III, King of England, 180, 213, 214, 244
Edward IV, King of England, 128, 129, 215, 244
Edward VII, King of Great Britain, 62, 80, 123, 124
Edward, Prince of Wales, (later Edward VII) 86
Edward, Prince of Wales, (later Edward VIII, Duke of Windsor), 137
Einaudi, Luigi, Pres. of Italy, 42
Eisenhower, General Dwight D., 213
Elena of Savoy, Queen of Italy, 66
Elephant, Order of the (Denmark) 210–213
Eligius, St., 163
Elijah, Prophet, 242

Elizabeth, St., 239, 240, 242, 257
Elizabeth, St., Queen of Hungary, 255
Elizabeth, St.
see also: Isabella, St. Queen of Portugal
Elizabeth (Sultzbach), Order of St. (Bavaria) 193
Elizabeth, Empress of Brazil, 66
Elizabeth II, Queen of Great Britain, 90, 121, 205, 218, 219, 229
Elizabeth the Queen Mother, Queen to George VI of Great Britain, 214, 223
Elizabeth, Queen of the Belgians, 66
Elizabeth Augusta, Countess, (Sultzbach), 193
'Emmissaries' 234
England 73, 87, 89, 124, 204–206, 213, 214, 218, 222, 227, 228, 244, 254
Ephemeral extinct Catholic Orders 177, 178
Equestres Ordines 27, 40, 50
Equestrian Order of the Holy Sepulchre
see: Holy Sepulchre, Order of
Equites Aurati 35
Equitissa 174
Ernest, Duke of Saxony, 212
Eugene III 254
Eugen, Archduke of Austria, 108, 110
Eugénie, Queen of France, 66
Europe 85, 87, 94, 203, 205, 209, 231, 248, 264
Council of 84
Nuncio to the Community of 118
Evora, Friars of 202
Ezechiel, Prophet, 260

Family Orders
see: Dynastic Orders of Knighthood
Familiars, Teutonic Order, 109
Farnese, Antonio, Prince, 145
Farnese, Francis, Duke of Parma and Piacenza, 145
Fatima, Shrine of Our Lady of 65, 66
Fatimid Caliphs 82
Faustin I, Emperor of Haiti, 194, 198
Faustin, Imperial Order of St. (Haiti) 194
Federations of Chivalry, self-styled, 231
Felix V, antipope, 137
Ferdinand I, Archduke of Austria, 108, 140
Ferdinand II, Emperor, 83
Ferdinand III, Emperor, 200
Ferdinand II, Grand Duke of Tuscany, Grand Duke of Würzburg, 192
Ferdinand III, Grand Duke of Tuscany, Grand Duke of Würzburg, 157, 158
Ferdinand II, King of León and Galicia, 161, 163, 220
Ferdinand III, King of Castile and León, St., 168, 252
Ferdinand I, King of Naples and of Sicily, 128, 129, 146, 195
Ferdinand IV, King of Naples and of Sicily, 151, 194
Ferdinand VII, King of Spain, 134, 164, 168, 169
Ferdinand, Prince, Duke of Calabria, (Duke of Castro), 147
Ferdinand, St., 134, 168, 194
Ferdinand, Order of St. (Spain) 168
Ferdinand and of Merit, Order of St. (Naples) 194
Ferdinand II the Catholic 163
Ferrars, Marquis of 37
Fidei et Virtuti Medal 71
Filastre, Bishop Gillaume, 143
Fiora, Dukes of S. 37
Flag of the Danes, Order of
see: Dannebrog, Order of the
Fleet, Order of the (France) 183
Florebert, Bishop, 255
fons honorum 3, 173
Fouad I, King of Egypt, 42
France, Kingdom of 137, 182, 183, 185, 187, 191, 198, 205
France, Republic of 175
Francis I, Archduke of Austria, Emperor, 108, 140
Francis II, Emperor, 140, 142
Francis II, King of Naples and of Sicily 151
Francis I, King of France, 130
Francis II, King of France, 130
Francis, St., 240, 252
Franciscans, (O.F.M.), 93, 94, 252, 255, 258
Custodians of Mount Sion 93, 94
Francis – Joseph I, Emperor, 140
Francis Xavier, Shrine of, Goa, 66
Franco Bahamonde, Francisco, Head of Spanish State, 33, 132, 134, 164, 165, 168–170, 172
François-Joseph II, Prince Sovereign of Liechtenstein, 143
Frankish Kings 37
Frederick III, Elector of Brandenburg, 188
Frederick III, Emperor, 186
Frederick VI, King of Denmark, 209, 210
Frederick IX, King of Denmark, 42, 43
Federick I, King of Sweden, 125, 225
Frederick, Prince of Wales, (later George IV), 134, 205
Frederick Wilhelm IV, King of Brandenburg, 188
Frederick William III, King of Prussia, 86
Frederick William IV, King of Prussia, 86
Furness, Viscount, 89

Gabriel, Archangel, 241
Galeazzi, Count, 104
Garter, the 213–215, 218, 253
Garter, Lady of the 214, 215
Garter, Most Noble Order of the 117, 128, 137, 155, 201, 213–219, 222
Garter Principal King of Arms (England) 214
'Garters', title 214
Gazelas Maria Yonnes, Doña, 161
Geistliche Schatzkammer, Hofburg, Austria, 142
Gelasian decree 253
Gentleman Usher
of the Black Rod (Garter) 214
of the Green Rod (Thistle) 223
of the Scarlet Rod (Bath) 205
George I, King of Great Britain, 205
George III, King of Great Britain, 205, 253
George IV, King of Great Britain, 134, 205
George V, King of Great Britain, 229
George VI, King of Great Britain, 214, 218
George, St., 24, 145, 150, 153, 186, 195, 218, 239, 240, 252–254, 267
George, Sacred and Military Constantinian Order of St. (Two Sicilies and Spain) 24, 35, 120, 139, 140, 145–151
George, Order of St. (Bavaria Wittelsbach) 153
George of Alfama, Order of St. (Spain) 162, 185, 186
George of Antioch, Order of St. 233
George of Austria, Order of St. 186
George of Burgundy (of Belgium, of Miolans), Order of St. 186, 232
George in Carinthia, Order of St. (Empire) 186, 232
George of Ravenna, Order of St. (Papal) 195
George of the Reunion, Order of St. (Two Sicilies) 195
George's, Chapel, St., Windsor Castle, 214, 217, 218
'George, The' 215, 218
'George, The Lesser' 215, 218
Gerard, Blessed, 82, 83
Gerhard V, Duke of Jülich-Berg, 153
Germany 182
Fed. Republic of, and self-styled orders 236
Gideon 143
Glastonbury 261
Glorious St. Mary, Order of 173, 177
Gluck, Christopher Willibald, 40
Goddard, G., 113
Godefroy de Buillon 93
Godfrey, Archduke of Austria, Grand Duke of Tuscany, 157, 158
Gold Cross of the Holy Apostle and Evangelist Mark 235
Golden Collar of the Order of Pius IX (Holy See) 44, 47, 50, 51, 115
Golden Fleece, The Noble Order of
general 24, 120, 126–132, 137, 155
the Austrian branch 126, 134, 140–143
the Spanish branch 120, 126, 132–134
Golden Knights, Order of the 145
Golden Militia, Const. Lascaris, Angelical order of the 232
Golden Militia, Order of the 21, 22, 26, 27, 35, 38, 40
Golden Rose, the (Holy See) 61, 63–67, 73, 115
Golden Spur, Order of the (Holy See) 24, 26, 27, 30, 34–37, 40, 50, 57, 113, 115, 116, 277–280, 306, 307
Gómez Fernandez Barrientos, Don, 161
Gonzaga, Eleanor, Empress, 156, 200
Grace, Princess of Monaco, 167
Grand Collar of the Orders of Christ and of St. Benedict of Aviz (Portugal) 224
Grand Collar of the Three Orders of Portugal 216, 224, 225
Great Britain 26, 73, 84, 86, 87, 116–118, 123, 124, 204, 205, 213, 216, 219, 222, 227–229, 265
Gregorian Reform 47
Gregory the Great, Pope, St., 52–54, 56
Gregory the Great, Order of St. (Holy See) 22, 24, 53–56, 72, 113, 216, 290–299
Gregory IX 106, 185, 188, 263
Gregory XIII 130, 137, 195
Gregory XV 264
Gregory XVI 26, 38, 53, 54, 57, 70, 84, 290, 292
Grey, Sir Edward, (later Viscount Grey) 215
Grimaldi, reigning House of Monaco, 166
Gronchi, Giovanni, Pres. of Italy, 33
Gaudalupe, Shrine of Our Lady of 66, 190
Guardian Angel 182
Gudmarsson, Ulf, 248
Gustav III, King of Sweden, 225
Gustav IV, King of Sweden, 225
Gustav Wasa, King of Sweden, 225
Gustav Adolf VI, King of Sweden, 47, 50
Guto'r Glyn 35
Gutur Owain 35
Gwaith Tudor Aled 35

Habsburg-Lorraine, Imperial and Royal House of 108, 110, 130, 140–142, 156, 200
Habsburg, H.I. and R.H. Archduke Otto von, Archduke of Austria, 140–142, 157
Hacha
see: Hatchet
Hailé Sellasie, Emperor of Ethiopia, 50
Haiti 194
Hatchet, Dames of the 173
Hatchet, Order of the (Spain) 173, 183

Heim, Archbishop B.B., 90
Heinemann, Gustav, Pres. of the Federal Republic of Germany 50
Helena, Empress, 65
Helena, M.M.M., Sr. 74
Henri, Prince, Count of Paris, 154
Henrik, Prince of Denmark, 211
Henry III, King of England, 229
Henry IV, King of England, 204
Henry VII, King of England, 130
Henry VIII, King of England, 86, 91, 130, 131
Henry III, King of France, 154, 155
Henry IV, King of France, 191
Henry VII, Emperor, 130, 182
Henry, St., 196, 239, 254
Henry, Military Order of St. (Poland-Saxony) 196
Henry, Royal Military Order of St. (Haiti) 196
Henry Christophe, King of Haiti, 196
Hermenegildus, St., 169
Hermenegildus, Royal and Military Order of St 169
Herod Agrippa 256, 257
Herodias 257
Heuss, Prof. Theodor, President of the Federal Republic of Germany, 42
Hiro-Hito, Emperor of Japan, 132
Hohenzollern, Royal House of 85
Holbein, Hans, the Younger, 131
Holy Cross Convent, Tulle, 63
Holy Ghost 155, 239, 240, 257
Holy Ghost, Order of the (Bourbon-Orléans) 154–156, 214
Holy Ghost of Montpellier, Order of the (France) 183
Holy Land Pilgrim's Cross 106, 111, 112
Holy Saviour, Order of the (St. Bridget) 248
Holy See 19–22, 24, 26, 33, 38, 40, 53, 61, 75, 81, 82, 84, 85, 87, 93, 94, 108, 109, 111, 116, 117, 119, 124, 126, 138, 139, 145, 147, 148, 150, 159, 173, 181, 185, 186, 191, 201–203, 208, 216, 231–237, 264
Holy Sepulchre (Jerusalem) 93
  Custodian of 93, 94, 106
  Basilica of 93, 94
Holy Sepulchre, Order of (general) 24, 81, 92–95, 98–100, 102–106, 112, 113, 117, 233
  Grand Master 92–95, 100, 106, 117
  Grand Magistry 92, 93, 100, 117
  Seat of Order 94, 102, 106
  Constitution 95, 102, 104
Holy Spirit 137
Holy Trinity 206, 239, 261
Holy Vial, Order of the (France) 183, 184
Holy Year 1925, *Benemerenti* Medal 71
Holy Year 1975 93
Holy Year 1975, Medal for meritorious services 70, 73, 74
Honduras 199
Honours List (Great Britain) 229
honours *sub specie aeternitatis* 269
Horn, Order of the 153
Hornes, House of 174
Hornes, Elizabeth, Mary and Isabella (sisters) 174
Horty de Nagybany, Nicholas, Regent of Hungary, 42
Hospitaller, title, 81–83, 88
Hubert, St. (St. Hubert-en-Ardennes) 153, 154, 187, 239, 255
Hubert, Order of St. (Bavaria Wittelsbach) 24, 153, 154
Hubert of Lorraine (of Bar), Order of St. (France) 187, 232
Hungary, Austria-Hungarian Empire 200
  Socialist Republic and Orders of
    Knighthood 176
Hungus, King of the Pitts, 222
Hussain I, King of Jordan, 42, 43
Hussites 182

Illtyd, St., 251
Image of the Holy Infant of Bethlehem, Shrine of the 66
Immaculate Conception (of the Blessed Virgin Mary) 38, 143, 153, 161, 163, 164, 239, 241, 242, 268
Immaculate Conception, Order of the 178
Imperial Society of Knights Bachelor (Great Britain) 227–229
India 124
Indies, Patriarch of the 164
Inner Temple, London, 179, 181
Innocent II 65, 179
Innocent III 163, 188, 202, 229
Innocent VIII 94, 185
Innocent XII 145
Inns of Court, London, 179
International Law 82, 84, 87, 106, 108, 109, 126, 142
International Military Order of St. James of Jerusalem 235
Investiture 94, 109
ipso facto, alleged recognition of self-styled orders 20, 237
Ireland 124, 204, 206, 261
Isabella, Infanta of Portugal, 126
Isabella II, Queen of Spain, 66, 132, 134
Isabella, Queen of Castile, 169
Isabella the Catholic, Order of (Spain) 169–171, 216
Isabella, St., Queen of Portugal, 27, 196, 197, 225
Isabella, Order of St. (Portugal) 196, 197, 216

Islam 83, 236
Italy (geographical) 160, 182, 187, 205
  Courts of Law 84, 135
  Crown of 138, 148
  State or Government of 62, 84, 106, 139, 148
  Hierarchy in 234
  Kingdom of 139, 147, 158, 195
  Mint of 75
  Republic of 135, 139, 148
Republic of . . . and self-styled orders 234
  ure sanguinis 119
Ius collationis 119

Jacob 143
James I, King of Aragon, 185
James II, King of Aragon, 162
James V, King of Scotland, 222
James I of England (VI of Scotland) 181
James II of England (VII of Scotland) 222
James Clemens, Duke of Bavaria, 198
James, St. Apostle, 226, 239, 256
James of Compostela, Shrine of St. 163, 240, 256
James of Compostela, Order of St. 163
James of Altopascio, Order of St. (Tuscany) 187
James, Order of St. (or of the Shell) 177
James of the Sword, Military Order of St. (Portugal) 220, 221, 224
James of the Sword, Military Order of St. (Spain) see: Santiago, Military Order of
Januarius, St., 151, 152, 256
Januarius, Royal and Illustrious Order of St. (Two Sicilies and Spain) 24, 120, 151, 152, 164
Jason 143
Jean, Grand Duke of Luxembourg, 30, 34, 42, 143
Jean–Adam, Crown Prince of Liechtenstein, 143
Jenkins, Douglas, 100, 101
Jerome, Prince of Thessaly, 145
Jerusalem 24, 81–83, 93, 94, 105, 107, 112, 126, 143, 184, 247, 251, 258
  Kingdom of 83, 93, 105
  Latin Patriarch of 93, 94, 102, 105
Jesus Christ, Militia of 177, 207
Jesus and Maria, Order of 178
Joachim, St., 247
Joan, Countess of Salisbury 213
Job 143
Johannes Wilhelm, Elector, Duke of Neuburg, 153
Johanniter Orden (Prussia, Austria, Germany, Switzerland, Finland, Hungary, France, Netherlands, Sweden) 85–87
John XXII 27, 162, 185, 207, 220
John XXIII 32, 73, 88, 94, 114, 148, 219
John III, King of Portugal, 203, 220
John IV, King of Portugal, 192
John VI, King of Portugal and Brazil, 191, 196, 203, 226
John II, King of Sicily, 128, 129
John Andrews of Drivastus 145
John at Jerusalem, Order of St. 138
John Lateran, Basilica of St. 66, 111
John Lateran, Order of St. 177
John of Acre, Order of St. 232
John of Austria 63
John of Jerusalem, "Sovereign" Order of St. 233
John the Apostle, St., 111, 240, 254, 257
John the Baptist, St., 82, 111, 239, 246, 256, 257, 260, 262
John the Baptist, Order of St. 232
John, Knights of St. 180
John Paul I 30, 78
John Paul II 2, 3, 34, 73, 78, 80, 92, 93, 102, 192, 219, 238
John and Thomas, Order of SS. 177
Johnah, Father of St. Peter, 262
Johnson, Dr., London, 245
Joseph II, Emperor, 140, 186
Joseph, St., 157, 241, 257
Joseph Order of St. (Hasburg–Lorraine) 157
Joseph Bonaparte, King of Naples, 195
Joseph Charles, Palatine Count, 193
Juan Carlos I, King of Spain, 30, 44, 50, 126, 132, 133, 134
Juan de Bourbon y Battenberg 132
Julian, Order of St. 161
Julian of Pereyro, Order of St. 161
Juliana, Princess of the Netherlands, (formerly Queen Juliana), 214
Julius II 27, 220
Julius III 145
Jurists's attitude to self-styled orders 231–238
Jus Patronatus 252, 264
Justo, Augustin P., Pres. of Argentina, 33

Karl, Duke of Würtemberg, 143
Karl, Prince of Prussia, 86
Karl–Theodor, Palatine Elector, 198, 199
Kekonen, Urho, Pres. of Finland, 50
Kettler, Gothard, 189
Killrule 246
Keys of St. Peter 263
Kings of Arms, Great Britain, 205, 214, 223
Klein, Dr. Norbert J., Bishop of Brno, 108
Knight

inauguration of a 205
induction of a 99
dubbing of a 94,115
"knightly orders" (self-styled or autonomous) 234
Knights Bachelor 117, 227–229
Knights Bachelor, the Imperial Society of 227–229
Knights, ceremonial dress of (Great Britain and Holy See) 30, 40, 51, 56-58, 113, 216, 218
Knights Hospitaller 180, 181
Knights of Columbus, Association of 237, 238
Knights of Emperor Constantine 35
Knights of St. John and of Rhodes 94
Knights of St. Julian of Pereiro 161
Knights of the Collar 170
Knights of the Garter 214, 216, 218
Knights of the Golden Collar 44, 47, 50, 51
Knights of the Golden Spur 34, 35, 41, 43
Knights of the Lily 21
Knights of the Spur see: Knights Bachelor
Knights of the Thistle 223
Knights of the Two Swords 189
Knut IV, King of Denmark, 212
Kulturkampf 62

Lady, use of title, 104, 228
Laetare Sunday 66
Lambert, St., 255
Lambruschini, Card. A., 282
Langues 83, 88, 90, 91
Lateran Cross 111
Lateran Council, fourth, 163
Lateran Treaty 40
Laura Bacio Terracina 215
Lauretan Cross 111, 112
Lauretan Knights 21, 111
Lauretta, Lady, 21
Lazarus of Bethany, St., 139, 257, 258
Lazarus of Jerusalem, Order of St. (France) 137, 138, 191, 232, 258
Lazarus of Jerusalem, Our Lady of Mount Carmel and St., Order of (France) 138, 183, 191
Lazarus the Leper 258
Lebrun, Albert, Pres. of France, 33
Lech I, Prince of Poland, 189
Ledochowski, Card. M., 311
Legal personality of Orders of Knighthood 82, 84, 85, 87, 106, 108, 119, 148, 231–238
Légion d'Honneur 144, 175
Legion of Honour of the Immaculate 233
Legitimacy, juridical, of Orders of Knighthood 233, 234, 236
Leguia, Augusto B., Pres. of Peru, 33
Lemnos 185
Leo IX 63
Leo X 21
Leo XIII 33, 45, 60–62, 67, 73, 74, 94, 111, 112, 308
Leo, Associate of St. Marinus 171
Leopold I, Emperor, 156
Leopold II, Emperor, 140
Leopold I, King of the Belgians, 62, 217
Leopold III, King of the Belgians, 132
Letters Patent of Nobility 223
Levant 83
Lily, Knights of the 21
Lion as an emblem (St. Mark) 260
Lion of Holstein-Limbourg, Order of Merit of the 182
Lion of the Black Cross, Order of the 232
Lithuania 188, 190
Litteris suis 47
Liturgical calender 240, 242, 253, 258
Liverzani, Mgr., 99
Livonia, Knights of 189
Lomas, Lady Mary Frances, 94
Longevous extinct Catholic Orders of Knighthood 177–200
Lopez, Joaquin Marie, Pres. of Spain, 132
Lord Lyon, Scotland, 223
Loredan, Francis, Doge of Venice, 63
Loreto, Holy House of 21, 112
Loreto, Order of 112, 178
Loreto, Shrine of Our Lady of 66, 112, 240
L'Osservatore Romano 87, 111, 231, 233, 234, 238, 267
Louis, Duke of Bar, 187
Louis, St., King of France, 155, 183, 258
Louis VIII, King of France, 63
Louis IX, King of France see: Louis, St. King of France
Louis XI, King of France, 156
Louis XIV, King of France, 130, 155, 156, 183, 245
Louis XV, King of France, 155, 187
Louis, XVIII, King of France, 155, 156, 186, 187, 191
Louis, Order of St. (Parma) 155, 197
Lourdes, Shrine of Our Lady of 66
Ludwig, King of Bavaria, 199
Luke, St., Evangelist, 257
Lusignian Kings 83
Lutheranism 189, 213, 225
Luxembourg, Grand Ducal Family, 67
Lyon King of Arms, Lord, Scotland, 223

Macchi, Card, Aloisius, 275, 276, 279, 280, 289, 297, 299, 302, 305
Magisterium of the Church 82

Maglione, Card. A., 286
Magnus, I, King of Sweden, 125
Magnus IV Eriksson, King of Sweden, 125
Malta 83, 84, 87, 262
Malta, Order of see: Sovereign Military Order of Malta
Manuel I, King of Portugal, 63, 207
Manuel II, King of Portugal, 208
Margaret, St., 198, 258, 259
Margaret, Order of St. (France) 198
Margrethe II, Queen of Denmark, 211, 214
Maria Christina, Queen of Spain, 66
Maria Grazia Pia, Princess of Bourbon and of the Two Sicilies, 66
Maria Luisa, Duchess of Parma, 134, 146
Maria Luisa, Royal Order of 134, 135
Maria Mercedes, Princess of the Asturias, Infanta of Spain, 147
Maria Theresa of Sardinia 66
Maria Theresa, Empress, 200
Maria Pia, Princess of Sardinia, 66
Marie I, Queen of France, 198
Marie de Bourgogne 128
Marie Emmanuel, Margrave of Meissen, Duke of Saxe, 143
Marie Henrietta, Queen of the Belgians, 66
Marina, St., 258
Marino, Civil and Military Order of San 171, 172
Marinus, St., 171, 172, 239
Mark, St., Evangelist, 260, 262
Mark, Order of St. 177, 233
Martin of Tours, St., 261
Mary, Blessed Virgin, 24, 28, 38, 63, 126, 136, 143, 188, 201, 218, 239–243, 246, 250, 256, 257, 264, 268
Mary (Blessed Virgin), Patroness and Queen of Portugal, 192
Mary, Queen of England, 86
Mary, Queen of Portugal, 203, 204, 208, 220, 221, 224
Mary, Queen of Scots, 222
Mary, Queen to George VI of Great Britain, 214
Mary Magdalene, St., 198, 260
Mary Magdalene, Order of St. (Haiti) 198
Mary of Bethlehem, Militia of 138
Mary, or Our Lady of Bethlehem, Order of St. 232
Mary, Order of St. (Denmark) 212
Mary, Order of the Glorious 173, 177
Mary, sister of Lazarus of Bethany, 257, 260
Martha, sister of Lazarus of Bethany, 257, 260
Masonic Societies 181
Matthew, St., Apostle, 257
Maurice, St., 261
Maurice, Order of St. 137, 138
Maurice and Lazarus, Order of SS. 24, 120, 135, 137–139, 147, 148
Maximilian, Archduke of Austria, 128, 130
Maximilian IV, Elector of Bavaria, 192
Maximilian I, Emperor, 186
Maximilian I, Emperor of Mexico, 190, 193
Maximilian Emmanuel, Elector of Bavaria, 153
Maximilian Joseph, King of Bavaria, 153, 199
McGivney, Fr. Michael J., 238
Medal, Pontifical 73, 75–79
Medal *Sede Vacante* 75, 78, 79
Medal *Sede Iterum Vacante* 78, 79
Medina, D. José Maria, Pres, of Honduras, 199
Mercy, Order of 177, 232
Merit of the Lion of Holstein-Limbourg, Order of 182
Merit, Order of (Great Britain) 117
Merit, Orders of
  Pontifical 115
  Religious 88, 97, 98, 104, 105
  Catholic, stage-founded, 159, 160, 164–172
  Secular 175, 177, 201, 203, 205, 220
Mesa 143
Mexico 190
Michael the Archangel, St., 53, 155, 156, 199, 239, 240, 244–246
Michael, Order of St. (Bavaria) 198, 233
Michael of France, Order of St. 155, 156
Michael's Wing, Order of St. (Portugal) 188
Michaelmas Day 246
Michael and St. George, Order of St. (Great Britain) 244
Middle Temple, London, 179, 181
Miklas, William, Press, of Austria, 33
Military Cincture, Order of the (Sicily) 184
Military Order of St. George of Antioch 235
Military Order of St. Michael and St. James of Holland 235
Military Order of the Holy Saviour and St. Bridget of Sweden 235
Militissa 174
Militia of Our Lady 174
Militia of Jesus Christ or of St. Dominic, Order of 177, 207
Militia of Jesus Christ, Royal Military Order of the 27
Miolans, Order of 186, 232
Mohamed II, Sultan of Turkey, 145
Mohamed Reza Pahlavia, Shainsha of Iran, 42
Monaco, Principality of 166–168
Monckton, Viscount 89
Montesa, Military Order of (Spain) 160, 162, 185, 186
Montfrac, Order of (Spain) 184
Montgomery of Alamein, K.G., Field Marshal Viscount 213
Montjoie, Order of (Spain) 184
Moors 161, 162, 183–185, 202, 203, 207, 240,

252, 263
Moretto, Order of the 21
Mothering Sunday 66
Motu Proprio 22, 30, 38, 113, 114
Mozart, Wolfgang Amadeus, 40
Multum ad excitandos 22, 27, 38, 57, 269
Murillo, Bartolomé Esteban, 165, 242, 243
Muslims 83, 93, 142, 159, 160, 176, 183, 185, 195, 252, 258, 263
Mussolini, Benito, 40

Naples and Sicily, Kingdom of 137, 140, 145–148, 151, 194, 195
Naples, Cardinal Archbishop of 150
Napoleon Bonaparte 84, 106, 132, 134, 142, 144, 164, 180
Nassalli Rocca di Corneliano, Mgr., 47
Nazareth 242
Nazarus, St., 258
Nero, Roman Emperor, 262
Nicaea, Council of 57
Nicholas IV 166
Nicholas V 75, 137
Nicholas I, Czar of Russia, 190
Niedballa, Rudolf, 56
Nobility titles 22, 35, 38, 47, 61, 82, 107, 117, 118, 173, 174, 223, 228
Noblesse of Scotland 223
Norfolk, Duke of, Earl Marshal of England, 214
Nuncios 37, 61, 67, 118

Oesch, Mgr. Albert, 104
Official Statement by the Holy See 231, 233, 234
Olav V, King of Norway, 47, 50
Olybrius, Roman Prefect, 258
Order *Al Merito della Rupubblica Italiana* 139
Order of the Hospitaller Knights of St. John the Baptist of Spain 235
Order of Knighthood of Christ the King 235
Order of St. George and Victor 236
Order of St. John of the Lateran 235
Order of the Knights of St. Andrew of Serravalle 235
Order of St. Lion of Vitanval 235
Order of the Corps of Knights of SS. Sebastian and William 236
Order of the Holy House of Loreto 235
Order of the Most Holy Trinity and of Villedieu 235
Order of the Redeemer of Jerusalem 235
Orders, Honarary 160, 178, 207
Orders of Knighthood, Autonomous 20, 86, 87, 173, 177, 181, 191, 231–237
Order of Knighthood, Catholic, Merit
Pontifical 115
Religious 88, 97, 98, 104, 105
state-founded 159, 160, 164–172
Orders of Knighthood, Catholic, state-founded 159–172
Orders of Knighthood, Dynastic 119
Secular 121–125
Catholic 126–143, 145–158
Orders of Knighthood, *ephemeral* Catholic, extinct 177, 178
Orders of Knighthood, formerly Catholic 122, 201–229
Orders of Knighthood, *longevous* Catholic extinct 177–200
Orders of Knighthood, Monastic–Military 119, 159–164, 177, 178, 186, 201
Orders of Knighthood, Pontifical 19, 21–61, 72, 113–118, 216, 273–307
Orders of Knighthood, Religious 80–110, 117, 118
Orders of Knighthood, self-styled 20, 87, 173, 177, 181, 186, 231–237
Orders, use of term 21–26, 81, 82, 84, 85, 87, 107, 231–238
Orthodox Church, Register of Saints, 241
Orthodox Churches and Orders of Chivalry 86, 87, 236
Our Lady, Militia of 174
Our Lady of Bethlehem, Order of (Papal) 185, 187, 242
Our Lady of Guadalupe 190
Our Lady of Guadalupe, Order of (Mexico) 190
Our Lady of Loreto, Order of 178
Our Lady of Mercy, Sacred Military Order of (Spain) 185, 263
Our Lady of Montesa (Spain) 162
Our Lady of Mount Carmel, Order of (France) 138, 191, 242
Our Lady of Mount Carmel and St. Lazarus of Jerusalem, Order of (France) 138, 183, 191
Our Lady of Peace, Order of 232
Our Lady of Vila Viçosa, Order of (Portugal) 191, 192

Papal Bull 77, 106, 119, 207, 214
papal documents used illegally by self-styled and autonomous orders 181, 186, 191, 231, 233
Papal Knights 21–59, 115, 117, 118
Papal Knights, Association of (Great Britain) 113

Papal Legates, 37, 45, 61, 166
Papal Secretariat of State 20, 22, 111, 113–115
Papal States 21, 40, 45, 53, 71, 166, 185, 195
Paris, Treaty of 84
Paris Temple 180
Parma, Duchy of 197
Paschal II 82
'Passion of St. George' 253
Patriarchate of Jerusalem 93, 94, 102, 105
Patriarchs 37
Patrick, St., 261
Paul, Apostle, St., 67, 111, 176, 260–262
Paul II 186
Paul III, 21, 111, 195
Paul VI 27, 33, 40, 42–44, 47, 50, 65, 68–71, 73–76, 78, 102, 231, 233, 234, 248, 264, 306
Paul, King of the Hellenes, 42
Paul, Prince of Yugoslavia, 42
Paul, Tzar of Russia, 84
Pauvres chevaliers du temple see: Knights Templars
Pedro, Duke of Bragança 226
Peter I, King of Portugal 203
Peter II, King of Aragon, 185, 255
Pelagius II 53, 251
Pepin, King of the Franks, 255
Peter, Apostle, St., 67, 111, 162, 185, 239, 246, 255, 260, 262, 263
Peter's Basilica, St. 66, 93, 262
Peter, King of Portugal, 203
Peter Nolascus, St., 185, 263
Philibert of Miolans 186
Philip, St., 182
Philip II, King of Spain, (Philip I of Portugal) 130, 203
Philip III, King of Spain, 130
Philip IV, King of Spain, 128, 130
Philip V, King of Spain, 130, 145
Philip I, King of Portugal, (Philip II of Spain) 130, 203
Philip the Fair, King of France, 180, 181
Philip the Good 126, 127
Philip the Handsome 130, 131, 143
Philip d'Anjou 130
Pian Knights, Order of 21, 45, 47
Piast, Dynasty of 190
Picchioni, Mgr. A., 294
Pii patris amplissimi 45
Pilgrim's Cross, the Holy Land 106, 111, 112
Pilgrim's Shell 98, 112
Pius II 138, 185, 187
Pius IV 21, 35, 45, 250
Pius VI 70, 71, 146, 164, 208
Pius VII 21–23, 35, 38, 169
Pius IX 21, 45, 47, 48, 51, 66, 71, 94, 268, 281, 283, 285
Pius IX, Order of (Holy See) 22, 24, 30, 44–47, 50, 51, 61, 72, 113, 116, 216, 281–289, 307, 308
Pius X, St. 22, 24, 27, 33, 38, 39, 42, 53, 57, 67, 74, 94, 105, 269, 274, 277, 300
Pius XI 62, 67, 94
Pius XII 22, 47, 49, 51, 64, 65, 72, 73, 84, 95, 102, 104, 231, 286
Poland 189, 190
pontifical documents see: papal documents
Polish government in exile 190
Pontifical Knights see: Papal Knights
Pontifical Medal 73, 75–79
Poor Knights of Christ and of the Temple of Solomon See: Knights Templars
Portugal
First Magistrate of 224
Kingdom of 159, 160, 164, 188, 191, 192, 196, 197, 202–204, 207, 208, 220, 221, 224, 226, 227, 254
Republic of 191, 197, 204, 208, 216, 221, 224, 226, 227
Prammatica 145
Primatial Authority of the Bishop of Rome (St. Peter) 262
Prince of the Apostles 262
Pro Ecclesia et Pontifice Cross 61, 67, 68, 73, 74, 113, 115, 308–311
Pro Petri Sede Medal 71
Protonotary Apostolic 26, 37
Prussia 85, 86, 107
public law, recognition by 173, 202, 231–238

Quod singulari Deo concessu 67
Quod summis quibusque 53

Ramalho Eanes, Antonio, Pres. of Portugal 50
Rainier, Prince Sovereign of the Principality of Monaco, 167
Ranieri Maria, Prince of Naples and of the Two Sicilies, Duke of Castro, 147, 148
Raymond Berengarius, Count of Barcelona, 183
Raymond de Puy 83
Raymond of Peñafort, St., 172, 263
Raymond of Peñafort, Order of St. (Spain) 172
Real Illustre Y Muy Noble Confradia del Santisimo Christo de Perdon 235
Red Eagle, Order of the 233
Reformation 85, 89, 108, 109, 181, 201, 209, 225
Registrar of Companies, orders of knighthood and associations registered with the 237
Regulus, priest, 246
Religious and Military Order of Bethlehem 235

Renier, Prince and Duke of Castro see: Ranieri Maria
Res publica christiana 159, 160, 202, 268
Revolution, French 108, 142, 155, 156, 158, 186, 187, 191, 203
Revolution, Great Britain, 222
Rhodes 81, 83, 91, 136
Richard I, King of England, 213
Richard II, King of England 204
Rita of Cascia, Order of St 232
Robert, leader of the Norman Crusaders, 254
Roger I, Grand Duke of Sicily, 184
Roman Rite 240
Romanis Pontificibus 45
Rome, Bishop of (St. Peter) 262
Rosary, Order of the Celestial Collar of the Holy 178
Rose of Lima, St., 239, 263
Rose of Civilisation, Order of St. (Honduras) 199
Rothesay, Duke of 233
Round Church see: Temple Church
Royal Victorian Chain (Great Britain) 124, 125
Royal Victorian Order (Great Britain) 121, 123, 124, 216
Royal Warrant 116, 229
Rudolf I, Emperor, 130, 186
Rudolf II, Emperor, 83
Rue, Order of the See: Thistle, Order of
Rules to accept and wear chivalric decorations 24, 26, 116–119, 139, 148, 234, 236

Sacred and Military Constantinian Order of St. George (Two Sicilies and Spain) 24, 35, 120, 139, 140, 145–151
Sacred Congregation for the Propagation of the Faith 53
Sacred Congregation for the Religious 104, 109
Sacred Congregation of Rites 253
Sacred Heart, emblem of the 204, 208, 221, 224
Sacred Imp. and Angelical Order of the Cross of Constantine the Great 235
Sacro Militare Ordine Constantiniano de San Giorgio see: Sacred and Military Constantinian Order of St. George
St. John, Royal Prussion Order of 86
St. John of Jerusalem in the British Realm, Most Venerable Order of the Hospital of 86, 87, 90
  sub-prelate of 90
St. Mary Major, Basilica 66
Saints, official Register of (Catholic) 241
Salisbury, Bishop of 214
Salome 257
Sancho I, King of Portugal, 202
Sancho III, King of Castile, 161
San Marino, Most Serene Republic of 165, 166, 171, 172
Santa Anna, President of Mexico 190
Santa Maria del Fiore, Shrine of 66
Santiago, Military Order of (Spain) 24, 160, 163, 164, 220
Saracenes 93
Saragat Giuseppe, Pres. of Italy, 33
Saul see: Paul, Apostle, St.
Savoy, Royal House of 66, 120, 135, 136, 138
Saxony 151, 196, 212
Schnyder von Wartensee von Segesser
  Dr. Hans 104
  Mme. Hilde 104, 105
Scotland 73, 124, 206, 222, 223, 227, 246, 261
Sebastian, Order of St. 233
Secretariat of State (papal) 20, 22, 111, 113–115
Secretary of State (papal) 115, 238, 267
Secularisation of Orders 27, 164, 175, 201, 208, 220
Secularism 160
Sede Vacante 75, 78, 79
  Medal, and *Sede Iterum Vacante* Medal 75, 78, 79
Segni, Antonio, Pres. of Italy, 32, 33, 42
self-styled orders of knighthood 20, 87, 173, 177, 181, 186, 231–237
Seraphim, Royal Order of the (Sweden) 122, 125
Sforza-Cesarini, Dukes, 37
Sicilies, Kingdom of the Two see: Naples and Sicily, Kingdom of
Sicily 184, 185, 194, 195
Sigismund, Emperor, 182
Sikorski, General, Polish Prime Minister in exile 190
Simon, Cephas, see: Peter, Apostle, St.
Simon Magnus, magician, 262
Simon the Pharisee 260
Sir, use of title 117, 227, 228
Sixtus IV 66, 138, 186
Sixtus V 21, 169, 174
Slaves of Virtue, Order of the (Empire) 200
Solomon, Temple of 178, 179
Sostituto 115
"Sovereign and Military Order of the Temple of Jerusalem" 234
Sovereign Military Order of Malta 24, 80–91, 96, 97, 108, 109, 113, 117. 148, 185, 233
  Diplomatic relations 84
  Prince and Grand Master 80, 83, 84, 91, 117
  Seat of government 84, 91
  Solemn Profession 89
  Sovereign Council 88, 117

Sovereignty 82–85, 108
"Sovereign Order of St. John of Jerusalem" 233
Sovereign Order of St. John (Russian Orthodox) 86, 87
Soviet Union see: U.S.S.R.
Spain 134, 159–165, 168–172, 183–185, 216
Council of Ministers 134
Cortes 134
National Junta of Cádiz 134
Republic of 132, 160, 164, 168–170
Special Missions to the Holy See or the reigning Pontiff 114, 116
Spur, Knights of the Golden see: Knights of the Golden Spur
Spur, Order of the Golden see: Golden Spur, Order of
Starry Cross, Dames of the and Order of the 156, 157, 200
Stephen Order of St. (Tuscany) 158, 187
Stephen, St., King of Hungary, 200, 264
Stephen of Hungary, Order of St. (Empire) 200
Sublime Porte 94
Suero, Don, 161
Sunday of the Rose 66
Supernatural in the Orders of Knighthood, the 239–265
Supreme Order of the Knights of Peace 235
Swan, Order of the (Brandenburg) 188
Sweden 122, 125, 225
Sword, Military Order of the (Sweden) 225, 226
Sword Bearers, Order of the (Lithuania) 188, 189
Sylvester, Pope, St., 35, 57, 58
Sylvester, Order of Pope St. (Holy See) 22, 24, 38, 40, 57–59, 72, 113, 300–305
Sylvia, Queen of Sweden, 122

Tasso, Torquato, 94
Templars, Order of the Knights 27, 83, 162, 178–181, 188, 207, 234
Templars, seal of the 179
Temple Church 179–181
'Temple, Order of the' 233, 234
'Temple of Jersualem, Sacred and Military Order of the' 234
Temple of Solomon 178, 179
Teutonic Knights 106, 107, 108
Teutonic Knights of St. Mary's Hospital at Jerusalem see: Teutonic Order
Teutonic Order 24, 81, 106–110, 188
High/Grand Master 107–110
Sovereignty 107–109
Teutonic State 107
Thatcher, Rt. Hon. Margaret, Prime Minister of Great Britain, 229
Theban Legion 261
Theodore, Bishop 261
Theresa of Avila, St., 239, 264
Thistle, Lady of 223
Thistle, Most Ancient and Most Noble Order of the (Great Britain) 117, 201, 222, 223
Thomas, Apostle, St., 265
Thomas, Acts of St. 265
Thomas, Order of St. 232
Thomas More, Sir, St., 62
Thomas, Patriarch of Jerusalem, 105
Three Golden Fleeces, Military Imperial Order of the (Napoleonic) 144
Tiberius II of Constantinople 53
Titles, use of 24, 35, 38, 47, 61, 104, 105, 109, 117–119, 173, 174, 218, 223, 227–229, 231, 232, 269
Torquati Aurati 184
Tower and the Sword, of Valour, Loyalty and Merit, Military Order of (Portugal) 216, 226–227
Trent, Council of 45, 251
Troyes, Council of 179
Truxillo, Order of (Spain) 184
Turks 158
Tuscany, Grand Duchy of 158, 187
Two Moons, Order of the (France) 183
Two Sicilies, Kingdom of see: Naples and Sicily, Kingdom of
Two Sicilies, Royal Order of 195
Two Swords, Knights of the 189

Umberto II, ex-King of Italy 40, 132, 135, 139
United States of America 84, 87, 181, 231, 238
U.N.E.S.C.O. 84
U.N.O. 84
Urban II 63, 106
Urban VII 264
Urban VIII 83, 145
U.S.S.R. and Orders of Knighthood 176
Utrecht, Treaty of 130

Valerian, Roman, 250
Vasco da Gama 265
Vatican City State 102, 106, 219
Vatican Council
First 45
Second 70, 73, 240
Venice, Republic of 145
Versailles, Treaty of 140
Victor Amadeus I 136

Victor Emmanuel II, King of Italy, 139, 217
Victor Emmanuel III, King of Italy, 33, 40
Victoria, Queen of Great Britain, 61, 62, 86, 123, 205
Victoria Eugenia, Queen of Spain, 66
Victorian Chain, Royal (Great Britain) 124, 125
Victorian Order, Royal (Great Britain) 121, 123, 124
Vienna, Council of 180
Villot, Card. Jean, 79

Wales 35, 73, 251, 261
Wales, the Prince of 205, 214, 223
Walsingham 21
Wellesley, Arthur see: Wellington, Duke of
Wellington, First Duke of, Duke of Ciudad Rodrigo 134, 137, 256
Weltliche Schatzkammer, Hofburg, Austria 142
Wenceslaus, Duke of Bohemia, St., 265
Westminster Abbey, London, 205
White Eagle, Order of the (Poland) 189, 190
White Eagle, Royal Imperial Order of Russia 189, 190
William, Order of St. 233
William the Conqueror 254
Winchester, Bishop of 214
Windsor
  Castle 214
  Dean of 214
  Royal House of 121
  St. George's Chapel 214, 217, 218
Wittelsbach, Royal House of 143, 153
Wladislav I, King of Poland 190
Women and Orders of Knighthood 61, 88, 94, 104, 105, 163, 171, 173–175, 183, 192, 193, 196, 197, 200, 205, 210, 212, 214, 215, 218
Worshipful Company of Musicians 250
Würzburg, Bishop of 192

Xantus, Prince of Certicu 251

Yellow Ribbon, Order of the (Sweden) 225, 226

Zebedee, father of St. James the Apostle 257
Zechariah, father of St. John the Baptist, 257

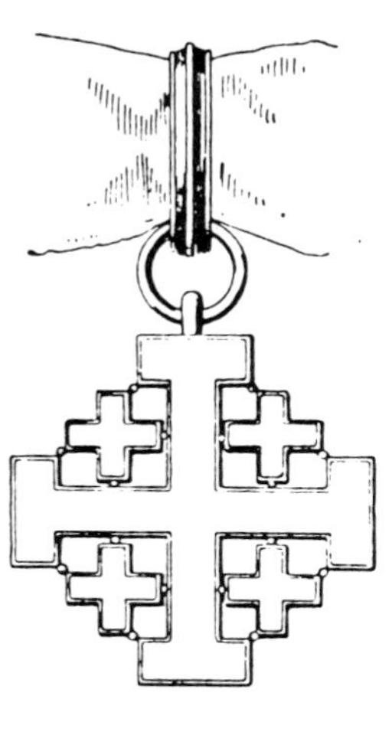